de Gruyter Studies in Organization 8

Alvesson: Organization Theory and Technocratic Consciousness

de Gruyter Studies in Organization

An international series by internationally known authors presenting current fields of research in organization.

Organizing and organizations are substantial pre-requisites for the viability and future developments of society. Their study and comprehension are indispensable to the quality of human life. Therefore, the series aims to:

– offer to the specialist work material in form of the most important and current problems, methods and results;
– give interested readers access to different subject areas;
– provide aids for decisions on contemporary problems and stimulate ideas.

The series will include monographs, collections of contributed papers, and handbooks.

Mats Alvesson

Organization Theory and Technocratic Consciousness

Rationality, Ideology and Quality of Work

Walter de Gruyter
Berlin · New York 1987

Dr. Mats Alvesson
Department of Management and Economics, Industrial Organization Group
University of Linköping
Department of Applied Psychology
University of Lund, Sweden

Library of Congress Cataloging in Publication Data

Alvesson, Mats, 1956–
    Organization theory and technocratic consciousness.
    (De Gruyter studies in organization ; 8)
    Translation of: Organisationsteori och technokratiskt medvetande.
    Bibliography: p.
    Includes index.
    1. Industrial sociology. 2. Industrial organization. 3. Work—Psychological
aspects. 4. Criticism (Philosophy)
    I. Title. II. Series.
    HD6955.A44313 1986   306'.36   86-24057
    ISBN 0-89925-165-X

CIP-Kurztitelaufnahme der Deutschen Bibliothek

Alvesson, Mats:
Organization theory and technocratic consciousness : rationality, ideology, and quality of
work / Mats Alvesson. – Berlin ; New York : de Gruyter, 1987.
    (De Gruyter studies in organization ; 8)
    Einheitssacht.: Organisationsteori och teknokratiskt medvetande ⟨engl.⟩
    ISBN 3-11-010574-8
NE: GT

Preface

This book constitutes an attempt to carry out a broad study of a number of problems in the field of organization theory and working life research. In this way I wish to contribute to reflections in these fields. This is desirable not least because there is considerable research activity currently evident in the field of working life and organization problems, which may naturally be regarded as evidence of their significance.

By far the greatest proportion of this research is concentrated on somewhat narrowly defined problems which supposedly can be solved with the aid of various techniques which are based on the knowledge gained. This book concerns itself with the problems from a broad perspective and critically examines approaches which suggest that complicated problems can be solved by the simple application of organization principles based on the assumption that expert and management control can solve them.

The emphasis of the book is on the critique of ideology in the scientific and systematized thought on organizations and on people in them. It deals more with organization theory than with organizations and thus has a meta-theoretical orientation.

The basic structure was originally developed between 1980 and 1982 and a first version of the book was published in Swedish in 1983 by Natur och Kultur. The present book is a completely revised and expanded version of the earlier work. In most chapters there are entirely re-written sections, Chapters 7 and 8 being for the most part absolutely new. Minor parts of the book have been previously published in English. This applies to Chapter 10 which is a slightly revised version of an article published in *Organization Studies*, 1985 (6/2) and to Chapters 7.5, 7.6 and 8.1 which have been published in a somewhat different form in an article in *Scandinavian Journal of Psychology*, 1985 (26/2).

A number of people have assisted me by reading and commenting on various working reports and drafts of this book. For this I wish to express my thanks to, amongst others, Göran Alsén, Leif Christer Andersson, Ingeman Arbnor, Gibson Burrell, Pippa Carter, Philippe Daudi, Claes Edlund, Göran Ekvall, Olof Henell, Norman Jackson, Kristian Kreiner, Anders Nilsson, Bengt Sandkull, Howard Schwartz, Sven-Erik Sjöstrand and Gunnela Westlander. I want also to thank David Hickson for arranging the contact with Walter de Gruyter and the Swedish Council for Research in the Humanities and Social Sciences which financed the translation of this book. The translation is by Gordon Elliott, Stockholm, with the exception of Chapter 10, which is the work of Marianne Thormählen, Lund.

Finally, I wish to express my gratitude to Yvonne Billing, who in addition to supporting my research und writing projects has made me better realise that not all the good things in life come from intellectual work.

1986   Mats Alvesson

Contents

0. Introduction

0.1 Problems

The shaping of working life and the way of organizing work in industrial companies and other organizations constitute an important field of research. Research in this broad field, as in the case of organization theory in general, has increased enormously in recent years.

On the basis of several academic disciplines and of different perspectives I have become interested in research on working life, organization theory and social theory. What has particularly impressed me are the differences in ideas conveyed by different traditions and theories with regard to the relationship between individual, work and organization. A comparison between the management-orientated organization theory and working life research indicates that in basic respects there are contradictions and weakly integrated (synthesized) assumptions and results. By organization theory in this book I mean descriptions and theories about work organization and other elements in the structure of organizations which take account of the dominant aims of organizations, usually economic efficiency. Here it is mainly management-orientated organization theory which is treated. By research on working life I mean theories and descriptions which primarily shed light on the individual's (and to some extent the collective's) working situation, mainly with regard to job content. Whereas the organization theory dealt with is for the most part business administration orientated, the research on working life in this book is generally concerned with problems of interest with regard to the employee's perspective (concern for his well-being). One type of organization theory with the latter orientation is taken up and developed, chiefly in Chapter 10. Authors on management organization theory and working life research take up to some extent the same kind of questions, e. g. the individual at work and the organization, but they often do so in different ways. For the person involved in both types of research the result can appear to be somewhat confusing. I shall give an example of contradictory theses which I will try to clarify in this book.

An important assumption in large areas of organization theory is that the long-term efficiency which companies normally have as the predominant bench-mark of their activities "demands" that the personnel have satisfactory and motivating working conditions which stimulate qualitatively good performances and personal development. From this we may expect that working conditions have been changed in the course of time so that they have become still more satisfactory and motivating.

An important – but controversial – thesis in research on working life is that for large groups of workers and lower salaried employees the work has been dequalified and impoverished as the result of an increased division of labour. If this theory is correct, and there is much to suggest that it is, we may draw the conclusion that long-term efficiency does not necessarily "demand" that the personnel should enjoy satisfactory and motivating work conditions. This conclusion assumes both that companies act in accordance with long-term efficiency as their objective, generally succeeding rather well in achieving this, and also that dequalified and impoverished work conditions are not satisfactory nor motivating. I shall introduce detailed discussions of this point at a later stage.

That these theses have been drawn up independently, without being confronted with each other to any considerable extent, is a serious shortcoming. The task of confronting, possibly also of integrating various subdisciplines with each other within the overall field of research – research on organization and working life – therefore appears to be highly desirable.

Another problem I deal with is the lack of critical reflection in large areas of organization theory. In my opinion little has been done to tackle problems concerned with rationality and ideology, especially in management-oriented research on organization. A critical examination on the basis of the critical theory of the Frankfurt tradition and closely associated aspects should be able to shed light on important sides of problems in work and organizations, and how research relates to these problems.

Inspired by this tradition, I shall take up two forms of rationality typical of this ideal and study how these are related to each other in practice and in research. One of these is based on optimizing the output of people's working life in economic terms. Here productivity and efficiency are central targets. The other is based on attaining maximum well-being in and from work in terms of mental health, self-actualization, etc. This form of rationality is founded on humanistic values and ignores economic aspects. An overall theme in this book is to study how organization-theoretical research relates to these types of rationality. I offer the thesis that an understanding of this relationship requires consideration of the *ideological* element. By ideology here I mean an outlook influenced by the needs of a dominating elite to legitimize prevailing social conditions rather than one embodying intellectual independence and tolerance. (See further Chapter 7.)

The study of this overall set of problems includes the posing and answering of a number of other questions such as: Can we talk about a dominating rationality in organizations (on an abstract level)? If so is the case: What good and evil does it bring about? What interests are behind it and what are against it? Are there any conflicts and contradictions (negations) in relationship to the dominating rationality? What elements in current practice, development lines and general possibilities for a new type of practice in organizations point towards an integration between the two rationalities mentioned above? How do the ideologies of the predominant practice and the ruling elite as reflected in systematized thought (in public debate, organizational and management text books etc) relate to the basic issue of rationality?

With these questions and attempts to answer or at least comment on them in relation to organizational practice as my starting point, I shall then proceed to make a critical review and interpretation of organization-theoretical texts and analyses in a more or less meta-theoretical manner. The aim is to contribute to a more reflective attitude to thinking in and about (i.e. research on) organizations and the organization of work. Such a reflective attitude is virtually the opposite of the technocratic way of thinking now characteristic of so much organization research. In this technocratic way of thinking basic questions of aims and rationality are ignored and the dominant form of rationality is accepted as a matter of course.

Very much organization theory is characterized by the discussion of various problems within the framework of this form of rationality. Thus no attention is paid to the value, meaning, content and alienation of work except as problems of social engineering which can be handled by techniques for job redesign, participative management and increased motivation. A basic line of thought in the present book is, in accordance with the critical theory, to attempt to contribute to an attitude which ensures that basic, potentially political and philosophical problems are *separated* from the instrumental attitude which more or less barely aims at solving the problems (or perhaps rather their symptoms) without regard to the context or without relating the problems to other kinds of social rationalities. To put it the other way round, we may say that problems which are now often (amongst other things in organization theory) formulated as minor problems, well suited for action with the aid of problem-solving and management, of the type dissatisfaction in work and low motivation, will be re-defined in this book so that they can also be regarded as philosophical and political problems.

Theories which are inadequately confronted and integrated in addition to the absence of a critical organization theory constitute research problems which are associated with inadequacies and problematic conditions with regard to the *understanding* of work, working life and organizations.

That importance is ascribed to these problems of knowledge is naturally due to problems which have arisen in practical reality. The forms assumed by the individual's job and job content add up to a question of the utmost importance. Working conditions are of great importance to the life of the individual, and from the point of view of society much significance must be attached to the development and nature of working life. To obtain reliable and all round knowledge of the mechanisms, considerations, action alternatives and restrictions which determine the internal structure of organizations and the organization of work is therefore a vital task.

0.2   The Structure of the Book

The book is made up as follows: in the first chapter I take up certain general points of departure for my study. The chapter deals with metatheoretical and methodological aspects. References are made to the Frankfurt school and to other writers who can be claimed to belong to the critical tradition and the relationship between these and what I call critical organization theory is made clear. In addition, certain problems concerned with critical/emancipatory versus empirical/analytical knowledge are treated.

In the second chapter I discuss how work is designed and organized. I take up research results relevant to Braverman's theses on the degradation of work in the twentieth century (in "Labor and Monopoly Capital", 1974) and discuss the debate which arose after the publication of his work.

In the following two chapters I deal with what work and different kinds of working conditions mean to the individual and – indirectly – to the community.

The fifth and sixth chapters are concerned with the relationship between the individual and work/organization from the perspective of management. The problem of motivation and its relationship to job satisfaction is discussed. A basic organization theoretical thesis states that efficiency assumes good performance on the part of personnel, good performance assumes in its turn motivation and motivation assumes, finally, stimulating working conditions. This thesis means that humane job conditions can at the same time generate job satisfaction and efficiency. In consequence the demands of efficiency should in the long term lead to a humanization of working life. But the question is whether it works out like this in practice.

In the seventh chapter I continue the discussion on the importance of organization theory. I put forward the idea that the "humanistic" organization theory lays a smoke screen over certain problems. In this context I take up the ideological and legitimizing functions of organization theory. I continue with this theme in Chapter 8, in which I treat some organizational culture and symbolism research which I find to be characteristic for the 1980's.

In the ninth chapter I sum up the earlier presentation. The following question is posed: can a community be better than its working life? I link up with the Frankfurt School and critical theory (mainly Marcuse) and discuss working life as the central "institution" in which the domination of technological rationality over society, working life and the individual is most clearly manifested. The ideological importance of organization theory is related to the legitimizing problems of technological rationality.

In the final chapter I give an outline of the main features of a critical organization theory. On the basis of the cirical study of the existing organization theory made in the previous chapters I draw up an alternative theory, inspired by the Frankfurt School.

The presentation may be said to consist of four parts. As previously mentioned, the first two chapters deal mainly with overall points of departure, i.e. critical theory and the development of working life according to the sociology of work research.

In the next four chapters attention is paid mainly to problems concerning the nature of job conditions, job satisfaction and personal development at work, in addition to the problem of motivation, from two aspects First (in Chapters 3 and 4) from a humanistic or employee perspective, and then (in Chapters 5 and 6) from an instrumental or management perspective.

What the opposition between these two perspectives looks like and how it is treated in organization theoretical research and literature is interpreted in the three chapters which follow.

The final chapter provides points of departure for a critical alternative framework for organization theory and research on working life. Now and then throughout the book I touch on theories and fields of research which are dealt with in greater detail further on in the text. It may be worthwhile for the reader who is not so familiar with the areas where I refer to later chapters, to go forwards and backwards through the book.

1. Metatheoretical and Methodological Points of Departure

In this chapter I shall present some basic theoretical points of departure. In addition to the critical theory of the Frankfurt School and the organization research associated with the types of questions characteristic of that school, I shall also give an account of the procedure of my inquiry and the levels of interpretation which it covers.

1.1 Critical Theory I: The Frankfurt School

The Institute of Social Research at the University of Frankfurt, generally known by the term "the Frankfurt School", was founded in the early 1920's. The most familiar names in the first generation of the school were Horkheimer, Adorno and Marcuse. In the 1930's Fromm also belonged to the Frankfurt School. When the Nazis came to power in Germany the members of the school left the country, finally reaching the United States where they continued their research. After the war Horkheimer and Adorno returned to Frankfurt, where they rebuilt the institute. Marcuse remained in the USA and in connection with the student revolt at the end of the 1960's he attracted much attention.[1] During the 1960's a new generation made its appearance in the Frankfurt tradition. To this group naturally belongs above all, Habermas and – it is sometimes claimed – Offe as well as Negt and Kluge. A work by Max Horkheimer, "Traditional and Critical Theory" (1937), is generally regarded as a declaration of the programme of the Frankfurt School. In this work Horkheimer criticizes traditional, "neutral" research. As a research ideal he offers a science which is not content to describe prevailing reality as a legitimately established and unalterable structure but analyses critically the negative conditions in that reality with a view to abolishing them. Horkheimer's ideal is the critical theory which aims

---

[1] As is evident, I deal extremely briefly with the history of the Frankfurt School. For a more detailed account of the development of the school, see e.g. Held (1980).

"... to transcend the tension and to abolish the opposition between the individual's purposefulness, spontaneity, and rationality, and those work-process relationships on which society is built." (p. 220)

The Frankfurt School's Concept of Critique

The central importance of the concept of criticism to the Frankfurt School motivates a brief discussion of the subject. According to Connerton (1980), we should speak of two forms of criticism *(critique)* in order to understand the critical theory's application of the concept, namely "reconstruction" and "criticism". Between the two forms of criticism there are some important differences. "Reconstruction" is based on data regarded as being "objective" such as opinions, acts or cognitive insights, on conscious operations from the human actor. "Criticism", on the other hand, is focused on conditions and experiences in which the "objectivity" is open to question:

"... criticism supposes that there is a degree of inbuilt deformity which masquerades as the reality and it seeks to remove these distortions and thereby to make possible the liberation of what has been distorted. Hence it entails a conception of emancipation. (Connerton, 1980: 26)

Further, "reconstruction" explains what is regarded as being "correct" knowledge, e. g. the knowledge required to follow rules in a competent manner. "Criticism", however, aims at changing or even abolishing the conditions for the false or distorted consciousness. This form of criticism strives to initiate a self-reflection process in individuals and groups aimed at liberation from compulsion and dominance. It is with this latter meaning that the Frankfurt tradition applies the critique concept.

The Research Orientation of the Frankfurt School

The overall research tasks of the Frankfurt School and at the same time its development can be divided into four rather broad themes (phases), according to Connerton (1976; 1980). The choice of issues is based partly on a basic theoretical interest in the Marx-Hegel tradition, partly on the problematical conditions which have subsequently been created by social developments.

1. The importance of ideology. The background to the interest in ideology was, amongst other things, that the border between the economic (public) and private spheres characteristic of the liberal epoch were abolished in the 1930's by both German Nazism and organized capitalism. Political propaganda and marketing psychology invade individuals, exploiting them and creating artificial needs which harmonize with and support the existing social order. In this way the overall social structure is fixed to the individual's personality in a systematic manner, although outwardly the individuals may appear to be more independent than ever. Adorno (1951):

"Culture has become ideological not only as the quintessence of subjectively devised manifestations of the objective mind, but even more as the sphere of private life. The illusory importance and autonomy of private life conceals the fact that private life drags on only as an appandage of the social process. ... the task of criticism must be ... to decipher the general social tendencies which are expressed in these phenomena and through which the most powerful interests realize themselves." (p. 271)

This led to representatives of the Frankfurt School extending the originally Marxist critique of ideology, which was concentrated on political economics, into the field of social psychology. The well-known study on the authoritarian personality (Adorno et al., 1950) can also be referred to this phase.

The Frankfurt School took up and emphasized the subjective side of the "objective" class conflict by focusing attention on the socio-cultural dimension. Even if it was assumed that Marx's criticism of political economy was on the whole correct, already in their earliest publications the members of the school were doubtful as to whether the development of capitalism could create not only the objective conditions for a classless society but also the subjective conditions for the emancipation of the working class. The Frankfurt School stressed the importance of paying regard to the relationship between critique of the political economy and Marx's theory of revolution by systematically examining the sociocultural dimension which "mechanical" Marxism had neglected. In time the first generation Frankfurtians began mainly to take up the cultural dimension, i. e. they moved from the substructure to the superstructure.

2. The repressive elements in the Enlightenment and technological rationality. Horkheimer and Adorno's principal work, "The Dialectic of the Enlightenment" (1947), is introduced as follows:

"In the most general sense of progressive thought, the Enlightenment has always aimed at liberating men from fear and establishing their sovereignity. Yet the fully enlightened earth radiates disaster triumphant."
(Horkheimer and Adorno, 1947: 3)

The enlightened rational domination of Nature with the help of science and technology tends to develop into domination of social life and individuals. The "rationally" planned and governed world means that the demands of science and technology for efficient administration, division of labour and disciplining of social relation are given supremacy. Horkheimer and Adorno consider, as a commentator expressed it, enlightenment.

"as subject throughout history to a dialectic wherein it all too easily gives itself an absolute status over and against its objects, thereby constantly collapsing into new forms of primeval repression which it earlier set out to overcome." (Bradley, quoted in Held, 1980: 151)

The focus for analysis and criticism here is not, as in (traditional) Marxism, political economy and class supremacy but that form of rationality which permeates modern, mainly capitalist, society as a result of the culmination of the Enlightenment. Enlightenment changed in time into a positivistic and technocratic view of knowledge, subordinate to capitalism and possessing totalitarian features. (See further e. g. Connerton, 1980, Ch. 5; Held, 1980, Ch. 5).

The thoughts expressed in "The Dialectics of Enlightenment" are markedly influenced by the idea that the working class was incorporated into the advanced capitalist community rather than constituting a negative force within that community. This view was shared by Marcuse who, in "One-Dimensional Man" (1964) and elsewhere, speaks of the domination of technological rationality over thinking, and the satisfaction of needs in the advanced industrial society. Here his point of departure is the idea of a basic antagonism between this rationality (sometimes also termed instrumental reason) and its negation. The latter can consist of a subject (e. g. a political movement such as the Student Movement in 1968) or of latent human needs. Sometimes "practical reason" is mentioned as the opposite of technological rationality – mainly, however, in Habermas' texts. With some risk of indiscriminately tying together writers whose works span an intellectual tradition of two generations, we may say that an opposition between these two forms of reason is the point of departure for large parts of the analysis of the Frankfurt tradition. The concepts are not very clearly defined and cannot without difficulty be nailed down in a simple formal definition of two lines. Practical reason can be briefly and simply said to be aimed at attaining a "good" life through liberation from domination and external social restrictions.

". . . the self-emancipation of men from the constraints of unnecessary domination in all its forms." (McCarthy, 1976: xviii)

Technological rationality is based instead on technological or instrumental control of Nature, resources and even of social life and individuals. According to the Frankfurt School this rationality has increasingly begun to dominate practical interest and has been extended to include far-reaching domination and control of the individual.

These matters are treated in greatest detail in the works of Marcuse, which I deal with mainly in Chapter 9.3, but Horkheimer and Adorno and Habermas also take up this central theme. The former comment, for example, on the way this form of rationality penetrates the cultural sphere in the mass-consumption society:

"Marked differentiations such as those of A and B films, or of stories in magazines in different price ranges, depend not so much on subject matter as on classifying, organizing and labeling consumers. Something is provided for all so that none may escape; the distinctions are emphasized and extended. The public is catered for with a hierarchical range of mass-produced products of varying quality, thus advancing the rule of complete quantification. Everybody must behave (as if spontaneously) in accordance with his previously determined and indexed level, and choose the category of mass product turned out for his type." (Horkheimer and Adorno, 1947: 123)

Habermas takes up various political and moral problems which should be discussed on the basis of practical reason, but are formulated instead as technical problems to be solved with the aid of technocratic efforts subordinated to technological rationality as the general emblem for social and individual action.

"The power of technical control over nature made possible by science is extended today directly to society: for every isolatable social system, for every cultural area that has become a separate, closed system whose relations can be analyzed immanently in terms of presupposed system goals, a new discipline emerges in the social sciences. In the same measure, however, the problems of technical control solved by science are transformed into life problems." (Habermas, 1971: 56)

By broadening the analysis and re-aligning the focus from ownership and the capitalistic sphere of circulation to the domination of instrumental reason the representatives of the Frankfurt School can be said to have transformed criticism of political economy to a more general criticism of technical civilization (Schroyer, 1973: 136).

This does not mean that criticism of political economy was wholly abandoned. Instrumental reason cannot be regarded as disengaged from the economic system. To the Frankfurt School critique of technological rationality also meant criticism of the capitalist economy. The former is closely linked to the latter and constitutes the predominant line of thought in a capitalist society. But technological rationality *can,* of course, obviously dominate other economic systems, not only the capitalistic.

3. The search for negation. The original idea in the research programme of the Frankfurt School was to seek knowledge of relevance to the further development of historical materialism and thereby – even if indirectly and mainly in philosophical form – to the working class. This idea was given up in practice rather soon, due, amongst other things, to the weakening of the working class as a revolutionary proletariat during late capitalism. This reduced class struggle and the chance that it could lead to a transgression of the prevailing circumstances. The target of the criticism mainly became technological rationality in industrial society and not, to the same degree, capitalism. The development of the Frankfurt School from focusing on political economy toward a sociologically related metapsychology, based on

Freud, continued and found expression in, amongst others, Marcuse's "Eros and Civilization" (1954). Members of the Frankfurt School during the 1930's and 1940's had made much use of psycho-analysis to obtain an understanding of the social-psychological roots of fascism. Unlike Horkheimer and Adorno, who during the post-war period adopted a more pessimistic view on the transformation of society and considered individuals to be well integrated into the social machine, Marcuse saw, in Freud's theoretical argument on civilization, the urges of the individual as a kind of basis for the negation of the technological-capitalistic community. From the dominant "performance principle" of this society, which is a special version of the "reality principle" governing man's behaviour in civilization in general, there follows a "surplus repression", i.e. a stronger repression of urges than that which civilization in general should demand. Against this surplus repression there is a tense relationship with human erotic needs. In later works Marcuse has, amongst other things, pointed to the Student Movement and to art as possible sources of negation of the prevailing social order.

4. Hermeneutics and communication. The fourth main theme (or phase) in the development of the Frankfurt School is represented by Habermas. In his theory of communication mention is made, amongst other things, of *instrumental* action, which is concerned with technical control and the solution of problems, as well as of *communicative* action which aims at understanding. Habermas believes that a scientific-technical society can only be regarded as rational if the development and application of science and technology are the objects of public control. The attainment of this requires a dialogue about the aims and objectives of social existence. Communicative action must exist parallel to the instrumental. The former means, ideally, that the communication is undistorted, i.e. free from obstacles. This requires, however, that all participants should have effective and equal possibilities of joining in the dialogue. The conditions for an ideal communicative situation are thereby such that the conditions for an ideal discourse are related to the conditions for an ideal form of social life. Rational communication in this sense might be seen as the prerequisite for the rational society.

This survey bears a certain historical stamp, but it should not convey the idea that the first themes were only of current interest during the earlier phase of the school. Rather the later themes have gradually taken their place beside the earlier ones. In this study it is mainly the first two themes which are of interest, and this is why I have devoted more attention to them.

This brief description of some important themes on which the Frankfurt School worked during its development will be supplemented by a brief account of the views of the school on science and knowledge. This is marked by the adoption of an anti-positivistic stance in the broad sense. The ideal science should not be limited under the guise of neutrality with respect to values to producing surveys and establishing relationships of the existing reality. Research with a 'pure' empirical orientation easily results in the development of knowledge being subjected to the aims, the basic rationality and the direction characteristic of the society. Thereby research is also subjected to the dominating interests and to the elite, and is made to contribute to the reproduction of the social order – all this under the guise of objectivity and neutrality. The critical research worker must maintain his independence with respect to the current observable social reality, something which is taboo according to a traditional empiricist view of knowledge:

"For the scientific mind, the separation of thought from business for the purpose of adjusting actuality, departure from the privileged area of real existence, is as insane and self-destructive as the primitive magician would consider stepping out of the magic circle he has prepared for his invocation; in both cases the offense against the taboo will actually result in the malefactor's ruin. The mastery of nature draws the circle into which the criticism of pure reason banished thought." (Horkheimer and Adorno, 1947: 26)

This quotation touches on another important element in the Frankfurt School which lies close to the antipositivistic line, namely criticism of technocracy, which also includes science developed to bring about social engineering. Problems arising in different sectors of society ought to be related to the totality in which they are expressions and not be met by knowledge and technological development aimed at the better functioning of particular components.

The contribution of critical theory to the unsatisfactory state of affairs and problems characteristic of society is to shed light on the irrationality and on the conditions of domination which make it difficult for people clearly to recognize the core of the problems as well as to make, on the basis of their "true" interests, rational choices. The latter is made difficult by a number of social circumstances, including artificial needs, created or at least reinforced and controlled by, amongst others, cultural and consumption industries. Critical theory opposes those ideologies and illusions which work against the individual's independent and free choices. In capitalist society people often appear to be free at the same time as the social institutions, supported by positivistic and technocratic research, penetrate people even at the level of urges. Awareness of this is restricted in consequence of the strong influence of technological rationality and its ideology. In order to counteract this, various circumstances of domination will be studied. This domination is extended not only to Nature (where maximum exploitation is the governing principle of capitalism) and to the individual in the working process, where discipline and control are necessary for the exploitation of Nature, but also to the individual's own personality and nature (Marcuse, 1970).

The aim of critical theory is to counteract tendencies in favour of "false consciousness" by means of criticism of domination, ideology and social arrangements and to stimulate critical reflection on the subject of social life. This will contribute to the conditions for emancipation, for liberation from the repressive social and individual circumstances which the dominating social ideology systematically generates in terms of needs and forms of awareness and which are subordinated to the prevailing instrumental rationality and which describe deviations from this as impossible, sheer lunacy or – which is most problematical – as inconceivable.

I shall revert to the Frankfurt School's concept of knowledge in Chapter 7, in which the concept of ideology is discussed in greater detail, and in Chapter 9.3, in which some themes from Marcuse and Habermas are examined.

Current Interest in the Frankfurt Tradition

In recent times the Frankfurt School has attracted increased interest. Two reasons mainly account for this (Connerton, 1976).[2])

The first concerns philosophy of science/methodology, and is connected to the criticism of positivism. Dissatisfaction with this research tradition has caused many young research workers to turn to the long anti-positivistic tradition of the Frankfurt School. The other reason is political and is concerned with the increased influence of science and technology. From having earlier exercised a rather limited influence as a phase in the production process, these have now become important production forces.

Related to this, we have economic expansion and the problems associated with it, e. g. social problems and the pollution of the environment. The legitimacy of technological rationality appears doubtful in the light of environmental and social criteria. Like the representatives of the Frankfurt tradition, many people ask questions of the type:

"What is the nature of the "necessity" for increasing rationalization of society in order to stimulate economic growth? What are the material *and* social costs of

---

[2]) Thus numerous examples of the early works of the Frankfurt school have been translated for the first time into English. In recent years an increasing amount of secondary literature on the Frankfurt tradition has made its appearance. The keen interest taken in Habermas who appears to be one of the most notable sociologists of the 1980's indicates that the Frankfurt tradition is of current interest.

alternative models of development? What are the technical means and options available to groups who want to control their own production and/or drop out of the consumer society? Until we have a social science that treats these questions as seriously as organization for greater economic growth is treated, we will not have an *objective* (there is no *neutral*) social science." (Schroyer, 1973: 24)

1.2 Critical Theory II: The Radical Humanist Paradigm

Critical theory in my opinion can be defined in at least two ways. The concept can be given rather a narrow meaning which is identical with the Frankfurt tradition. It is usually the case that critical theory is regarded in this way. But we can, however, speak of critical theory in a wider sense. This is necessary if it should be possible to create a critical theory as a broad alternative to positivistic and other "bourgeois" as well as "orthodox" Marxist research. A critical theory which only embraces the Frankfurt tradition would be too exclusive to be capable of constituting a third standpoint which, regarding volume and weight of research, could vie with the other two. I shall therefore attempt to give a wide definition of critical theory. This is based on Burrell and Morgan's (1979) determination of sociological paradigms.

Burrell and Morgan classify sociology in terms of two dimensions: "the subjective – objective dimension" and "the regulation – radical change dimension". The first is concerned with the philosophy of science standpoint and the other with the view of society.

The Philosophy of Science Dimension

In the philosophy of science dimension Burrell and Morgan distinguish between a "subjectivist" and an "objectivist" element. Social science based on the former *subjectivist orientation* is anti-positivistic, i.e. it regards the social world as being constructed of individuals, and considers that it can only be understood on the basis of a position where the individual participates and is involved in the activities which are being studied. Social science is a subjective rather than an objective activity. According to this view objective and neutral knowledge is not possible. The subjectivistic element also emphasizes the voluntary characteristic in human nature and prefers research methods which permit the analysis of subjective ideas and experiences in connection with mental and social phenomena.

The *objectivist element,* on the other hand, is positivistic in the sense that it is based on an epistemology which attempts to explain and predict social events and phenomena by seeking regular patterns and causal relations between different components. Representatives of this point of view assume that the expansion of knowledge takes place cumulatively, i.e. that fresh knowledge, obtained by the application of strictly scientific methods, is added to existing knowledge. The objectivistic view assumes that the behaviour of the individual is largely determined by factors in the situation and the environment. (For a detailed discussion of the above concepts, see Burrell and Morgan, 1979, Ch. 1.)

The Social-Theoretical Dimension

Burrell and Morgan's social-theoretical (sociological) dimension is characterized by two different basic views of society. One of these is called *sociology of regulation* and is distinguished by, amongst other things, society being regarded as a stable, well-integrated social structure, bearing the stamp of elements and functions which help to hold society together and to avoid conflicts. It is assumed that there is a basic consensus with regard to the dominant values. Burrell and Morgan call the other view *sociology of radical change*. This is characterized by the emphasis on the process and change aspect of society rather than on its stability. Society is regarded as being affected by opposition and conflicts of interest between different social groups and classes, by the domination of different groups or classes over each other, as well as of different, contradictory values. The two views have much in common with the consensus and conflict views of social relations in society. However, Burrell and Morgan develop these and formulate their "regulation – radical change dimension" in the following way:

Sociology orientated towards *regulation,* focusing on:	Sociology orientated towards *radical change,* focusing on:
a) Status quo	a) Radical change
b) Social order	b) Structural conflict
c) Consensus	c) Forms of domination
d) Social integration and adjustment	d) Contradictions and conflicts
e) Solidarity	e) Emancipation
f) Satisfaction of needs	f) Deprivation
g) Actuality (that which exists)	g) Potentiality (that which can be attained)

(After ibid, p. 18)

Some of Burrell and Morgan's concepts call for a brief explanation. By "consensus" the authors mean voluntary and "spontaneous" agreement on values. "Solidarity" stands for the view that fellowship between individuals and groups is primary, while "emancipation" stresses the importance of certain individuals and groups being interested in liberating themselves from prevailing social and hierarchical conditions of domination. The "satisfaction of needs" stands for the concept of the regulation view that different kinds of social arrangements and phenomena can be explained on the basis of the "needs" of individuals or the system, i.e. that society is primarily structured as a reflection of such "needs". The interest of the radical change view in "deprivation" reveals the standpoint that the existing social system prevents the satisfaction of human needs.

Burrell and Morgan's Social Science Paradigms

Burrell and Morgan interweave the two dimensions and produce a fourfold table in which each field stands for a sociological paradigm.

Sociological dimension / Philosophy of science dimension	Sociology of regulation	Sociology of radical change
Objectivism	Functionalist social science	Radical structuralism
Subjectivism	Interpretive social science	Radical humanism

(After ibid. p. 29)

The four paradigms can be summed up as follows:

- *Functionalist paradigm.* This is characterized by an "objectivist" scientific theory, including amongst other things a positivist epistemology and a deterministic view of human nature and social events as well as a social-theoretical focusing on consensus, social integration and status quo. To this paradigm are referred Comte, Durkheim, Weber and Parsons, amongst others.
- *Interpretive paradigm.* The social theory is the same as that of the functionalistic, while the philosophy of science standpoint is different. Burrell and Morgan speak of a "subjectivistic", anti-positivistic (e. g. hermeneutic, phenomenological) view on knowledge and stress the scope for free action. To this paradigm belong Schutz and the eth-nomethodologists Cicourel, Garfinkel and Goffman. Proponents of this orientation normally focus on sociological micro situations.
- *Radical structuralist paradigm.* As in the case of the functionalist, the philosophy of science is "objectivistic" whereas the social theory em-phasizes structural conflicts, conditions of domination and the possibility of overcoming the existing social system. The majority of the representa-tives of Marxism belong to this paradigm.

- *Radical humanist paradigm.* The scientific view for this paradigm is "subjectivistic", while the social view like that of the radical structuralist paradigm focuses on conflict, conditions of domination and radical change. The radical humanist paradigm is thus almost the opposite of the functionalist paradigm. To this paradigm belong, amongst others, the representatives of critical theory (Marcuse, Habermas et al.), Sartre, Illich, Lukács and Gramsci.

Burrell and Morgan's radical humanist paradigm corresponds to my view of critical theory in the wider sense of the concept, i.e. over and above the Frankfurt School a number of authors whose standpoint is not far removed from that of the school.

Burrell and Morgan apply the concept critical theory in a sense which lies between the two which I apply. To this line are referred the Frankfurt School as well as Lukács and Gramsci. The common denominator is that they lie close to the works of the young Marx.

In common with other attempts to construct typologies, Burrell and Morgan's classification can be criticized for being schematic, oversimplified and fabricated. In every one of these paradigms there are authors whose theoretical views differ considerably. In the radical humanist paradigm, for example, representatives of the Frankfurt School have expressed severe criticism of writers whose works have a more obvious humanist emphasis (e. g. in the sense of assumptions concerning a human nature with – at least potentially – good characteristics and stressing the human subject as the creator of society), e. g. Erich Fromm in his writings after left the Frankfurt School at the end of the 1930's (Jay, 1972). In a book on the paradigms of sociology Brante (1980) is of the opinion that there are two established paradigms – a Durkheimian and a Weberian. This classification of paradigms is thus quite different from that made by Burrell and Morgan. In the latter both Durkheim and Weber are referred to the functionalistic paradigm, and there are three other paradigms, all of which are lacking in Brante. This indicates that the formulation of sociological paradigms is a discretionary enterprise. A further problem of the typology is the different character which the dimensions acquire when combined with each other. Thus "subjectivism" means something different when we have a view of society in accordance with "sociology of regulation" compared with the meaning it would have if our notion of society was the opposite. As far as the Frankfurt School is concerned, they largely overstep the dichotomy between subjectivism and objectivism. Not least Habermas has large elements of objectivism in several of his writings. The difficulties in seeing the Frankfurt School as subjectivistic are also indicated by Burrell and Morgan who, along a continuum, refer the school to the furthest bounds of the subjectivistic field close to the objectivistic.

Even if a number of objections can be raised to Burrell and Morgan, I still consider that they do point to some basic aspects and indicate their importance. Their typology possesses an obvious analytical value. This is perhaps most evidently the case when the typology is related to the various organization theoretical groupings which is the main purpose of Burrell and Morgan's typology of the sociological paradigms.

1.3 Critical Organization Theory According to Burrell and Morgan

Burrell and Morgan tie up their study of the paradigms with organization theoretical research and theories. They relate different authors and schools in organization theory to the four different sociological paradigms. The greater part of all organization theory belongs, according to Burrell and Morgan, to the functionalistic sociological paradigm. It was not until recently that other organization theories were formulated. In this context what is of greatest interest is that organization theory which they refer to as radical humanist paradigm. This is called "anti-organization theory". The choice of name is motivated as follows:

"It is anti-organisation in that it stresses the importance of the *mode* of organisation reflecting a particular totality, rather than the importance of organisations as discrete middlerange units of analysis worthy of attention in their own right. It is anti-organisation in the sense that it views the reified social constructs labelled 'organisations' as alienating 'intermediaries', which serve to mystify human beings in their attempt to comprehend and appreciate the nature of the totality in which they live." (Burrell and Morgan, 1979: 311)

Thus Burrell and Morgan define the anti-organization theory by seeing it as the negation of the prevailing functionalist organization theory. They present a number of aspects of the organization theory/anti-organization theory, the most important of which in my opinion I reproduce below:

	Organisation theory	Anti-organisation theory
Paradigmatic location	Functionalism	Radical humanism
Conceptual level (level of analysis)	Organisations	Mode of social organisation
Focus of ontology	Structures	Consciousness
Predominant socio-economic problem	Widespread lack of job satisfaction	Universal alienation
Generic term for contemporary society	Industrial society; post-industrial society	Capitalism, One dimensional society, corporate state, managerial fascism, etc.

	Organisation theory	Anti-organisation theory
Concern for maximisation of	Productivity	Human creativity
Current status of production	Universal scarcity and shortages	Widespread economic surplus available within capitalism
Human behavior in accord with	Purposive rationality	Value rationality
Ethico-political stance	To understand: possibly to alter the system	To understand: certainly to induce a new totality

(ibid, pp. 322–323)

Burrell and Morgan summarize the research task of the anti-organization theory as follows:

"... anti-organisation theory seeks to demonstrate the sources of *alienation* inherent within a *totality*, which converge in an organisation context. It provides a systematic critique, in the tradition of critical theory, by identifying the factors which impinge upon and dominate human *consciousness* in the form of seemingly objective social forces over which man appears to have no form of direct control." (Ibid, p. 323)

Burrell and Morgan refer to a few studies which belong to the anti-organization theory. Since the book was written some interesting literature has appeared on the subject, to which some references are made in the present book. Regarded as tradition, this kind of organization theory is very young and still undeveloped. From the critical theory (in both the narrow and the broad senses of the word) to work on organization theories is to set off into what is still unexplored territory.

1.4   Critical Sociology According to J. Israel

Joachim Israel speaks of critical sociology. His views are related to those of the Frankfurt School.

He rejects the empirical doctrine in sociology. (This doctrine lays down that only empirically established knowledge is of value.) He motivates this by declaring that the 'world order' which sociological research deals with is constructed of people and possible to change.

"To accept the social 'world order' as given and to leave the empirical study of this to sociologists will therefore have the following consequences, amongst others:

1. It will lead to the study of problems of change being supplanted or neglected.
2. It will prevent a *critical* analysis of the prevailing 'world order' or make it not worthwhile.
3. A discussion about and an analysis of alternative 'world orders' is regarded as non-legitimate." (Israel, 1972: 99)

For Israel the research interest of critical sociology is emancipatory. Its task is to "sketch the final condition which means liberation from the world 'as it is now'."

Israel believes that critical sociology has three functions:

1. It can facilitate the choice between alternative models and theories.
2. It can criticize ideas, thoughts and theories which are accepted and often regarded as self-evident and therefore no longer open to question.
3. It can discuss and clarify the ideological basis of empirical sociology. (Ibid, pp. 170–171)

Israel defines ideology as follows:

"By ideology I mean a scientific or quasi-scientific theory which consciously or unconsciously, directly or indirectly, attempts to defend prevailing social conditions." (Ibid, pp. 141–142)

I adhere to Israel's view of critical sociology. However, I should like to make a few comments. Israel's definition of "ideology" can seem a little slanted and possibly oversimplified. A scientific theory which attacks prevailing social conditions may also surely be regarded as "ideological" in some sense. (Perhaps we could speak of counterideologies in such cases.) Now, however, it is not the latter type of theory which is the object of research for my study, nor is it Israel's. For my research problem Israel's definition of ideology is adequate for the time being. The concept of ideology is dealt with in greater detail in Chapter 7 in connection with the interpretation of ideology in organization theory.

Israel's view of critical theory implies that he emphasizes the theoretical work:

"A critical theory assumes and can only function in relation to empirical (or other speculative) theories." (Ibid, p. 164)

An important task for critical theory is to work metatheoretically. This is not least important bearing in mind that social and behavioural sciences have had and still have an empirical bias. Naturally we can also conceive that critical theory works empirically on the basis of the above-mentioned research interest and does not restrict itself to dealing with criticism of research and ideology.

1.5 The Author's Approach and Method

I shall now try to collate the aims stated in the introduction and the points of departure referred to in the previous section. The various aspects of critical theory which I have taken up constitute the overall terms of reference on which this book is based.

By regarding critical theory in a broad sense, in which the Frankfurt School constitutes *one* important theory structure, conditions are created for a wider perspective. With my point of departure from the critical theory of the Frankfurt tradition, I leave when required, the framework of the school and introduce aspects from authors who may be regarded as belonging to the same overall paradigm as the school (the radical humanistic paradigm).

Israel's view of the functions of critical sociology is well adapted to the context and is applicable to a clarification of my work. By translating these from a general level to the problems I am trying to work on, my research objectives can be formulated as follows:

1. To facilitate the choice between alternative theories and terms of reference in working life research and organization theory.
2. To criticize ideas, thoughts and theories which have been accepted and which are regarded as self-evident and are therefore no longer open to question in (mainly) social psychologically orientated organization theory.
3. To discuss and clarify the ideological foundations of the prevailing organization theory.

By attempting to solve these three tasks I contribute to the two overall aims of this work, i.e. integration of knowledge and critique of ideology. The border between the tasks and the aims is therefore not absolute. For more information on the relationship between aims, research tasks, etc., see p. 25)

Furthermore, both aims are mutually supporting. The integration of knowledge can in fact be applied in such a way as to reveal hidden meanings in research and theory and thereby constitute a phase in a critique of ideology process. By confronting different theories, research results, etc., with each other (integration of knowledge), light can be shed on their inadequacies. These shortcomings, once proved, can thereafter provide a basis for critique of ideology in which the aim is to show how the existing research activities and theories fulfil ideological and legitimizing functions. (See further Chapter 7.)

But at the same time ideological criticism may be regarded as a method of attaining integration of knowledge. An interpretation of theory and research on the basis of a position of critique of ideology is capable of facilitating the choice between alternative theories. By interpreting the ideological elements in a certain theory we obtain conditions for judging the "purely"theoretical virtues of the theory in question. (More on this subject in Chapter 7, in which the relationship between theory and ideology is discussed.)

On Levels of Interpretation

Five different levels of interpretation can be distinguished in my presentation. The borders between these are, however, by no means clearly drawn. There are two reasons why I wish to indicate, and give a brief account of, these levels:

- To facilitate the reading and understanding of the presentation.
- The use of the five levels of interpretation and the relations between them are important to my method. A discussion of the way I have worked may possibly make a methodological contribution to critical research.

The *first* level consists of "empirical reality" or perhaps rather descriptive research on this. The reality in question is the development and actual structure of working life, mainly with respect to qualification and control aspects, as well as the mental and social effects of this reality on individuals. I take an interest in overall conditions characteristic of the job situation of broad categories of wage earners. I utilize and base my work on empirically orientated research, not least research connected with job content and its mental consequences.

The *second* level, like levels three-five, is theoretical. Here I deal with theories of explanatory and/or normative type concerning the empirical reality which was treated on the first level. The theories examined lay claim to reveal conditions, mechanisms, etc. which control how organizations and working conditions are structured and/or indicate guiding lines for the way they should function in order to achieve certain targets, e. g. high efficiency in the long term. Theories concerned with personality, adjustment, job satisfaction, motivation, work organization, etc., are dealth with. My interpretation on the second level is based upon the first and is aimed at a criticism of certain theories and ideas, amongst other things, in which the claim to function in a guiding capacity for practical application stands in a problematical relationship to reality – the empirical level does not appear to be what it ought to be according to these theories and ideas.

Both the third and fourth levels of interpretation are concerned with ideological aspects of organization theory. The interpretation of the *third* level is based on the relationship between the first and second levels and is focused on conflicts and incongruences between empirical reality and certain theories on that subject. I interpret the incongruences between both levels on the basis of a critique of ideology standpoint.

The *fourth* level of interpretation sheds light on ideological aspects from a different point of departure than the third. Ideological elements in organization theory are not interpretated on the basis of a relationship of tension between theory and practice, but with the point of departure in organization literature as such. I attempt to show how the formulation of problems, announcements, assertions, conclusions, etc. in organization theoretical texts is influenced by ideological and legitimizing elements. At this level of interpretation I leave empirical reality and focus exclusively on the texts. The philosophy of science orientation of the book is more apparent here than at the other levels of interpretation. We may say that here organization theoretical literature constitutes empirical objects for analysis and interpretation. In principle this type of critique of ideology is disengaged from the third level. In relation to the latter, the fourth level of interpretation can be said to be an attempt at independent "validation" of the central thesis that parts of organization theoretical literature fulfil ideological and legitimizing functions.

The *fifth* level, finally, may be regarded as an overall "result interpreting level". It is *not* the case, however, that conclusions and contents of the continuing discussion and interpretation are assembled here, but it is once again a question of a new level, a level which does not supply additional knowledge to, for example, the second level of interpretation which aims at determining the practical value of certain organization theories. At the fifth level the discussion is raised to the sociological or social philosophical level. On the basis of the critical theory, and in particular Marcuse's views on technological rationality and its domination in advanced industrial societies, results are interpretated from all the four other levels. Amongst other things ideology in organization theory is regarded as an expression of the prevailing rationality and the need for dominating interests to legitimize this.

Problems – Aims – Methods

The relationships between problems, aims, research tasks and methods will be briefly treated here and may be seen in the following figure which is a summary of parts of what I have so far taken up.[3])

Corresponding to the two overlapping problems of research which this study is based on there are thus two aims which indicate what I am endeavouring to attain in my work. The aims are, however, expressed in relatively general terms, which has to do with the character of the problems I deal with. The stated research tasks may be regarded as an alternative, supplementary formulation of what I want to achieve in the book. They contribute to some extent to defining my objective.

---

[3]) This summarized method applies to the presentation in Chapters 2–9. The final chapter is of a different character to the others.

	Criticism and integration of knowledge	Critique of ideology
Research problems	Contradictory ideas and poorly integrated results in working life research and organization theory	Absence of "critical theory" in organization theory. Need for critical examination.
Aims	Integration of knowledge. Criticism and evaluation of various theories and subdisciplines aimed at obtaining coherent knowledge.	Critique of ideology. Interpretation of theories and subdisciplines to show how ideological functions influence the content of theories.
Research tasks	– To facilitate the choice between alternative theories and points of view	
	To criticize ideas, thoughts and theories which are accepted and not put to question.	
		To discuss and clarify the ideological foundations of the prevailing organization theory.
Method, "general"	"Critique of ideology"	"Criticism and integration of knowledge"
Method, "explicit"	Interpretation at different levels.	Interpretation at different levels.
Level of interpretation 1	Interpretation of "empirical reality"	
Level of interpretation 2	Interpretation of the theory of "empirical reality"	
Level of interpretation 3		– Interpretation of incongruences between levels 1 and 2.
Level of interpretation 4		– Interpretation of ideological elements in theory on the basis of critical examination of text.
Level of interpretation 5	– Overall interpretation of levels 1–4 on the basis of the critical theory, above all Marcuse's views on technological rationality.	

On a general level the two aims can be regarded as each other's methods. Thus critique of ideology, facilitates the integration of knowledge, while the ambition to attain the integration of knowledge provides good grounds for attaining the aim of critique of ideology. Possibly this may sound a little like a merry-go-round, but in practice this is no problem as the two aims are not the only methods applied in the analysis, but are methodologically limited to assisting one another. To put it more precisely my application of methods may be said to consist of interpretation at five levels. Of these, the first two are mainly associated with the integration of knowledge aim and to the research task of facilitating choices between alternative theories and points of view. Through the interpretation of empirical reality and theories about this, some theories and points of view receive support, while others are rejected, the good theories being accorded recognition in more or less coherent bodies of knowledge in a field of research which will stand up to critical examination, while other, unsatisfactory theories are eliminated.

Levels of interpretation three and four are concerned with the ideological aspect and assist in the achievement of the second aim, i.e. a clarification of the ideological foundations of the organization theory. This is effected partly on the basis of comparison between empirical reality and various theories on that subject, partly on textual studies of relevant literature.

One level of interpretation, the fifth, is of an overall nature and common to both aims.

1.6   The Critical Approach and Empirical/Analytical Knowledge

I shall now take up the kind of knowledge which is compatible with the critical effort. The most important question is to what extent empirical/ analytical knowledge is applicable to and compatible with the points of departure outlined above.

Habermas (1966) speaks – possibly in rather a catchphrase manner – of three types of knowledge interest: empirical-analytical, historical hermeneutic and emancipatory. Of interest in this context are the first and last. The empirical scientific theories are guided, according to Habermas, by a striving for knowledge utilizable for instrumental actions which can be controlled through their success. We can speak of an interest in knowledge which takes the form of keeping objectified processes under technical control.

Emancipatory knowledge is described by Habermas as follows:

"... it tries to discover which (if any) theoretical statements express unchangeable laws of social action and which, though they express relations of dependence, because they are ideologically fixed, are in principle subject to change. ...

Self-reflection is influenced by an emancipatory concern with know-ledge, and it is shared by the critically oriented sciences and philosophy." (p. 294)

Many research workers who believe they represent critical effort in some sense and who are sharply critical of positivism are, however, prepared to use what is often loosely referred to as positivistic knowledge in a critical context (e.g. Aubert, 1970; Nygren, 1979). Nygren criticizes Habermas' classification of interest in knowledge referred to above and believes that even as an empirical-analytical research worker one can give critical "information" (Nygren, 1979: 15).

C. W. Mills expresses another opinion. Mills is more sceptical towards the narrow empirical-analytical research being compatible with a critical and liberating expansion of knowledge. Amongst other things Mills writes that the style and methodological inhibitions of abstract empiricism are unsuitable for a democratic and emancipatory science. Mills believes that empirically organized research which follows "bureaucratic" research rules prevents people from becoming independent and substantial thinkers. Empirical regular research leads to the following consequences, writes Mills:

"... the style of abstracted empiricism (and the methodological inhibition it sustains) is not well suited for the democratic political role I am describing. ...

To tell them that they can 'really' know social reality only by depending upon a necessarily bureaucratic kind of research is to place a taboo, in the name of Science, upon their efforts to become independent men and substantive thinkers. ...

It is, in effect, to encourage men to fix their social beliefs by reference to the authority of an alien apparatus, and it is, of course in line with, and is reinforced by, the whole bureaucratization of reason in our time. The industrialization of academic life and the fragmentation of the problems of social science cannot result in a liberating educational role for social scientists. For what these school of thoughts take apart, in very tiny pieces about which they claim to be very certain. But all they could thus be certain of are abstracted fragments, and it is precisely the job of liberal education, and the political role of social science, and its intellectual promise, to enable men to transcend such fragmented and abstracted milieux: to become aware of historical structures and of their own place within them." (Mills, 1959: 209)

Mills' standpoint is not an absolute denial of the thesis that empirical-analytical knowledge can serve as a basis for a critical line. What he does recommend, however, is caution with regard to experiments of that kind.

Critical theory is based on an anti-positivistic standpoint. From this there follows a restrictive attitude to empirical-analytical knowledge. Positivism is an idea tradition which is in harmony with and reinforces a consciousness which reproduces the prevailing social conditions. To pursue positivistic research of this kind and lean heavily towards such knowledge therefore includes always a moment of social reproduction, even if an effort is made to apply this knowledge in a critical context. This is consequently far from unproblematical. Rigorous methodology in the spirit of critical theory thus implies a critical and restrictive attitude to empirical-analytical knowledge. This is the ideal and one must strive to attain it.

Now ideals can only be fully attained in exceptional cases, and compromises are inevitable. In the present study I frequently refer to research results which emanate from survey studies, i.e. a method considered to be in harmony with a positivistic view of science. I take up and criticize some of these studies, others I refer to in support of my analysis. This is inevitable because there as yet exist only a few results (in some cases none) from studies in the spirit of the critical tradition in several of the fields with which I am concerned. By trying to treat the empirical-analytical results within the framework of a critical context I hope I can adequately meet the demand for methodological rigour.

1.7   Some Problems with the Approach

In this chapter I have described my metatheoretical points of departure and have discussed general methodological considerations including considerations for applying empirical-analytical knowledge in a critical effort. Further aspects of methods are discussed in the later presentation.

The terms of reference for this study are critical theory in a broad sense in which the Frankfurt School constitutes the nucleus. With regard to the specific research task, I adopt Israel's view of the functions of critical sociology.

There are two basic problems with my contribution. The first is that the critical effort, as defined here, has been applied only to a limited extent in the research field in question.

Due to the rather early development stage in which the critical organization theory still finds itself, I am forced in part to base my work on the prevailing functionalist paradigm and much of the remaining presentation is based on its definition of reality, conceptual apparatus, etc. This means that it is difficult to keep strictly to the critical effort. In consequence of this problem in certain sections I shall hold discussions which are only indirectly connected with my overall framework.

I wish to emphasize that I have *no* ambition to attempt to create a finally formulated Frankfurtian organization theory. (Incidentally such a theory would in some sense conflict with the basic dialectical view of critical theory.)

"to embrace radical humanism involves the rejection of organisation theory as a naive, misconceived and politically distasteful enterprise. It involves entering

another paradigm, another intellectual world – indeed, an alternative reality."
(Burrell and Morgan, 1979: 324)

My study aims at making a contribution to this "alternative intellectual world", i.e. to the formulation of a critical organization theory. The ambition in connection with this can be not only to maintain a position on the intellectual ("idealistic") level but also to give a knowledgeable basis to concrete work for change and to state certain normative guidelines for the functioning of organizations (e.g. in connection with alternative production, wage-earners cooperatives and other forms of activity having targets other than maximum profits on a market). These guidelines include cooperation, undistorted communication and domination-free interaction. A primary task for a critical organization theory is, nevertheless, to create, on an intellectual level, critical understanding of the rise, functions and ideological bias of the prevailing forms of thought and of the part of the dominating organization theory in this context. And it is above all for this problem that the present study attempts to find a solution.

The other problem is of a methodological-philosophical nature. It is far from unproblematical to relate demarcated, concrete, empirical study objects to the critical theory. It is difficult to retain the critical effort when one takes on such study objects. Empirical work is least of all the strenght of the critical theory:

"I am inclined to say that critical theory has performed a so-to-speak constructive-destructive part in the debate of the last decade on "the crisis of science" by contributing to the self-awareness of modern science, wholly in accordance with the ideological-critical, hermeneutic method. According to the critics they have been reduced to *mandarins* with lofty cultural criticism mainly with regard to repertoire and they have not succeeded in offering an alternative type of research which can be made applicable. Here Marcuse is illustrative when he rejects the verification criteria of modern positivism, which are "available from the establishment" without offering anything else instead." (Eliasson, 1980: 15)

This criticism of criticism is not unjustified.[4] I believe, however, that it does not apply primarily to the incompetence of the representatives of the Frankfurt School as research workers as to the problem of integrating empiricism and criticism. Empirical studies require that the object of research is demarcated and concrete. It is difficult within one and the same effort to be demarcated, concrete and empirical as well as critical-

---

[4] I do not go into the criticism which from different quarters but mainly (orthodox) Marxist circles has been directed against the Frankfurt school. This has been expressed for example by Slater (1978) and Therborn (1970, 1971) who amongst other things attack fiercely the unwillingness of this tradition to involve itself in political questions and to develop knowledge of direct interest to the working class. Discussions on this criticism are to be found in e.g. Connerton (1980, Ch. 7) and Held (1980, Ch. 13).

philosophical. This is illustrated by the fact that representatives of critical theory have found it difficult to apply the critical effort when attempting to work empirically. This type of cogency problem is characteristic of my own study when I deal with empirical, demarcated problems. Inspiration from critical theory becames more apparent in certain chapters (above all in the four last chapters of the book), rather than as a consistent line which permeates every sentence.

These problems notwithstanding, I believe that the critical theory can function as framework for organization theory and research on working life. This study is an attempt to illustrate this, or at least to find out whether this can be the case.

2. Work Conditions in Modern Society

2.1 Braverman's Thesis

As I pointed out in the introduction, Harry Braverman's book "Labor and Monopoly Capital" (1974) is of great importance to my study, even if I agree on many points with the severe criticism which has been levelled against him. Braverman's book is a comprehensive and very broadly based study of the development and degradation of work during (above all) the Twentieth Century. The underlying thesis in Braverman's work is that job content during the present century has been broken down into simple, monotonous, strictly controlled and narrowly specialized work phases which to a high degree are lacking in demands on professional skill, mental activity and judgment on the part of the worker:

"Thus, after a million years of labor, during which humans created not only a complex social culture but in a very real sense created themselves as well, the very cultural-biological trait upon which this entire evolution is founded has been brought, within the last two hundred years, to a crisis, a crisis which Marcuse aptly calls the threat of a 'catastrophe of the human essence.' The unity of thought and action, conception and execution, hand and mind, which capitalism threatened from its beginnings, is now attacked by a systematic dissolution employing all the resources of science and the various engineering disciplines based upon it. The subjective factor of the labor process is removed to a place among its inanimate objective factors. To the materials and instruments of production are added a 'labor force,' another 'factor of production,' and the process is henceforth carried on by management as the sole subjective element. This is the ideal toward which management tends, and in pursuit of which it uses and shapes every productive innovation furnished by science." (Braverman, 1974: 171–172)

According to Braverman such a development has not only characterized the job conditions of production workers. Corresponding changes have also affected many office workers. Braverman believes that the development towards large-scale production, mechanization, automation and computerization means that a very large number of office workers

"... are subjected to routines, more or less mechanized according to current possibilities, that strip them of their former grasp of even a limited amount of office information, divest them of the need or ability to understand and decide, and make of them so many mechanical eyes, fingers, and voices whose functioning is, insofar as possible, predetermined by both rules and machinery." (p. 340)

Braverman states that a similar trend also applies to a majority of commercial and service employees, whose working and wage conditions have basically begun to be similar to those of production and office workers. According to Braverman the "real" proportion of the working class in the population has increased considerably during the Twentieth Century, provided that office workers and service employees, etc., with working and wage conditions similar to those of production workers are referred to the category worker – which Braverman considers more reasonable than to apply the traditional division into salaried employees and workers.

What, then, lies behind this development? Here technological progress naturally plays an important part. According to Braverman this is not a dominating force in itself, but an instrument which business leaders and capitalists exploit, not only to achieve efficiency in some technically neutral sense but – in order to accomplish this – also to check and control their employees:

"This attempt to conceive of the worker as a general-purpose machine operated by management is one of many paths taken toward the same goal: the displacement of labor as the subjective element of the labor process and its transformation into an object. Here the entire work operation, down to its smallest motion, is conceptualized by the management and engineering staffs, laid out, measured, fitted with training and performance standards – all entirely in advance. The human instruments are adapted to the machinery of production according to specifications that resemble nothing so much as machine-capacity specifications." (p. 180)

Braverman's influence on working life research has been, and is, very considerable. Gunnarsson (1980) writes that "few books have met with such a positive reception as his". The book has also been the subject of much criticism, but as a source of inspiration for modern research on labour process theory it has no counterpart, at least not in the English-speaking world. During the 1960's the majority of working life sociologists believed that technological development and changes in the vocational structure would lead to a demand for generally higher qualifications. During the last fifteen years, however, quite different positions have come to be at least as widespread, implying that a more or less extensive dequalification has taken and is taking place for numerous office, industrial and service jobs.

In his extensive work Braverman takes up a large number of aspects which are worth noting and discussing.[1] In this chapter, however, I shall deal exclusively with Braverman's principal thesis, i.e. that the job content has been dequalified, degraded and more strictly controlled for large numbers of workers and salaried employees during this century. Braverman is not

---

[1]) Extensive discussions of various aspects of Braverman and of the debate which he inspired are to be found in Nichols (1980) and Thompson (1983).

the only person who has advanced this argument, but on account of his great influence and for practical reasons I sometimes speak of it as "Braverman's thesis".

From Braverman's work I shall start by taking up three "sub-theses" or aspects, which it can be rewarding to discuss one after another when evaluating his book. The first aspect concerns the nature of work in modern society. Braverman states that the jobs of the working class and the lower salaried employees are monotonous, unqualified and remote-controlled. The other aspect is concerned with *the development of work* during the Twentieth Century. The dequalification thesis which asserts that job conditions are being generally developed in the direction of lower qualification demands is central here. The third aspect is *the driving forces behind the development of job conditions* and their current formation. For me the most interesting is the first and second aspects i.e. the contemporary work and the historical development. The driving forces behind this are only dealt with to a limited extent in the book. They are treated in greater detail in Alvesson (1986). My discussion of Braverman's book corresponds to these three aspects. In the following section I take up some studies which attempt to show how usual tightly controlled, monotonous and unqualified job conditions are in modern working life. In the next two sections I discuss the development trend. Here I deal with both empirical studies as well as assessments of Braverman's historical writing to be found in literature on the subject. Thereafter references comments are made to the most important criticisms of Braverman, in which problems concerning his empirical thesis and to some extent his views on the driving forces behind the development and actual nature of work are dealt with.

2.2   Some Results of Investigations of Swedish Working Life[2])

On the basis of some Swedish quantitative studies I shall attempt here to give some points of view on Braverman's thesis on the nature of modern working life. I shall concentrate on three dimensions – self-determination/

---

[2]) The reason why I concentrate on some studies of Swedish working life is that I am most familiar with these and that it is an advantage to demarcate the field in such a way that different studies can be compared in a better way than if studies from different countries are taken up. I believe that conclusions concerning Swedish working life can be largely generalized to apply to other countries with a similar level of industrialization. However, there are probably some differences depending on political and cultural circumstances, which suggests some caution before generalizing from the results of these Swedish surveys.

control, monotony/variation and qualification demands – which are central
to an assessment of Braverman's presentation.

Korpi (1978) concluded that machines or other equipment wholly or partly
controlled the rate of work of 40% of the Swedish metal workers questioned. (His data was collected in the end of the 1960's.)[3]) Bolinder and
Ohlström's (1971) study which was based on a questionnaire from the
Swedish Trade Union Confederation to about 4000 members, revealed that
7% of the members of the Swedish Trade Union Confederation[4]) considered that their rate of work was entirely governed by a conveyor belt or a
particular machine, while 16% believed that this was partly the case.

The study of living conditions carried out by the Central Bureau of Statistics
(SCB, 1978) concluded that about 13% of all employees had no influence
on their rate of work, 31% had "a certain influence" while the rest, 56%,
had "considerable influence" on their rate of work. For the category
production and distribution employees, i.e. largely corresponding to the
Trade Union members, the corresponding results were 17, 35 and 48%.

Bolinder and Ohlström's questionnaire, like the CBS study, put the question as to what planning and assessment on the part of those questioned was
required at jobs. The answers were distributed as follows:

- 16% replied that they had "mainly one-sided, monotonous work".
- 60% replied that their jobs required "a certain amount of planning and
  assessment on their part".
- 23% considered that their work demanded "a great deal of planning and
  assessment on their part".

The CBS study yielded the following result: of all the employees, nearly
one-quarter had no influence on the planning of their own work. In the case
of production and distribution employees the corresponding proportion was
one-third. According to SCB (1985) the possibilities for influence on the
work situation in Swedish working life have increased somewhat between
1975 and 1979. Both Korpi and Bolinder and Ohlström inquired concerning
the time a novice needed to learn his job. Bolinder and Ohlström concluded
that 6% of those asked believed that the job took less than 3 days to learn
and that 23% believed that the job required a learning period of 3 days – 8
weeks. This means therefore that about 30% of all the members of the
Swedish Trade Union Confederation have jobs which they believe require a

---

[3]) The investigation is a questionnaire study and is concerned with metal workers. Since this
group, beside the municipal workers, is the largest member group of the Swedish Trade
Union Confederation, the working conditions of this category are of great interest.

[4]) The questionaire and consequently also the results referred to here apply to all members of
the Swedish TUC (with the exception of seamen and musicians), thus not production
workers only.

maximum of two months to learn. About 57% were of the opinion that it took more than 6 months to learn the job. Korpi concluded that about one-third of the metal workers consulted considered that their jobs demanded more than one year's training. Two-thirds of the workers expressed the opinion that their jobs could be performed by anyone at all.

In an inquiry undertaken by the Swedish Central Bureau of Statistics in 1984–85 is transpired that of all men in employment 19% had jobs which had no demands on education and training time, while 20% had jobs which they believed required some months' to two years' education/training time. For women the corresponding figures were 30 and 24% respectively. If less than two years' education/training time is regarded as a criterion of a low degree of qualification, it follows that 39% of the men and 54% of the women belonged to this category. (This inquiry included all gainfully employed and thus a series of professional groups apart from those of primary interest to this book, type teachers, officers, professionals, etc.)

This type of results probably underestimates the extent of low qualification requirements, since the Swedish Trade Union questionnaire was limited to Swedish-speakers, while Korpi's study also included Finnish-speakers. Naturally it is probable that employees who cannot speak Swedish are primarily given jobs which make low demands. The dequalification of the work can therefore be even more marked than is indicated by the above data. Because many people are probably unwilling to admit that their jobs are very simple and unqualified, it is conceivable that there is a tendency to "revalue" the learning period in the above-mentioned data. There is also a tendency for questionnaire studies and similar "superficial" methods to generate answers which "gloss over" the issues with a faintly positive bias (Björkman and Lundqvist, 1981). Having discovered that attempts to pin down working environment aspects with the aid of questionnaires resulted in the answers being in poor accord with "objective" conditions, Björkman and Lundqvist draw the conclusion that one must have recourse to detailed interviews to overcome the defence which makes people answer superficial questions positively in order to maintain their self-respect.

The types of questionnaires referred to here are scarcely a reliable instrument to shed light on the questions which are of interest here. We can ask ourselves what "a *certain* amount of planning and assessment" means. Also "a rate of work *partly* governed by machines". The scope for variation in the formulation of the meaning of these questions is so great that it appears to be difficult to draw any conclusions from the answers. This applies to a still greater extent to the CBS study which for the majority of the questions only permitted to alternative answers – yes or no.

With regard to the control/influence dimension, the studies referred to yielded somewhat contradictory results. The Swedish Trade Union questionnaire concluded that not quite one-quarter of the members had their rate of work entirely (7%) or partly (16%) governed by a conveyor belt or a machine. The CBS study (SCB, 1978) found that slightly more than half (52%) of, largely, the same category lacked (17%) or had only "a certain" influence (35%) on their own rate of work. It seems difficult to draw any conclusions from such different results. The varied answers in both studies point to severe problems with respect to methods.

The methodological problems implicit in the use of questionnaires are naturally also present in the matter of qualification requirements, but are probably not so marked as when people are asked whether they have "a certain" influence on their situation. Admittedly there is wide scope for the determination of meaning also in questions of the type "How long do you think it would take to learn your job in the case of a novice straight from the comprehensive school?" But the possibilities of making a fairly reasonable judgment are somewhat better for those required to answer this question: a period of learning can be stated quantitatively, which an assessment as to what extent a job requires planning by the worker himself can scarcely permit. With regard to jobs with an assessed learning period of considerable extent, the scope for different judgments is great because the work may be expected to be relatively difficult and it is much harder to assess the demands of qualified jobs than of unqualified. However, I can imagine that a certain concord and reliability can be attained in assessing unqualified jobs. I therefore believe that conclusions can be drawn with a certain degree of reliability from assessments of jobs with short learning periods which Bolinder and Ohlström and Korpi have obtained, even though also the conclusions from this material can only be drawn with great caution.

Bolinder and Ohlström's study revealed that nearly 30% of the Trade Union members asked judged that their jobs would only require a learning period of a maximum of 8 weeks for a novice straight from the comprehensive school. As observed above, two-thirds of Korpi's subjects considered that anyone at all could perform their jobs equally well. These statements give some support to Braverman's thesis about low qualification requirements. However, we can scarcely regard this as a clear and unmistakable indication that Braverman is right. Nor do they say anything about how the qualification requirements have developed.

To sum up I should like to state that Braverman's standpoint is difficult to judge against the background of the material referred to here. The methodological problems are very serious. Not least there is reason to suppose that the subjects of the questionnaire studies express too optimistic a view of the conditions in order to adjust to jobs characterized by a low level of qualifications and strict control. With this reservation we can at the very most draw the conclusion that Braverman is to a certain extent supported by data indicating that very low qualification requirements are common, whereas data on control emerge as uncertain and difficult to judge. The material referred to possibly suggests that Braverman is a little too categorical in his presentation.

2.3   Research on Qualification/Dequalification

I shall now discuss some research and assessments on the direction of changes in the level of qualifications of job content in industry and other activities in recent times. This research has studied current or recently implemented changes and draws from these conclusions as to the validity of various testimonies concerning the development of job content with respect to qualifications.

Most research workers in this field believe that this type of research demands highly detailed studies if reliable results are to be obtained. Data of the type branch statistics with respect to skilled workers, unskilled workers and semiskilled workers at different times are to be considered as virtually worthless sources of information (Berggren, 1982, Braverman, 1974). The need for accurate empirical investigations means that most of the research is of case-study character. Subjects studied are one or several workplaces/companies, a branch or part of a branch, or workplaces typical of different branches. Individual studies shed light on large sectors of industry. A study by Kern and Schumann (1970), the most extensive in the field I am aware of, is based on data comprising 32 organizations/factories and 981 interviews with workers (referred to by Bergman and Helgeson, 1983).

Today, more than ten years after the publication of Braverman's book, there is a very large number of studies of labour processes. Since my book is not within the field of labour process theory, but only intends to utilize some important conclusions from research on this subject, I will content myself with referring to some of these studies before going on to discuss what conclusions can be drawn from this research with regard to the development of job content. An extensive review of research, mainly in the English language, is to be found in Thompson (1983). References to numerous German studies are made in Haug et al. (1978).

In the following short review of some studies I start with research on industrial work and then mention a couple of studies on clerical work.

- Kronlund and Wigblad (1981) studied job conditions at a small steelwork before and after the introduction of a new technique. Among their conclusions it may be noted that the proficiency of some workers became superfluous as a result of the change of technique and mechanization, and also that the workers were given less freedom as the new production required each to devote himself to his specialized task.

- Noble (1979) has studied various considerations which lay behind the design of automatically controlled machine tools. (Machine tools are machines used for cutting metal.) He does not treat the qualification conditions in much detail, but devotes his analysis to comparing two possible technologies for changing the labour process. Of these two preference was given to numerical control. According to Noble the reason was that not only was this technique economically more efficient than the other, but also the control interest was of great importance. Noble refers to an interview with a consulting engineer who, amongst other things, remarked:

> "Look, with record-playback the control of the machine remains with the machinist - control of feeds, speeds, number of cuts, output; with N/C there is a shift of control to management. Management is no longer dependent upon the operator and can thus optimize the use of their machines. With N/C, control over the process is placed firmly in the hands of management – and why shouldn't we have it?" (Noble, 1979: 34)

The introduction of numerical control in the form it has been applied at the companies Noble has studied, resulted in stronger control and the dequalification of job conditions in relation to both earlier conditions as well as to alternative technologies which have come under consideration.

- Zimbalist (1979) reveals in a study of the American printing industry that the introduction of new technology in recent decades, which was preceded by a long period of successful resistance by the printers, resulted in highly developed skills becoming useless. A similar tendency in Sweden is described by Ehn and Sandberg (1982).
- In their extensive study of the relationship between technical development and various types of industrial jobs from the end of the 1960's, the West Germans Kern and Schumann (referred to in Bergman and Helgeson, 1983) conclude that the continuing mechanization and automation lead to the parallel growth of conventional repetitive sub-jobs alongside new qualified jobs. Only a small part of the proportion of jobs in partly-automated industrial plants involve automation work in its qualified form. An increasing proportion of industrial jobs are concerned with repairs and maintenance, which are relatively often fairly well qualified. At the side of these, however, at automated workplaces, there are a great many jobs characterized by lack of freedom and low qualification requirements.
Kern and Schumann's study indicates that technical development leads to a polarized job structure in which the number of jobs involving both high

and low qualifications is on the increase (at the cost of the intermediate group). This view is known as the polarization thesis.

- In a later study, with empirical facts collected 15 years after the implementation of the first investigation, Kern and Schumann (1984, quoted by Broady and Helgeson, 1985) find that the unskilled pole tends to shrink in certain areas of work in which modernization has advanced far.

"If we were previously forced to speak of the polarization of production work, of the contrast between the relatively skilled plant control job and the unskilled employment in partly automated machine systems, so during this time one of the poles have nearly melted away." (Kern and Schumann, 1984: 89)

Kern and Schumann find that business managements, instead of trying to make themselves independent of the workers' skills, make far-reaching attempts to utilize the skills better. They speak of re-professionalization of industrial work and believe that this has tended to be upgraded during the 1980's.

- Another West German research programme, performed by Projektgruppe Automation und Qualifikation (Haug et al., 1978), reaches the conclusion that many of the low qualification jobs which technical development created in recent times have been withdrawn or will be withdrawn as a result of continued automation. They believe that a majority of the occupations which have been referred to as evidence of the dequalification tendency have been replaced or are able to be replaced by mechanical systems. The routine job of card punching is disappearing, for example, as new machines are being produced for the purpose.

- A study by Glenn and Feldberg (1979) deals with changes in office jobs. Like Braverman, these authors believe we can speak of the proletarianization of office workers and by this they mean that office work has begun increasingly to resemble work in a factory. Glenn and Feldberg describe the general development as follows:

"... the general outline is clear. New office systems will use a technology based on subdivision and standardization. Choices among different work structures now available to workers will be considerably narrowed for those working in large organizations.

... old skills have been made trivial and opportunities to develop new skills have been reduced. Such traditional specialities as stenography and bookkeeping, which required extensive training, have been displaced or simplified beyond recognition. The skills now required are more *mechanical,* as in operating a xerox machine, *lower level,* as in typing addresses on automatically typed correspondence, and/or *more technical and narrow*, as in the administrative support center." (Ibid p. 61)

Similar observations have been made by Crompton and Reid (1982). However, the above-mentioned study by Haug et al. (1978) points out that current technical development is leading to the automation of many routine jobs.

- Another study of changes in office jobs deals specially with the insurance business, de Kadt (1979) declares that the division of labour and standardization of routines and labour processes have led to an impoverishment of job content for large numbers of insurance employees. As an indication of the job dequalification de Kadt mentions that, whereas fifteen years ago aspirants were required to take a seventeen-week introductory course, nowadays the training is given either directly at work or by means of a two-week course.
- In agreement with de Kadt's presentation is Brunander's (1979) study of an insurance company where computerization resulted in numerous proficiencies becoming superfluous.
  Yet another field in which division of labour and dequalification are documented is computerized data processing. Braverman himself takes up this case (Braverman, 1974: 285 ff). His views are confirmed by studies by Greenbaum (1976), Sandberg (1979) and Cooley (1980).
- On the basis of secondary data from the 6–7 years recurrent standard of living investigations in Sweden, Åberg (1984) has studied how the distribution of the working population in various types of jobs has changed between 1968 and 1981. The classification into job types is based partly on the educational requirements which different vocational tasks are associated with, partly on questions of mental strain and monotony in jobs. (Monotony is considered to mean low demands with regard to qualifications, whereas mental stress combined with non-monotony is interpreted as an expression of demands for intellectual involvement in the job, which can be compared with relatively high qualification requirements.) Of all Swedish blue-collar workers in 1968, 29% had relatively qualified jobs (which were considered to require at least two years' vocational training and which were not considered by the employees to be monotonous) whereas about as many, 28%, had the same in 1981. The proportion of relatively unskilled jobs was thus constant between these years. (64 and 67% respectively had jobs which required less than two years' vocational training and on both occasions 7% had jobs which required at least two years' vocational training but which were regarded as monotonous in character.) The qualification level for Swedish blue-collar workers should thus, according to this information, have been constant throughout this period. For salaried employees the proportion of relatively unskilled jobs had fallen from 30% to 22% during the period. The relative proportion of skilled jobs had risen to a corresponding extent.

Åberg concludes that this information contradicts Braverman by showing that no degrading of jobs has taken place. In the case of salaried employees there has been a certain amount of upgrading. Whether the latter is due to the creation of a number of expert appointment, etc., in industry and commerce and of jobs in the public sector of the type administrator and teacher, this information is not, however, incompatible with Braverman's views. Nor does it tell us anything about the way the various types of jobs have changed with respect to content. A further point which should be considered is the possibility that the borders between the various types of jobs may have shifted in such a way that several jobs tend to be coded as requiring a longer period of training. The training expansion of recent decades (which is probably largely influenced for employment reasons and more severe competition on the labour market) is leading to more jobs being held by people who have at least a couple of years' education over and above compulsory schooling. This can mean that the assessment of educational requirements for various jobs has been influenced. (Between 1968 and 1981 the average educational time for individuals with the least skilled jobs increased by rather more than one year.)

• Some information in a statistical survey of working conditions (SCB, 1985) is also of relevance in this context even though it only indirectly sheds light on changes in job content. According to this, the proportion of those who work on automated machines in Sweden who have "very repetitive tasks and a maximum of some months' training period (the same tasks and movements being repeated many times per hour during at least half the working hours)" amounts to 42% (SCB, 1985: 128). This indicates that the technological development should not only or even mainly create skilled tasks.

So far we have referred to some direct empirical studies. Literature on the subject contains also numerous analyses and views based on materials other than direct studies of qualification development in industry and offices, e.g. theoretical analyses, studies of work organization forms or other themes of relevance to the question of qualifications and studies of research on labour process theory. I shall refer briefly to some studies of this kind.

A book which reveals a great many similarities to Braverman's is Mendner's "Technologische Entwicklung und Arbeitsprozess" (1975). Mendner's work is largely based on Kern and Schumann's extensive empirical work on West German industry. Like Braverman, Mendner emphasizes control from above (exercised through technology) and dequalification of job content. However, he does not generalize quite so much, nor is he so deterministic, as Braverman, but points to limitations in the possibilities of controlling the workers and the possibilities of increased influence on their part which this can mean. In the main, however, Mendner's views agree with those of Braverman.

Support for Braverman's thesis is also to be found in Sandberg (1978) and Sandkull et al. (1981; 1982).

"The direction in which the work organizational changes have proceeded is well known. Division of labour, mechanization, specialization and planning have resulted in ever simpler, shorter and more monotonous tasks." (Sandberg, 1978: 37–38)

A similar view is formulated by Sandkull et al. who have studied the employees' possibilities of exercising influence on the technological development of various companies:

"The division of labour in modern companies, both in industry and in commerce, both on the factory floor and in the office, has resulted in the majority of employees performing standardized and limited tasks over and over again. These conditions apply also to companies which are owned by the state, local government, trade unions, consumer-cooperatives or farmer cooperatives. Almost all of these have followed the privately-owned companies' management model." (Sandkull et al., 1981: 1)

Several authors emphasize, however, that there are several different kinds of work organization in existence and that these are in the course of development. Therefore we cannot merely generalize and regard those which are based on farreaching division of labour and control – often with accompanying dequalification – as the most widespread. Variations on this theme are expressed, amongst others, by Edwards (1979), Friedman (1977), and Wood (1982). Friedman believes, for example, that a form of work organization based on responsible autonomy has become more common, above all in the economically more robust sectors of industry. Kern and Schumann (1984) also propose that a new "production concept", based on holistic, integrated and flexible structuring of work have become more common since the end of the 1970's. A discussion expressing scepticism of the scope of this type of development is to be found in Thompson (1983, Ch. 5).

In his extensive study and analysis of research on labour process, in which both studies which support and studies which criticize Braverman are dealt with, Thompson reaches the following summary conclusion on the development of job content in relation to qualifications:

"Evidence does now show that factors such as labour markets and worker resistance operate as constraints on the divisibility of skills. It is also the case that there are cycles of deskilling, related to the conditions of capital accumulation, that manifest contradictory tendencies between and within industries. These constraints and variations are important, and question the rather one-dimensional and unilinear approach of writers like Braverman. Workers' skills, however, *are* normally an obstacle to the full utilisation of the means of production by capital. *How* that obstacle is modified or removed depends on the specific circumstances. But the fact that variation of circumstances between and within sectors negates a crude deskilling thesis has unfortunately been used to construct an overly 'agnostic' perspective, as in Wood's introduction to his (1982) collection of articles. Deskilling remains the major *tendential* presence within the development of the capitalist labour process." (Thompson, 1983: 118)

The West German studies, however, tend to point in the opposite direction, which may indicate that there are differences between the Anglo-Saxian countries and West Germany.

2.4 Braverman and Simon

Most of the authors who have shown interest in the question of the development of work are sociologists. Many of them, like Braverman, are inspired by Marxism. As a rule they are also "Post-Bravermanian" and keep Braverman's book as a valuable source of inspiration, which may have meant a certain cognitive and theoretical control. Something of this kind is also characteristic of my presentation. On these grounds it is interesting to note that Herbert A. Simon, psychologist, economist, etc., who in most respects has adopted a position which is very far from Braverman's, in a book on automation describes a viewpoint which is remarkably close to Braverman's principal thesis.

One of Braverman's most important points is that the work organizational principles which have been traditionally applied to production have been developed and spread to include the job situation of office personnel also. Simon expresses the same view:

"Both the factory and the office, then, are rapidly becoming complex man-machine systems with a very large amount of production equipment, in the case of the factory, and computing equipment, in the case of the office, per employee. The clerical department and the factory will come more and more to resemble each other." (Simon, 1965: 34)

Braverman states that office workers are being proletarianized. A tendency towards impoverishment and control from above/mechanical control of job content is, according to Braverman, characteristic of higher and higher professional levels in companies to an increasing extent.

This view is also represented by Simon:

"... there is reason to believe that the kind of activities that now characterize middle management will be more completely automated than the others, and hence will come to have a somewhat smaller part in the whole management picture." (p. 47)

However, Simon goes still further than this: he believes that in future the work of top management will also be programmed. Simon thus drives the thesis of distinguishing between planning and thinking on the one hand and execution on the other hand very far. To Simon computerization and other techniques for programming human activities are taking over control from human beings.

"Companies are just beginning to discover ways of bringing together the first two of these developments: of combining the mathematical techniques for making decisions about aggregative middle-management variables with the data-processing techniques for implementing these decisions in detail at clerical levels." (p. 75)

"An important principle of organization design that has emerged over the years has been called facetiously 'Gresham's Law of Planning.' It states that programmed activity tends to drive out nonprogrammed activity." (p. 67)

This trend makes it essential to set up special departments in companies in order to produce non-programmed thinking activities.

"The creation of organizational units to carry on these activities allocates brain-power to nonprogrammed thought, and provides some minimal assurance that such thought will occur in the organization." (p. 67)

Thus from entirely different positions Braverman and Simon agree on a very similar description of job/organizational development, even if Simon's views go, if possible, still further than Braverman's. Towards the consequences of this development Simon adopts an entirely different attitude to Braverman's. Simon believes that

"We must be cautious, then, in inferring, because managerial work will be more highly programmed in the future than it has been in the past – as it almost certainly will – that it will thereby be less satisfying or less creative." (p. 98)

Instead

"... they seem to me changes that will make it easier rather than harder for the executive's daily work to be a significant and satisfying part of his life." (p. 111)

But how, then, is the situation changed for the person who is not a business leader? Here Simon makes a somewhat contradictory impression. On one and the same page (p. 97) he writes, obviously with the aim of making the reader positively disposed to the programming and automation of work, that automation

"... has probably tended to make work less, rather than more, routine ..."

And also that routines are positive in themselves:

"Routine is a welcome refuge from the trackless forest of unfamiliar problem spaces."

(The psychosocial consequences of planned routine jobs will be dealt with in the following chapter. I shall therefore leave this subject for the time being.)

Despite their different views concerning the effects of the development on individuals, Braverman and Simon have similar ideas on the development tendency as far as job content is concerned. Actually they do not really have the same time perspective – Braverman is mainly concerned with the historical trend, while Simon is looking to the future – but both claim to capture the development trend characteristic of the 1960's and 1970's. Simon's standpoint can therefore be said to offer sound support for Braverman's dequalification thesis.

2.5 Criticism of Braverman

It is now time to deal with the criticism which has been directed against Braverman. I start with an article by Berggren (1982) who states that Braverman's presentation is founded on three basic postulates:

- Control of the labour force is a central aim of capitalists and business management.
- It is possible to derive a general form of work organization out of the capitalistic production system, namely the Tayloristic one.
- The position of power of capitalism is such that its intentions can for the most part be realized in practice.

These postulates express the factors behind the dequalification process. Berggren does not reject these postulates directly but considers that they must be qualified and modified. Amongst other things he believes that Braverman carries the control interest too far, that he does not take account of the fact that the costs of far-reaching control (e.g. through MTM) are considerable, and that far-reaching division of labour entails losses, e.g. in the form of low motivation. It may be added that corporation leaders for the most part have scope for action permitting them to choose between different principles of organization and that there can be considerable differences between managers with regard to the choices they make. They differ with respect to values, background, style of leadership, etc. It should also be noted that companies differ with regard to size, marketing, type of production, etc., and that this has consequences for the question of control which Braverman does not take up. This point of view is relevant to the second postulate, i.e. whether there is a general capitalist work organization. This cannot be derived theoretically but must be treated as an empirical question. A general thesis requires a general verification. Braverman's material is limited to case studies of individual of important occupations. Berggren refers here to Edwards (1979) who believes that the Taylorist organization principles in certain companies, mainly research- and salaried employee-intensive corporations such as IBM and Polaroid, have given ground to what Edwards calls "bureaucratic control". This form of control implies control by means of highly differentiated job category divisions, thoroughly differentiated and individualized salary scales, evaluation and promotion procedures, etc. bureaucratic control has been developed for higher organization levels but has worked its way down the hierarchy. According to Edwards bureaucratic control means an overstepping of Taylorism. Edwards' conclusion is open to question as he does not have much empirical material to support him. I cannot really see why bureaucratic control necessarily implies a break with Taylorist principles. Rather the former may be looked upon as a complement to the latter. (Cf. Thompson, 1983: 146–150) However, we can say that there are at least considerable efforts to create other forms of work organization than the Taylorist. (See further Chapter 6.)

Taylorism does not suit all forms of industrial activity. Taylorist techniques are difficult to apply to important and uncertain variations in raw material or production processes (Wood and Kelly, 1982: 86). The same applies to numerous works on automated production. Evidently Braverman grossly exaggerates the spread and inevitability of Taylorism.

The third postulate has been criticized by numerous authors, e.g., Edwards (1979), Friedman (1977) and Littler and Salaman (1982). Braverman describes the development as though the intentions of capital can be put into practice without problems. Against this view Berggren writes as follows:

"... the concrete forms of application of technique are formed in an *entire field of force,* determined by the structuring of capital (and possibly fragmentation), the organization (respectively splitting) of labour, and the relations between capital and the workers." (Berggren, 1982: 12)

From the latter assumption it follows that we cannot reckon on developments in the USA and in Sweden or Great Britain and West Germany, for example, where relations between labour and capital are somewhat different both nationally and locally, being entirely the same.

Some of the viewpoints expressed in the criticism will be treated from time to time later in this presentation, and I therefore leave these for the moment. This applies, amongst other things, to the motivation problem. With regard to Braverman's stressing of a specific capitalistic interest in a narrow detailed form of control, I agree that he goes much too far (cf. Alvesson, 1986). Whether it is the control or the profitability interest which is the primary reason for the development of work is not, however, of decisive importance to the correctness of Braverman's description of the actual development of work during the Twentieth Century, and since it is the latter which is of interest in this book I shall not delve further into the question.

To me the most interesting problem is, however, to what extent work has generally been developed as Braverman describes it. Before I go into the criticism of Braverman's general thesis I shall deal briefly with a couple of problems in connection with the determination of the development of qualifications.

One major problem is associated with the difficulty of defining and empirically measuring qualification. How shall we compare, for example, "knowledge" with "responsibility", "attentiveness" with "manual dexterity"? Often the degree of qualification is defined as the time of training plus learning required, on average, to attain normal performance. (In this book the concept of qualification has approximately this meaning.) It is a rather simple definition and at its best it yields a somewhat rough and ready measurement of qualification.

Another problem, prior to assessment of the development of qualification, is concerned with determining which vocational categories are to be included. Karlsson (1982) writes that development has probably gone in the direction of increased vocational proficiency in consequence of the more and more complicated technological, commercial and administrative structures implicit in the development of society. But here are included all kinds of gainfully employed, including top managers and specialists. The average level of qualification for all categories in society is not of interest in this context, since this is partly determined by the addition of some specialist and management appointments. Braverman's thesis does not include the latter. For him, as for me (and the majority of research workers on working life), what is of interest is the large employee groups at lower levels in industrial and office companies.

Braverman's postulate is that a general dequalification takes place and his failure to add any modifying statements has encountered severe criticism.

Berggren believes that

"It is impossible to derive a general tendency to dequalification of the labour force on the basis of capitalistic development and the spreading of Scientific Management in production and offices. The question of up and down grading of the collected labour force is in the highest degree an empirical problem which has not yet found its solution." (Berggren, 1982: 14)

Berggren expresses doubt as to whether the spread of Taylorism and subsequent dequalification are applied to existing activities and tasks in such a way that craftsman-type jobs are broken down and turned into fragmented detail work. Berggren believes – and refers to certain empirical material in support of his views – that this is only taking place to a limited extent and that dequalification for the most part results from the appearance of new activities, in which Tayloristic principles are applied from the start. However, here it may be noted that dequalification does often happen when new technologies replace older ones in one and the same field of activity.

Other authors express even more severe criticism of a general dequalification thesis. They point out that even if some occupations and jobs undergo dequalification, there are also cases of requalification and the raising of qualifications (see e.g. Karlsson, 1982; Wood and Kelly, 1982). Differences with regard to the development of qualifications can also be found in the same type of work between different companies. Jones (1982) studied the use of NC (numerical control) in five manufacturing industrial companies and found that the qualification level varied considerably, even if the introduction of NC in several cases implied a certain amount of dequalification. Jones concluded that NC technique does not necessarily have to imply dequalification and increased control.

Kern and Schumann's first study (1970) indicates that, alongside a development in the direction of dequalification for many jobs, continued technical development can also imply that the qualifications for many jobs are raised. Their second large study (1984) points towards a tendency towards increased qualifications. Haug et al. (1978) believes that

"The empirical studies on the development of qualifications are clearly contradictory. There is no thesis which will not permit itself to be supported by an empirical study, whether it is a case of the raising, lowering or polarization of qualifications." (pp. 141–2)

Haug et al. refer to studies from the same branch of industry which yield different results and believe that the contradictions in the results cannot be traced back to differences between the places of employment in different branches of industry and activities. They name five studies which point out that office automation leads to the polarization of the qualification structure for office workers and two studies which cite higher qualifications. Regarding metal industry, references are made to two studies which state that automation does not lead to any significant changes, one which points to higher qualifications and one which concludes that dequalification will be the result. Haug et al. observe that these studies are concerned with approximately the same time period so that the differences in the results can scarcely be referred to the time factor.

Some of the rather disparate results which the studies referred to in this chapter present may nevertheless be to some extent due to the various time at which the studies were performed. Another dimension which probably plays some part is the nations in which the various investigations took place. Whereas the West German studies indicate increased demands for skill, most of the British and American studies support the degrading thesis. To some extent this reflects actual differences in development, which can in turn be due to, amongst other things, political, cultural and labour market factors. In a comparative study of British and West German manufacturing firms on the impact of micro-electronics on the quality of working life it was shown that in Britain the new technology leads to greater de-skilling of blue-collar workers, much more so than in Germany where blue-collar workers (craftsmen) tend to be trained to handle and understand CNC-technology (Hartmann et al., 1984). In countries with sharp conflicts between capital and labour the representatives of the former can have an interest in trying to reduce the power base of the workers which a qualified job content brings about. This is, however, a complex question and I shall content myself with merely pointing it out.

Furthermore it is possible that various attitudes of researchers play a part in the way they conceive of and report their results. Different criteria, different ideas and interests lying behind the selection of what is to be presented may also play a part here. Haug et al., for example, are interested in stressing the possibilities in development and warn against "miserable discourses" on the degrading of work, which can be taken as a reason for cutting down training and in this way prove to be a fulfilling of their own prophecies (Broady and Helgeson, 1985). The interest of Braver-man and many others, on the other hand, is to express criticism.

These types of explanations, however, probably account for only a small part of the heterogeneous character of the research under review. We must note there is no dominant trend but that there are examples of both degrading and upgrading of job content and that these differ among various places of employment, companies, epochs, branches of industry and countries. On these grounds it is understandable that a common reaction to Braverman's generalizations is sceptical.

Wood (1982) writes that a "rough and ready dequalification thesis" must be rejected" and argues for the need for detailed empirical studies. It should, however, be observed that the named critics are also positive about Braverman in a number of respects. Berggren believes that Braverman's considerable influence is justified and Karlsson (1982: 13) writes that

"Harry Braverman pointed out quite rightly a very important fact when he declared that the vast majority of workers, in both industry and offices, were engaged in jobs which lay below their mental capacity."

There is extensive material supporting this view. The criticism cited means that the scope of Braverman's thesis on the dequalification of work must be questioned. The criticism indicates that Braverman's presentation is far too categorical, lacking nuances and reservations as to how far the thesis can be driven. Obviously there are many examples of working conditions which have requalified or have had their qualifications raised, while many companies avail themselves of forms of work organization other than the traditional, inspired by the scientific management philosophy. At the same time many empirical studies and a number of research scholars support Braverman on the whole. There is reason to believe that not only does technical development often lead to dequalification of job content for large groups, but also that the opposite development takes place.

2.6   Conclusion

Harry Braverman's book is an important work. Perhaps it is one of the most significant contributions to sociology in the 1970's. But this is not to say that it is undisputable. Statements of the following kind appear to be open to doubt:

"Like a rider who uses reins, bridle, spurs, carrot, whip, and training from birth to impose his will, the capitalist strives, through management, to control." (Braverman, 1974: 68)

What is interesting here, however, is mainly Braverman's principal thesis: has job content been generally developed in the direction of dequalification and increased external control? Is the job situation for the majority of people in modern industrial and office work impoverished?

I have tried to discuss whether it is possible to answer these questions on the basis of studies of a quantitative nature concerning job conditions in working life. Different studies point to partly different conditions: Korpi's study of metal workers points to extensive dequalification, while the Swedish TUC questionnaire does not point so clearly in the same direction. The CBS study (SCB, 1978) suggests far fewer possibilities of influence than those indicated in the Swedish TUC study. These studies probably tend to underestimate the extent of unqualified job conditions.

The empirical studies of the Korpi, Bolinder and Ohlström and CBS type are characterized by extensive methodological problems which add to the difficulties of reaching reliable conclusions based on the material. There is reason to be sceptical with regard to studies of this kind, as Björkman and Lundqvist (1981) amongst others, point out in their study. Conclusions from these can thus only be reached with great caution.

The qualitative, historical and/or development-orientated studies to which I referred mainly in section 2.3 better capture the aspects which are of importance here. Several of these studies indicate a development in the direction of increased division of labour, standardization and dequalification of work content, but there are also extensive studies which point in the opposite direction.

Among research workers who represent a standpoint similar to Braverman's with regard to the aspects which are relevant here is Simon. Independently of Braverman and ten years before him, Simon describes a trend which in all essentials is in full agreement with Braverman's thesis. Subsequently, when it is a matter of what that trend "means" with regard to positive/negative aspects, Simon and Braverman are of different opinions. I shall revert to this later.

Braverman's book has, however, aroused considerable criticism, especially in recent years. Amongst other things the critics declare that the dequalification thesis is far too general, or even erroneous, and that Braverman exaggerates the spread of Taylorism. The critics object to excessively rough and ready generalizations and stress the need for detailed studies of different branches of industry, companies and skills. I am partly in agreement with these critics, but believe that it is important to produce descriptions and theses at various levels, even at aggregated levels. In this study the aggregated level is of principal interest.

With regard to the principles of the Taylorist work organization, these have not been developed uninterruptedly nor without alternatives, but, even so, much of current working life seems to be dominated by Taylorist ideas in one form or another. (See the section "Scientific management" in Ch. 6.)

An attempt to weigh up the material which I have gone through in this chapter in order to try to determine the reasonableness of Braverman's thesis reaches the following conclusion:

Braverman has shown that the previously generally accepted idea of the consequences of technical development for work, i.e. that increasingly more qualified and more interesting jobs would be created, is false at least in part. The current development means that in any case a number of jobs are dequalified and degraded. Subsequent research has mainly confirmed the thesis that such dequalification does in fact occur, even though the precise extent of this trend, and its significance in relation to changes resulting in requalification and the raising of qualifications for jobs, have not been surveyed in a manner which would make it possible to draw definite conclusions. Apparantly, a number of jobs have been upgraded during the recent decades. The surveys illustrating the general qualification level of industrial work indicate that this is often low. Unqualified work is common. This is in line with Braverman but as a theory on the general development of labour under capitalism his book displays considerable shortcomings. However, it is also possible to read his book in another way, namely from the point of view of critique of ideology.

The latter approach means that Braverman's book should be regarded above all as a powerful antidote to previous ideas about working conditions in the kind of society which Braverman calls monopoly capitalism. These earlier notions, which have come to be expressed in numerous works of research, were bound up with the idea that the increasingly advanced industrial society was rapidly approaching Utopia, even in the case of the working class. Kumar describes the sociological view of this matter in the 1950's and 1960's as follows:

"The worker may not always be satisfied and integrated, but the future trend will lead in that direction. The emphasis on the emergent 'utopia' of automation was a characteristic feature of writings in this period." (Kumar, referred to in Thompson, 1983: 17)

Against these idyllic pictures Braverman presents a powerful picture of the development of the labour process, in which degradation tendencies are placed in the centre. By bringing to the fore this aspect, he reveals the falseness of the views of previous labour and organization sociologists. Not seldom did these scientists place the workers' conduct and attitudes in the centre, presenting a generally idealized and misleading picture of the workers' situation, amongst other things, by not taking up seriously the nature of work, which must be regarded as the decisive factor in the working situation.

This reading of Braverman means that the degradation thesis should not mainly be regarded as something which must be hypothetically proved against an objective reality. The thesis constitutes rather a basis for criticism of authors who consistently emphasize positive features of development and of current conditions. And Braverman devotes considerable force and lucidity to the criticism of various authors, texts and presentations as having an ideological bias.

In the first instance it is in this critical sense that I make use of Braverman's book in my presentation. My point of departure is that Braverman and extensive research after him, are right when they emphasize that the continuous technical development in recent decades has resulted in the dequalification of many jobs, even if it is doubtful whether this constitutes a main trend. The occurrence of such a development provides me with an important point of departure for the discussion of different organization theories. This also yields for the fact that unqualified work is very common in contemporary working life.

Before embarking on my continued presentation, I repeat that I base my work not on Braverman as the father of a complete theory of the character of labour under monopoly capitalism, but content myself with the (much less ambitious) thesis in his book that technical development has brought about a more or less extensive but in academic literature before him largely neglected degradation of a considerable number of jobs.

Before proceeding I shall make a distinction. I shall speak of industrial and "quasi-industrial" jobs. By the latter concept I mean activities which are not to be found in industry but which are organized according to traditionally typical industrial principles of work organization, i.e. the Tayloristic. The spread of the industrial work organization form to other sectors of working life such as medical care and offices means that we can speak of a "quasi-industrial working life" and "quasi-industrial organizations" (cf. Ingelstam, 1980, Ch. 15). By applying these concepts I wish to make it clear that discussions which primarily concern industrial companies may also hold true of many other types of organizations. For this reason I also – intentionally – switch between speaking of companies and of organizations. As Braverman and other studies referred to have shown, an increasing part of working life has acquired this "quasi-industrial" character.

3. The Importance of Work to the Individual

In the preceding chapter I dealt with some aspects of modern working life. I shall now relate these working conditions to the individual's psychosocial job situation. The presentation is intended to answer questions of the type: What does work mean to the individual? Is it of decisive or limited importance to his general satisfaction in life and to his quality of life? What working conditions exercise the most negative effects on the individual's mental well-being? Are we justified in speaking of some working conditions as being, in general, mentally gruelling?

The aim of this chapter is to provide a basis for the judgment and analysis of the human being's job and life situation in relation to the form of rationality which governs working life and society.

Furthermore, at the end of the chapter I discuss some aspects of the sociology of science relevant to the field of research treated in the chapter. I offer an interpretation of the reason why the relationship job content – mental health came to be "overlooked" for a long time in research on working life and why it was subsequently "discovered".

3.1   The Concept of Mental Health

To give a definition of the absolute border between mental health and mental illness is impossible since such a border scarcely exists in reality. Westlander and Baneryd (1970) illustrate the concept of mental health by means of the following figure:

Mental sickness   ⟷   Mental health

←——————————————————————————————→

Psychopathology   "Normal" personality   Ideal personality
(according to socio-   (maximum health)
cultural standards)

This way of regarding mental health/illness is linked to the WHO concept of health which defines mental health as "physical, mental and social well-being and not just the absence of sickness".

It is difficult to give the concept a theoretically tenable definition. The problem is complicated by the fact that mental health is not a static characteristic but has to be related to the environment and the situation in which the individual finds himself. Lohmann (1972) treats this set of problems in considerable detail and observes that the theoretical difficulties are so comprehensive that it is tempting to consider mental health as a "will o' the wisp."

Katz and Kahn (1978) express a similar opinion, but consider that there is a certain convergence between authors who believe that mental health means freedom from distressing symptoms (gastric discomfort, anxiety, inability to sleep, etc.) and around positive affect towards self and towards life.

In occupational psychology mental health is often considered to be (operationalized as) the individual's subjective experience of well-being and mental satisfaction. The interesting point about this study is the way different job conditions generate different experiences of mental health.

How the individual feels about his mental health and his well-being is often sufficient to provide a "covering" picture of the question at issue. Most of the studies referred to in the next part attempt to pin down mental health in this way. The experience of mental health or illness does not cover the entire range of problems. This is obvious when we think of manic and psychotic people who, without necessarily feeling sick, are obviously suffering from mental problems. Over and above experienced poor mental condition and psychotic behaviour there is another set of mental problems, character problems (character neurosis or other disturbances of the personality). This often proves to be the source of at least temporary experiences of suffering, but the individual can feel quite well in a social environment which is so to speak in harmony with his psychology. The good adjustment of the individual to environments which generate distress for the majority of people can frequently be regarded rather as an expression of mental health than the contrary, e.g. the masochistic or the authoritarian personality in a repressive social system. This aspect can be relevant to work and organization contexts also. To experience pleasurable adjustment and satisfaction in many contemporary common jobs according to the survey in Chapter 2 can not thus immediately be identified with mental health. Socialization at work and changes of personality as a stage in this must also be taken into account, as I shall do to some extent in Chapter 4.

An understanding of the importance of work to, and its influence on, people must cover a wide spectrum of aspects from job satisfaction, experience of mental well-being in general and psychosomatic problems as well as understanding the job's influence on personality (and of course vice versa). Only to take up job satisfaction and to believe that thereby light is shed on the influence of work on individuals is quite wrong. Job satisfaction is but one, and by no means the most important, mental consequence of work (Kohn, 1980).

3.2 Job Conditions and Mental Health

During recent decades considerable research has been devoted, not least in Sweden, to the relationship between working conditions and mental health. How human beings are affected, purely from the point of view of experience, by job conditions has thus been relatively thoroughly surveyed. Some brief references will be made here to the results.[1])

Gardell (1977a) found that job conditions characterized by small possibilities of self-determination with regard to the person's own work and simple unskilled tasks (short training period), monotony and the feeling that the job is uninteresting are associated with a low degree of mental satisfaction.

Bolinder and Ohlström's (1971) study (see Chapter 2.2) led to broadly similar results. A clear correlation was established between experiences of mental stress and strain at work and psychosomatic symptoms. Among the causes which the workers themselves regarded as responsible for their mental strain could be noted the physical environment (e.g. noises), jobs involving physical exhaustion, forced rates of work, wages problems, dull and uninteresting work. In this study, on the other hand, social conditions at work were considered by the workers themselves to have relatively little effect on their mental stress and strain. However, social problems (restricted possibilities of contact at work, poor relations with foremen and fellow workers, etc.) correlated with psychosomatic problems.

Westlander (1976b) takes account of two dimensions of mental health, self-esteem and self-realization. She reached the conclusion that social factors at work (management, fellow-workers etc.) were highly significant for the dimension self-esteem – feeling of prestige. Job-content was of great importance to self-realization.

Karasek (1981) starts from two important dimensions in work, its demands (work load, stress factors) and scope for action (decision possibilities) to meet these requirements, and studied above all the combination of these two for a number of different aspects of mental health. He found that working conditions were of very great significance to depression (nervousness, anxiety and sleeping problems) and exhaustion (based on the respondent's report on severe exhaustion, inability to relax in the evening and difficulty in getting started in the morning). The proportion of individuals

---

[1]) I do not take up factors which can assist in influencing relations between working conditions and mental health, such as sex, age, individual qualities, etc. I am content to deal with general aspects. For an approach which relates work and mental reactions of work to e.g. the family situation, see Westlander (1976a). In Westlander (1976b) there is a survey of studies and discussions differentiating between various categories of employees with respect to the relationship work-individual.

out of a large number of employed males, who displayed symptoms of depression and exhaustion was greater the higher working demands and the lower the action and decision scope (control of their own working situation) they had. The strongest link between the job situation and these symptoms was found when both dimensions were combined at the job. From the two reported studies (one from Sweden, one from the USA) it turned out that the proportions with symptoms of depression were 45 and 47% respectively in the group with high working demands and low action scope for decision makers, while in the opposite group who thus had low working demands and considerable action scope for decision makers, about 8% had corresponding symptoms. In the intermediate groups, viz. those with either low working demands and little scope for action, high working demands and considerable scope for action, or with medium-high working demands and medium-high action scope, between 14 and 16% of the people reported symptoms of depression. Karasek's conclusion from the studies of both populations is that it is mainly workers having jobs which at the same time permit little freedom of action and also place high demands on the workers who report exhaustion after work, difficulties in waking in the morning, low spirits, nervousness, anxiety and sleeplessness or difficulties in sleeping.

According to Karasek, it is primarily scope for action and the possibilities of controlling the individual's own situation that are problematical and require remedial measures. High working demands admittedly constitute a stress factor for the individual but these can also have many positive consequences by exercising an activating influence. For this reason a combination of a high degree of control by the individual with regard to decision-making and rather high working demands is to be preferred.

Katz and Kahn (1978) sum up some research on various types of jobs and the consequences of these for mental health, amongst other things. On the basis of a division into four occupational clusters – blue-collar unskilled, blue-colour skilled, white-collar unprofessional and white-collar professional – it turned out that the occurrence of stress factors diminished in order from the first to the last. The greater the occurrence of stress factors, the more widespread were negative affective responses, especially boredom and dissatisfaction with the work role. Amongst other things Katz and Kahn concluded that.

"These negative reactions to the job are in turn associated with more general negative affects – feelings of depression, irritation and anxiety. These in turn are associated with somatic symptoms." (p. 607)

Gardell (1976) sums up the conclusions which can be drawn from behavioural scientific research on which job conditions exercise a negative influence on mental health:

"If we look to the international field, we can sum up by saying that psychological and sociological research has indicated that the following conditions are not compatible with healthy and dignified working conditions:

- authoritarian and detailed supervision
- tasks characterized by severe restrictions with respect to the individual's possibilities of utilizing his resources in an allround manner
- working conditions implying that the production system places little demand on the individual to contribute knowledge, responsibility and initiative
- working conditions permitting little possibility for the individual to exercise influence on the planning and organization of the job
- tasks which deprive the individual of self-determination of rate of work and working methods, and
- tasks which permit few or no human contacts during work."

As Westlander and Baneryd (1970) point out, much of the research pursued in this field has been somewhat schematic and oversimplified. Much use has been made of questionnaires. From the positivistic point of view, criticism can be directed against the reliability of the conclusions since it has not proved possible to maintain control of underlying or intermediate variables. As the majority of the authors referred to here declare, we cannot entirely exclude the possibility that states of low mental satisfaction have been caused by factors outside the job situation. There might be a possibility that experience of highly forced rate of working lead to mental strain is the result of low mental health instead of the other way round.

However, efforts have been made to test this "psychologizing" theory and the conclusion has been drawn that the associations referred to *cannot* to any considerable extent be explained with regard to recruiting/selection (Bolinder and Ohlström, 1971; Westlander, 1976b; Kohn, 1980; Oldham and Hackman, 1981). The quality of the job conditions is of greater importance than the employee's mental characteristics for satisfaction and mental health at work.

The importance of work to the mental health of the individual is a vital field of research, the individual's conscious experiences in relation to different job conditions constitute a rather well researched field, at least as regards survey technique. On the other hand there appears to be a lack of qualitative and theoretically qualified work in the field. Characteristic of the greater part of the social and behavioristic sciences has been and still to some extent is:

"... The advantages of survey studies do not stand in reasonable proportion to their actual spread. The mode of procedure for obtaining *other* types of information is on the whole underdeveloped and/or unexploited. Whoever attempts to practise alternative modes of procedure enjoys as a rule no academic prestige." (Asplund, 1979: 21)

Although the research referred to here is in certain respects open to discussion, there seems to be considerable unaminity on the broad lines of the results of the research carried out. Thunberg and others (1978) state, for example:

"... it is incontestable that highly mechanized or routinized jobs counteract the experience of identity and human dignity." (p. 145)

When it is a matter of theoretical understanding of why exactly this should be the case, attempts at formulating advanced theories are lacking to a great extent. In occupational psychology much more interest has been devoted to working empirically than to developing theories on mental health in relation to work. It now appears to be important to advance from this empirical position and take up other and broader problems than the quantifiable significance of job conditions to the experience of satisfaction measured by means of survey questionnaires. To work out theories on the human being in relation to the work content which deepen the empirical understanding would seem to be an important goal for research.

The lack of advanced theoretical work in occupational psychology is probably, in part, associated with the preponderance on the quantitative side and on the positivistically orientated view on science. When positivism is in the ascendant, the result is often quantitative and theoretically cautious work. Fjellström offers the following criticism of positivistically orientated research:

"The collection and classification of facts, the sorting of data have become the principal scientific activity – a kind of 'dataism'. Theory has been regarded as more secondary and involving a difficult element of speculation. The creative moment in scientific work has been overlooked, especially in the forming of concepts and theories. In this way positivism has come to function in an anti-theoretical direction in a manner which in the long run has had an inhibiting effect. Obsession with facts has resulted in concentration on superficial phenomena, more or less banal details which could be studied by means of collected data and processed with the aid of mathematics. Studies of this kind have a sort of fragmentizing effect: one obtains no perspective and no overall view." (Fjällström, 1975: 28).

I am aware of only a few works in this field of research which are of a more far-reaching theory-developing nature. It would take too long to go into these in detail and I shall merely briefly refer to a couple of studies which attempt to relate problematic working conditions to mental difficulties.

Frese (1978) speaks of fragmentized action, meaning by this an action which is not governed by the individual's own intellectual processes, but for which the execution and objective have been planned by other people who have thereby made the decisions. These actions are therefore characterized by the absence of intellectual control. By the concept of fragmentized action Frese means that it is identical with the control concept with respect to one decisive point: if the action is fragmentized, control of the individual's own activity lies outside his own person, instead of being guided from the intellectual level in the way corresponding to the usual pattern of action. Via the reaction pattern "learned helplessness" which means the feeling of the lack of control of the situation and which psychological research has demonstrated can generate depression, Frese explains how depression has been found mainly among people employed in jobs with limited possibilities of control.

Volmerg (1979) examines the meaning which broken-up monotonous working conditions have for the individual's identity concept. He believes that the division of labour and monotony in tasks are reflected in the mental structure of the individual. The repetitive character of the modern job gives rise to the mental state of monotony:

"In so far as the time structure is dispersed, the clear-cut contrast between subject and object is dissolved. A job action continously performed on the same object creates no registrable change; the object turns back the whole time in the same condition; the action is meaningless because it does not bring about any change." (Ibid, p. 43)

When the object of the work loses its demarcation, is deprived of its spatial uniqueness, its fixed contours are in a liquid state. The subject of the job process, i.e. the worker, has no basis to determine his place in time and space and can no longer feel a sense of identity with the object he is endeavouring to change. Volmerg writes that the action in the job process, i.e. the processing of an object, does not relate the worker as subject and object to each other. The action, subject and object stand meaninglessly alongside each other:

"The machine determines to the same extent subject and object. The subject can no longer distinguish his movements from those of the object. Also thinking as a possibility of creating his own reality is subjected to the object's movements. In this state the identity of the individual ceases to exist. The individual falls into a continuous state of apathetic indolence and emptiness. The meaninglessness and monotony of the job actions correspond to an emptying and unification of the senses." (Ibid, p. 44)

With the support of this argument Volmerg describes repetitive tasks or monotonous checking duties as being "instantly destructive to the identity".

Volmerg's reasoning is open to criticism on several points. For example he offers no clear definition of identity, nor are we told whether the identity-destructive effects are temporary or whether they change the personality more or less permanently. Nevertheless Volmerg's analysis – like Frese's – is an example of the way we can theoretically try to understand work – mental health in a much more profound way than is possible solely on the basis of empirical research results.

Other theoretically ambitious thoughts in this field may be found in, amongst others, Björkman and Lundqvist (1981, Ch. 9), Volpert (1979) and B. Volmerg (1977).

3.3 The Importance of the Organization

The "concrete" and, for the individual, specific job conditions discussed above which affect the individuals job situation cannot, of course, be disengaged from the overall structure of the organization in which he/she is working. The labour process and work organization link together the individual job situation and the overall organization and its structure. To that extent the individual's job conditions reflect the organization in its entirety. Nonetheless studies focused on work content and concrete job conditions, type machine control, do not always penetrate into all aspects of the individual's job situation which are generated by the overall organization.

The research devoted to the link between mental well-being and the job situation has often mainly been concerned with identifying the relevant job conditions for the individual. Among research workers who have emphasized the effect of the overall organization on the individual should be noted Argyris (1964a, 1973). As examples of important such factors he mentions organizational structure, hierarchy, standards, reward and penalty processes. Salaman (1981) speaks of two decisive sources of alienation. One of these, the more important, is the way in which work is designed and controlled, while the other is bureaucratization the systematic ordering and design of processes and organization in a manner rationalized from above. Also Brunander (1979) discusses the significance of organization conditions. In the company he studied, the overall organization formed a powerful instrument for control:

"Work is supervised and checked to a great extent by computer systems and other controlling systems outside the unit ... To be controlled externally was thus the pedagogical principle which characterized much of the routine work. It was, however, remarkable that this principle also left its mark on supervisors, not only on heads of groups but also on heads of departments ... It was not only economic questions and marketing questions which dictated the control but the entire organizational system." (p. 130)

One aspect of possibly large, significance, and apace with the triumphant procession of largeness as such in economy and working life growing importance, is the hierarchy of the organization and the individual's position in this.

In a large company the life's work of a particular individual may be of subordinate, not to say of negligible, importance to the company. At the same time the vital decisions are possibly made by a group management at the other end of the world, for which in turn the company in question represents a mere permillage of the annual turnover. Such conditions may be assumed to exercise a negative effect on meaning, involvement and satisfaction at work.

Another aspect is concerned with the degree of subordination. This is naturally reflected in the individual's job conditions. But very many aspects of an industrial or other working process cannot be controlled individually. It is then important to the individual if he participates in (institutionalized) collective control of the workplace or not (Frese, 1978). Self-determination and control of the job situation cannot thus be made into an individual question but the level of organization must also be brought into the picture. We must therefore study both organizational conditions, i.e. structures more or less common to the group as a whole, as well as job content, which is specific for every individual employee, in order to understand the psychological influence of the work (cf. e.g. Gardell and Svensson, 1981).

These aspects indicate how important it is that the field of vision should include not only job conditions at a "concrete" level, even if these are indeed significant, but must also take account of the overall structures. Here, of course, questions of power and democracy are introduced into the picture. The humanization of working life demands changes at both what might be called the mental/technical level, i.e. the individual's conditions in connection with the execution of his tasks, as well as at a social level which concerns the workplace as a whole. It is essential that none of these is overlooked so that both the work content as well as employee influence at high levels are developed and supplement each other.[2])

3.4   Mental and Physical Health

This book is not concerned with the physical working environment (apart from cases where it may be clearly important with regard to the psychosocial working environment). Thus I do not take account of the injuries and illnesses which job conditions can cause in the mental or physical way. Nevertheless it may be desirable briefly to refer to the interaction between physical and mental factors which are often at the root of a somatic health problem. Since the latter frequently influences mental health, it is difficult to cultivate a psychosocial aspect of health problems.

---

[2]) That we cannot regard the individual's job situation as isolated from the organization is illustrated in Lawler et al. (1973), who show how problems of job enrichment arise when tasks at other levels (e.g. foreman's level) are affected.

It is well known that mental stress often underlies or reinforces somatic ailments. Bolinder and Ohlström (1971) found, for example, that of people employed in jobs of a highly stressed mental nature 5% had no psychosomatic symptoms while 45% had severe symptoms. Of those who did *not* consider that their jobs involved mental stress 21% had no psychosomatic problems while 11% had severe ones. These figures can be compared with the total population: 14% had none, 18% had severe psychosomatic symptoms. For a survey of how psychosocial organization and job conditions influence somatic health, see for example Katz and Kahn (1978).

3.5   Other Effects: The Complexity of Work and Intellectual Development

Kohn and colleagues have studied the various effects of the complexity of the work content in a lengthy series of investigations (summarized in Kohn, 1980). By content complexity is meant the intellectual demands laid down by a job and which can range from reading instructions, following written instructions of a simple nature to synthetizing data for discovering new facts and/or developing knowledge, concepts or interpretations. Kohn has revealed a causal connection from the internal complexity of the work to the following mental functions and attitudes:

– work involvement and satisfaction
– the evaluation of self-determination contra conformity in the face of external authority
– anxiety and self-confidence
– receptiveness or resistance to change
– moral standards and authoritarian conservatism
– intellectual flexibility
– the intellectual content of leisure activities
– powerlessness, estrangement in relation to ego and lack of norms (which are all measurements of alienation)

Naturally an individual's mental resources influence the job he is given but the message in Kohn's study is that the reverse also applies. Of special interest, bearing in mind the stability which this function is usually regarded as possessing, is that the job requirements in question clearly affect intellectual flexibility and the thinking processes. Intellectual flexibility thus continues to be capable of being influenced by experiences late in life.

3.6 Work Situation and Life Situation

Having referred to and discussed some results of the influence of job and organization conditions on the individual, and having briefly touched on the psychosomatic aspect of this, I shall now proceed to discuss the importance of the work for the individual's life as a whole.

One can formulate a number of assumptions on the way work affects the general functioning of the individual. One is that the biological heritage possibly in combination with early development determines the personality in such a manner that capacities and conditions remain virtually constant during adult life. Another is that the individual has different roles and different areas of activity which scarcely affect each other and that no connection between what a person does or experiences at work and in his life situation outside work really exists. A third assumption is that the individual continues to develop during adult life and experiences at work exert a clear influence on his development. The research results which exist appear to support the third of these assumptions. Korpi (1978) reports data indicating a connection between the possibilities of exercising judgment at work on the one hand with on the other hand union activities, political interest and membership of sports associations. Westlander (1976a) reports results pointing to the fact that higher self-determination and competence development at work are combined with greater formal social participation, activities tending to encourage development and less indulgence in entertainment pastimes (e.g. watching television).

From his research results Karasek (1981) concludes that variety of leisure pursuits, totally active leisure and total political activity are clearly associated with considerable freedom of action in work and higher levels of psychological working demands.

Most of the literature and empirical thinking in the field suggests that work is of "significant" importance to the life of the individual. The research results referred to and discussed in the preceding part may also be regarded as a confirmation of this assumption: the dimensions of the mental health studied did not apply only to the feeling of satisfaction during working hours but also referred to the individual's "general" mental health/sickness. Amongst these we may note, for example, Westlander (1976b), who states that work conditions can account for between 14 and 25% (depending on the definition and operationalization applied) of mental well-being, and Kohn, whose results point to the importance of job conditions for a number of different aspects of the human environment.

Kornhauser (1965) found clear connections between job conditions and problems in family conditions. Of a factory workers group 21% were assessed as having difficulties in their family situation in the form of disturbances and disharmony, while 10% of the workers not employed in factories and 14% of the salaried employees had similar problems. The proportion rose to 28% for middle-aged people from the lowest vocational categories. A reasonable conclusion could be that frustrations in the job situation can create frustrations in the family.

Gardell (1977a) describes how so-called carry-over effects from the job to life otherwise can express themselves:

"The basic idea or hypothesis in this context is that severely controlled and monotonous tasks offering little scope for influence on the performance of the person's own job have a learning effect on people, the result being that people teach themselves to be passive, to avoid taking initiative, etc. Conversely people do not learn to communicate with each other, to analyse a situation or to accept responsibility or make decisions." (p. 109)[3])

Thunberg et al. (1978) draw a similar conclusion on the basis of the following reasoning:

"The person who works on bad and ugly premises, has uncomfortable and crowded rooms for breaks and meals, is strictly controlled by machines or supervision and whose presence is subject to constant checks, is often dealt with from above and is not credited with the capactiy for independent action, etc., the inferior position of that person is continually emphasized in his own eyes and those of others." (p. 145)

Occupational psychologists are not, however, completely agreed on the importance of work. Near et al. (1978) found, for example, that job satisfaction correlated to life satisfaction to a limited degree only. Naturally this suggests that the importance of the job for the life situation is restricted. Near's study is marked by a methodological weakness (even from the positivistic point of view): the attempt was made to determine job satisfaction and life satisfaction on the basis of a single closed question each (with four and five alternative answers respectively). Amongst other things Kornhauser's study indicates that employees have a tendency to answer differently, more positively and smoothly, to "superficial" standardized questions than is the case in deep interviews, thus revealing the difficulties involved in solving these problems by means of (excessively) simple methods.

A point of view which is sometimes expressed is that the importance of the job has diminished and is continuing to do so. Ahrne (1978) believes that this is the case with many men as a result of longer training periods, shorter hours of work, etc. Possibly fewer men than previously choose a job as "life

---

[3]) See also Karasek (1981) and Pateman (1970) who discuss the relation between participation at the place of employment and conditions for participation on the community politics level. Pateman's idea is that if the individual has small possibilities of learning to practise democracy in his day-to-day collectively organized situation, his chances to cope with practising democracy at the community political level are small.

style". This would seem to be reasonable against the background of the negative development to which work content has been subjected. In the case of women it is probably the case that the importance of working life is increasing in so far as more and more women are seeking employment.

Even if the interest in work in the total sense should be diminishing – which is by no means certain – this does not necessarily mean that the importance of the job to, for example, mental health, the development of the personality and life situations has diminished:

"Whether work is a central life-interest or not, it is emphatically a central life-fact." (Rose, 1975: 15)

Although there thus exist points of view and isolated empirical studies which suggest otherwise, considerable empirical material indicates that for the individual the job fulfils important mental functions and is of great significance to his existence.

"It operates as a great stabilizing, integrating, ego-satisfying central influence in the pattern of each person's life. If the job fails to ful fill these needs of the personality, it is problematic whether men can find adequate substitutes to provide a sense of significance and achievement, purpose and justification for their lives." (Kornhauser, 1965)

"... work is not only an indispensable need for Man. Work is what liberates him from Nature, his creator as a social and independent being. In the work process, that is to say in the forming and changing of Nature outside herself, Man forms and changes himself." (Fromm, 1955)

It is reasonable to assume that the job and working life are of great importance to the individual and the community. Their influence is not restricted only to those who come into contact with them. They probably also affect the rising generation. The way jobs affect people may reasonably be supposed to affect their ability to take care of and bring up children. In Chapter 9 I revert to this problem.

The conclusions of my research summary may be briefly summed up as follows:

– The job and the work situation are of great importance to Man's mental health and life situation. The quality of job conditions makes itself felt and influences Man's leisure and life situations and his entire way of functioning.
– Amongst those job conditions which counteract mental health and well-being the following may be mentioned: severe control of the job situation, simple, unqualified and monotonous tasks, and limited social contacts during working hours.

3.7   Job Satisfaction and Other Influences of Work

A somewhat different impression than that given by research on the various consequences of work for individuals may be found in some research on job satisfaction (e.g. Near et al., 1978). Mass studies of how satisfied (in the general sense) employees are usually points to their being only partially dissatisfied. Some scholars conclude that conditions are in general quite good, but consider that it is desirable to improve the working conditions for the 10–15% of the total labour force who, according to many surveys, express dissatisfaction (see e.g. Robbins, 1983). Some studies report that dissatisfaction has tended to increase during recent decades, which is also regarded as justifying efforts to reform working life (see e.g. Cooper et al., 1979).

The problem is that this type of research gives a very limited and also in part a directly misleading picture of the quality of working conditions and their effects on people. In the first place the concept of satisfaction has many different levels, from superficial adjustment and the absence of direct dissatisfaction to a deeper feeling of purpose and involvement with the work one really wants to do. Many quantitative studies of job satisfaction reflect people's resignation in the fact of job conditions and attempts by means of psychological rationalization to facilitate adjustment to a problematic work situation rather than more profound satisfaction/dissatisfaction (cf. Salaman, 1981). In the second place there is a whole series of other consequences of work than those which the individual consciously registers in the form of experienced job satisfaction. Kohn comments on the measurements of attitudes and satisfaction in work as follows:

"Such an approach ignores the possibilities that there can be a gap between the conditions to which a person is subjected and his awareness of those conditions; that the existence or nonexistence of such a gap is in itself problematic and may be structurally determined; and that conditions felt by the worker to be benign can have deleterious consequences, while conditions felt to be onerous can have beneficial consequences. The second limitation is the preoccupation of most occupational psychologists with job satisfaction, as if this were the only psychological consequence of work. I am less disturbed by the technical difficulties in measuring job satisfaction – a notoriously slippery concept – than I am by the assumption that work has no psychological ramifications beyond the time and place during and within it occurs. Work affects people's values, self-conceptions, orientation to social reality, even their intellectual functioning. Job satisfaction is only one, and far from the most important, psychological consequence of work." (Kohn, 1980: 194–195)

The widespread idea that if people are fairly satisfied with their work, then all is well, as expressed in a number of theses with some claim to scholarship, is thus grossly misleading. The following model illustrates the range of various mental consequences of working conditions in relation to what the individual has the possibility to observe and become aware of.

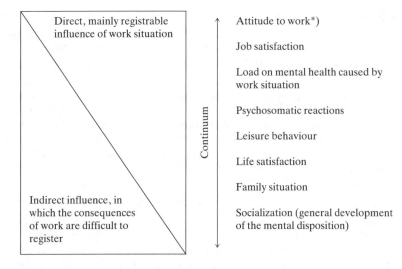

*) The precise nature of the psychological consequences of work in terms of the dimensions discussed here (direct/indirect) is difficult to assess. The ordering of the psychological reactions is of a very hypothetical character. The important point is the tendencies indicated by the figure.

The difficulties about becoming aware of the indirect consequences of the working conditions are partly associated with the fact that these are often relatively slight and continuously operate through time in a "stealthy" way, and partly because the influence of the job is only one of a large number of factors which play their part, it being impossible for the individual to trace the effects of these. Such derivations can only be performed in systematic investigations, in which even the minor but significant consequences of working conditions can be charted.

The above model sums up Chapter 3. The last-mentioned aspect, socialization, will be treated in the following chapter.

3.8   Digression: A Critical Reflection

One factor which may deserve thinking about is concerned with the great interest devoted to mental health in working life during the late 1960's and thereafter in Sweden. The empirical results concerning the relationship between job conditions and mental health produced after rather considerable research efforts in recent years are not particularly surprising. If we go back to the great social scientists of the Eighteenth and Nineteenth Centuries, Smith, Marx and Durkheim, we find that these scholars, who were able at close quarters to follow the development from crafts to the division of labour and industrial work, had understood and formulated the problem of industrial jobs in a way which in essential respects pins down what work psychologists one hundred years later had to devote much effort to discover:

"But the understandings of the greater part of men are necessarily formed by their ordinary employments. The man whose whole life is spent in performing a few simple operations, of which the effects too are perhaps always the same, or very nearly the same, has no occasion to exert his understanding, or to exercise his invention in finding out expedients for removing difficulties which never occur. He naturally loses, therefore, the habit of such exertion, and generally becomes as stupid and ignorant as it is possible for a human creature to become."

"The uniformity of his stationary life naturally corrupts the courage of his mind . . ."

"It corrupts even the activity of his body, and renders him incapable of exerting his strength with vigour and perseverance, in any other employment than that to which he has been bred. His dexterity at his own particular trade seems, in this manner, to be acquired at the expense of his intellectual, social, and martial virtues. But in every improved and civilised society this is the state into which the labouring poor, that is, the great body of the people, must necessarily fall . . ." (Adam Smith, 1846: 350)

Marx and Durkheim expressed similar points of view with regard to the break-up of job content and its consequences for the worker (Anthony, 1977).

These insights into the importance of work content appear to have been virtually forgotten until the 1960's:[4])

"The publication of Herzberg, Mausner, and Snyderman's monograph in 1959 signaled the beginning of a new trend which was to refocus attention on the work itself, a factor which had been ignored or de-emphasized by nearly everyone . . ." (Locke, 1975)

As an illustration of this phenomenon Segerstedt and Lundqvist's studies, discussed by Björkman and Lundqvist, from the early 1950's may be mentioned:

"The 'explanation', which they give that salaried employees in the firms studied display a more positive attitude to their work than the workers, is that the former are located closer to the company's source of norms, i.e. find it easier to identify with the company management and its aims. They do not discuss even the part the actual conditions can play for the experience, e.g. the fact that on the whole the salaried employees work in superior environments, have on the average better

---

[4]) The Hawthorne studies seem to have been of some significance to this. These laid emphasis on the social and emotional spects of the job situation and diverted possible working life research for a long time from observing the importance of the job content itself (Blumberg, 1968).

working hours, better forms of wages, which certainly applies to the companies studied." (Björkman and Lundqvist, 1981: 51)

This remarkable tendency to ignore the importance of work content is also to be found in more recent studies. I shall give one example. An American sociologist, Furstenberg (1974), discussed in a research summary the relationship between job situation and family situation. A series of studies reveals that the unemployed and individuals with unskilled jobs have more tensions and lower stability in their families than those of higher status in the occupational hierarchy. Furstenberg believes that this can be explained on the grounds that individuals with this job situation constitute "poor investments" with regard to socio-economic future prospects:

"Job careers and family careers are bound up with each other. Family members orientate their actual relations at least partly with regard to each others' role performance in the future. Concretely this means that if they are not looking forward to a successful working career, preparedness is lacking to initiate or maintain a family career." (Ibid, p. 355)

Since the lack of stability in the modern American nuclear family is thought to constitute a major social problem, Furstenberg argues in favour of a restructuring of job conditions so that anyone who wants to can take up a "career". This would then mean that employees in the main would start their careers with relatively low salaries and unskilled job conditions, which would then in due course be increased and upgraded respectively.

Much criticism and irony could be directed at Furstenberg's thesis with regard to both its points of departure as well as views on humanity and proposed measures. But I do not propose to take this up here. In this context what I wish to point out is that he almost entirely ignores job content and its significance for tensions and instability in the family. Working conditions which generate frustrations, low mental health and life dissatisfaction in addition to passive leisure are hardly the best breeding-grounds for harmony and satisfaction in the family situation. Because individuals from the lower socio-economic strata more often than others are subjected to such working conditions, it is reasonable to expect that disharmony is often to be found in these socio-economic strata. It is natural to reason in this manner and it is remarkable that Furstenberg does not do so, preferring to see, for example, the individual's actual and (even more) his anticipated salary as the determining factor for harmony in the family.

After these brief illustrations of how considerable sectors of the social sciences some decades ago and even in more recent times have ignored job content, I shall now formulate two questions which arise spontaneously:

1. Why did the insights on the importance of the job content and its effect on the worker, as formulated long ago by Smith, Marx and Durkheim so long ago, "disappear"?

2. Why were they "rediscovered" (by at least some sectors of the social sciences) mainly during the 1960's and thereafter?

The first question can probably be answered in part by referring to the obvious preference of early occupational research for the interests of those parties which possessed economic power (Rose, 1975; Gunnarsson, 1980; Björkman and Lundqvist, 1981). It was scarcely in the interest of capital owners and company directors to produce knowledge and information on the destructive effects of job conditions on human beings.[5])

The second question can obviously be answered by referring to some kind of general increased humanizing or (at least in Sweden) to the increased influence of the Trade Union Movement. A somewhat more cynical answer would be to refer to the economic interest which can be linked to the problems associated with mental illness in employment. What constitutes mental illness can often be the same as that which lies behind employee discontent with work and the corporation, turnover and absence due to sickness – phenomena having economic implications. In recent decades these problems have come to the fore and have probably acquired greater economic significance. Research on what causes mental problems in employment probably became increasingly economically motivated at about the same time as the research work in the field was actually carried out. In putting forward this hypothesis I do not wish to declare that the driving forces behind the field of research "mental health in work" should have been exclusively or even mainly economic. Instead it is rather the case, as I intend to point out in this study, that results from this research provide an excellent basis for severe criticism of the prevailing economic order. Interest in the problem field in question does not seem to have existed when divorced from economic interests. It was not until the research problem "mental health" had acquired a certain economic relevance that research scholars "discovered" the conditions which were well known as long ago as the Nineteenth Century.

---

[5]) Cf. Alvin Gouldner who writes:
"I am not saying that 'might makes right'. I am saying that viewpoints grounded in powerful social forces are taken more seriously than they might otherwise." (Gouldner, 1976: 6)
I agree with this and in various parts of this study (including Chapters 7 and 8) I shall illustrate this thesis.

4. Personality, Adjustment and Work Organization

4.1 On General Statements on Personality in Organization Psychology

The importance of work and the effects of certain working conditions on mental health and a series of different aspects of human functions have been illustrated from several points of view in the preceeding chapter, but one important aspect remains – the socialization possibly generated by working conditions. The concept of socialization here is defined slightly differently than often is the case in organization theory. In organization cultural research, for example, which deals largely – explicitly or implicitly – with aspects of socialization (see Chapters 6.5 and 8), emphasis is laid on how individuals adjust to, identify with or even internalize the specific values of the organization. In some branches of psychology/sociology socialization is bound up with the way behaviour patterns learned at work are transferred from the job to life in its entirety (Karasek, 1981: 75). Here I look upon socialization as as a more or less extensive change in the individual's mental dispositions, way of functioning and values in relation to organization and working conditions.

It cannot be taken for granted that socialization, in the sense of a change in the more profound or enduring mental dispositions, in consequence of experiences and incidents in the working situation, actually takes place. For example, it may be the case that the personality is determined in the first instance by biological heredity and early environmental influence and that only extraordinary influences in adult life can exercise an effect on the personality. This concept is to be found in some definitions of the personality. For example Johns (1983) writes:

"Personality refers to a relatively stable set of psychological characteristics that influences the way we interact with our environment." (p. 125)

A definition which provides the key to a socialization-theoretical approach could be that this relative stability applies above all to brief periods and in various situations, but that this "relatively stable set of psychological characteristics" can be changed through interactions with the environment in the course of time.

In connection with a discussion of work and mental health there are two kinds of aspect which require to be illustrated from the above point of view. The first is concerned with negative consequences of various working conditions on the personality of the individual. The second applies to the problem of generalizations about statements touching on negative consequences of working conditions. Is it reasonable to make statements of a universal nature? Naturally there are exceptions to general tendencies, but if they are few they do justify generalizations in any case. Or are the differences between individuals so great that they nullify or reduce the value of generalizations of the type referred to in Chapter 3 on job conditions which are not compatible with mental and somatic health?

In this section I shall discuss these questions, i.e. the possibility and reasonableness of starting with a "global" theory of personality in organization and working life research. The question has certain directly practical implications: can psychosocial problems in working life be largely solved by individual-centred measures of the type "right-man-in-the-right place" (as Berglind, 1976, proposes, for example)[1]) or should the emphasis be laid on general measures, i.e. to set up working conditions and organizations in accordance with definite principles? To keep the question within bounds I shall restrict myself to what is usually called "self-actualization". Can we regard manifest or latent orientation towards self-actualization as a universal characteristic?

Questions of this kind can hardly be answered except at the level of a psychological explanation. Social conditions must be taken into consideration. The question can also be answered in different ways, depending on the purpose the answer is to serve. For representatives of the management-perspective, which is mainly interested in the performance of the individual (primarily in the immediate future), the answers may have a somewhat different content than would be the case if the answers were directly focused on the personality and situation of the individual in the long term with the ambition of improving the possibilities of life. For my part I am chiefly interested in this second aspect. Unlike the majority of organization theorists, I do not discuss the problem for the purpose of facilitating forecasts of productive and efficient behaviour.

Schein (1980) deals with the question as to whether self-actualization can be regarded as a general characteristic. He emphasizes that we do not know

---

[1]) I find it difficult to understand to what extent this approach can solve any problems, because the number of individuals who are 'suitable' for jobs which just about anyone can do are considerably fewer than the number of jobs of this type (cf. Chapter 2).

"... if workers who are not actively seeking challange or self-actualization at the place of work either lack this need or they have not been given an opportunity to express it. This may occur because lower order needs have not yet been fulfilled or because the organization has "trained" workers not to except meaning in their work as part of the psychological contract." (Schein, 1980: 72)

This statement does not prevent Schein from declaring later in his book.

"By making broad generalization about people, managers not only run the risk of being wrong about the empirical realities, but, perhaps worse, such generalizations insult employes assuming that they are all basically alike." (Ibid, p. 250)

These quotations may seem to be contradictory, but this is not necessarily the case. The "empirical reality" which interests the business leader is really nothing else but the long-term development and inner growth of a limited number of individuals (and mainly those of managers and promising young executives). An individual who has been working for a long time in a monotonous and unqualified job is hardly likely to react immediately in a positive way to conditions which permit development and growth, i.e. conditions which require involvement – as contrasted with the non-involvement (Argyris, 1964a) to which monotonous work often gives rise and which the individuals has possibly taught himself. The consequences is that the individual's productivity is often likely to drop, at least in the short term, if for example control is reduced and the work made more qualified.

Schein's assertion that the employees would be insulted by the assumption of general traits seems reasonable only if the assumptions concerned are of a negative nature, e.g. that the employees are unreliable, lazy and must be checked, etc., or that the generalizations express a curt similarity. To assume that individuals in the main have a manifest or latent inclination towards "self-actualization" or that they are alienated by conveyor-belt conditions is surely hardly less insulting than to assume the contrary: that some employees are not interested in self-development or are suitable only for standing and repeating the same manual movements throughout the working day, not being required to use their judgment.

4.2 To Be or to Become

A shortcoming in many discussions on the individual in working life is that the personality is regarded as static (Brousseau and Prince, 1981). This is an oversimplification, at least according to research workers on socialization and interactionists who emphasize that the individual *becomes*, i.e. changes in a continuous social interaction:

"The individual may thus be regarded as both an active subject when he takes the initiative to interaction and as a passive object when he himself is the object of the actions of others. It is this interaction, i.e. his relations to others, which constitutes

him as an individual . . . 'Personality' is thus not a collection of characteristics. It is made up of his previous actions and the results of these, in addition to the actions of others of importance directed against him, the meaning of which he has incorporated within himself." (Israel, 1979: 71)

Israel uses the concept "relational" instead of interactionist in order to emphasize that the personality is not developed solely in interpersonal interaction:

". . . the individual does not relate himself only to other individuals but also to things, to groups and to society and its institutions. In order to emphasize this I use the term 'relational'." (Ibid, p. 102)

This point of view implies a risk of overemphasizing the changeableness of the personality and I wish to stress that the individual both is *and* becomes. He has characteristics, yet these are not static but are modified and developed in the long term in interaction with the social and socio-material environment.

In working life psychology, on the other hand, the personality is often regarded as more or less given. But the "level of expectations" is often regarded as a "dependent variable" (see e.g. Ekvall, 1969). This point of view is problematical from a relational or socialization theoretical standpoint. There also now exist a number of research results which show that the personality is changed by the influence of working conditions (Brousseau and Prince, 1981; Kohn, 1980). Here I shall tentatively discuss the importance of the relational aspect on the basis of the concept of self-actualization.

4.3   Self-actualization in the Relational Sense

Maslow (1954), in his view of the self-actualization concept, believes that even if all needs at the lower levels of the hierarchy of needs are satisfield, we often (if not always) find that a new case of discontent or of restlessness soon arises unless the individual does what suits him. A musician must make music, an artist must paint and a poet must write if he is to be totally happy with himself. What a person *can* do, he *must* do. Maslow calls this need self-actualization.

This definition is reasonable if not entirely clear. Maslow's needs theory has in fact not seldom been criticized for being "woolly" (see e.g. Locke, 1975; Schein, 1980). Maslow himself is aware of this but believes that sharper definitions are neither possible nor desirable (Maslow, 1955). One element in his self-actualization concept, which does not feature in the above definition, consists of so-called "peak experiences". These are quasi-mystical experiences which contain a feeling of being outside time and space and also that something extremely important and valuable has happened (see e.g. Shaw, 1972). This notion has inspired Johan Asplund to make the following ironical comment:

"Maslow's self-actualization model could – spitefully – be compared to a gearbox and motorway model. The human motivation engine is equipped with low and high gears: first, second, third, fourth *plus an overdrive*. With the last gear engaged, 'peak experiences' make their appearance. As long as we struggle along in low gear the rest of the traffic rushes past us. High gears enable us to overtake. When we engage overdrive we fly ahead in splendid isolation." (Asplund, 1979: 236)

Since I am not interested in self-actualization in the sense which comprehends peak experiences and similar exclusive exaggerations, I choose to define self-actualization as a profound effort for the individual fully to use and develop those capacities he feels to be must satisfying in relationship to productive and creative activity. In this there lies a wish to avoid working conditions which fall short of this. Self-actualization is thus primarily a question of qualification. The concept shall be understood in a relational and processual sense. Self-actualization states the relationship between the individual and his (external) work situation. Thus it is neither a question of a characteristic nor of an external condition, but is solely concerned with the relation and the interaction between the individual and his working environment.

The relation between work content and the employee is processual in the sense that a given work content in time generates an increase in the employee's capacity (i.e. provided that the working conditions make such demands that the employee's capacity can, and needs to be, developed). If the work content does not permit the utilization of this increased capacity, the result is "deprivation": the job content no longer corresponds to the employee's capacity. Thus self-actualization implies interaction between the individual and job content which is not static but always in a state of movement. "Balance" in some sense can only be attained if the working conditions give scope for the application of the continuous increase in capacity which ensues from job conditions which place demands on the individual and which therefore in the long term stimulate him to increase his competence.

If we compare this way of using the concept of self-actualization with Maslow's definition on the preceding page, we see that they do agree to some extent. The differences are that I emphasize the relational/interactionist instead of the individual, and also that the elements of exclusiveness which Maslow and his followers associate with the idea of self-actualization (and which find an extreme expression in the notion of peak experiences) have been removed. The fact that I emphasize continuous development of character does not, of course, mean that I look upon the stable characteristics of the individual through time as unimportant. My definition of the concept does not exclude these. When it is a matter of self-actualization in working life, I believe, however, that it is more constructive to emphasize the development of the individual rather than the biologically inherited, and after the earliest years of growth, stabilized characteristics, even if these are often of very considerable importance.

In working life literature it is often stated that the majority of individuals are orientated towards self-actualization in the above sense, have growth needs etc. At least from a superficial point of view this does not, however, seem to apply to all individuals. It appears as if some do not have such a leaning, but on the contrary can adapt themselves quite easily to monotonous and unqualified tasks. Should we recognise this is as a consequence of the fact that people *are* different, *have* different personalities? Or that it is an expression of their *becoming* different, *developing* different mental dispositions as a consequence of, amongst other things, interaction between the job situation and the demands it places?

One way of regarding self-actualization, growth, non-deprivation or whatever we wish to call it, is to assume that the individual is born with a possibility of retaining and developing such a "direction" or "aspiration". Whether this is subsequently upheld or withers away is a consequence of the manner in which the individual *becomes*. (Of course, parts of this becoming takes place prior to the individual's working life, e.g. through the primary socialization in the family and the secondary at school.) How does this approach agree with observable "reality"? Is it reasonable to look upon "personal development" as something of a restriction on movement and relate possible "deviations" to the way in which working life today contributes to the development of the individual, i.e. the socialization in and of work to which the individual is subjected.

4.4   Adjustment and Influence on the Personality

Studies by Walker and Guest and by Gardell indicate that 10 and 20–25% respectively of conveyor belt employees adjust relatively well to the job (Gardell, 1976). How does this agree with the assumption concerning personal development discussed above? Not particularly well, superficially, but the question is whether this state of affairs overthrows the assumption. If 75–90% do *not* adjust particularly well, we can still speak about a relatively general reaction with only a few exceptions. Gardell puts forward the view that those who do adjust to the conveyor belt would undergo a worse adjustment if the working conditions were changed in a humanizing direction (i.e. so that they correspond to human needs and generate possibilities of development).

In this section, however, my point is different. I assume that, in a certain situation to which an individual is subjected over a long period, his *personality* is also affected. A process of adaptation can be understood as a change of personality in relation to the influence of the social and physical environment. According to this view "adjustment" is thus somewhat "more profound" than, for example, the lowering of "pretensions" (the changing of an attitude) Adaptation to, for example, unskilled, monotonous and unfree working conditions may be assumed to be the result of, or may occur parallel to, a change of personality in the direction of qualities which harmonize with these working conditions. Self-actualization will no longer be a need or an important mental driving force, but instead a neglected possibility which the individual has been made to sacrifice in order to be able to adjust to the existing working conditions. According to this view it should be possible to retain the idea of orientation towards personal development as a possibility, which however is neither stable nor immune to the influence of the environment.

There are some empirical results which agree with this conception. For example, there appears to be a tendency that negative reactions to jobs offering little scope for self-actualization lessen in relation to the worker's ages – time spent at the job (Gardell, 1977a). Kornhauser (1965) found that among older factory workers with working conditions which hardly permitted self-actualization those who had kept alive their ambitions for utilizing their capacity and development enjoyed poorer mental health. He also discovered that employees for whom self-actualization was something important were often in a worse mental state than others.

This can be understood in different ways. *One* possible interpretation is that the degree of adjustment to these unfree and unskilled jobs stands in inverse relation to interest in self-actualization and nondeprivation. That is to say, the less interest in self-actualization, the less the problems of adjustment. Since adjustment appears to improve to some extent during the period an individual is engaged at a job, we may assume that interest in self-actualization generally declines in jobs which imply deprivation. This would then back up the assumption that the lack of, or only slight, orientation towards self-actualization *can,* at least partly, be regarded as the result of socialization at work.

4.5 On Adjustment to Unqualified Working Conditions

What has been said so far in this chapter can be related to a couple of themes in Chapters 2 and 3. The occurrence of a high frequency of jobs with impoverished content, no possibilities of self-actualization or development, in combination with the destructive consequences of such conditions which working life psychology has identified, as well as the fact that a considerable number of the employees according to studies of the entire labour force, report that they are contented with their work situation, results in a contradictory picture. This can only be understood if the socialization aspect is taken into consideration.

In organizational psychology, Argyris (1960, 1973) has analyzed the relationship between individual and organization from a development perspective, in which it is assumed that the individual is normally developed in the direction of more and more self-actualization and control of his own environment, in the direction of increasingly profound and enduring interests and to have a long-term perspective in his activities.

Argyris compares the qualities of the mature individual with the formal organization and believes that there is a conflict between the mature traits of the individual and the formal organization (at least in its bureaucratic form). The struggle for independence and self-actualization is frustrated by control, the struggle to develop and utilize many more profound qualities is frustrated by the principle of the division of labour, etc.

The working conditions and the demands of the formal organization, principally on individuals at the bottom of the organization hierarchy, and the working conditions discussed in Chapter 2, harmonize most readily with the qualities normally characteristic of an individual in a development terminated at an early stage. Good adjustment to the working situation characterized by control and checking, by fragmented and unskilled job content, can thus be assumed to be facilitated by undeveloped personality traits such as submissiveness, passivity, lack of skills and superficial interests.

Impressive empirical backing for this view on the way the working situation affects individuals in the long term, as laid down by Argyris, is to be found in a study by Karasek (1978). He investigated how workers with different kinds of jobs (in terms of qualification level) and with different times spent in working life (from 0 to 30 years) functioned in terms of active or passive leisure time. By active leisure time is meant participation in several kinds of leisure time activities (religious, sporting, political, intellectual, hobbies, etc.). The results are summarized as follows:

"'Newcomers' to the labor force (0 to 5 years) – regardless of their job content category – display relatively small systematic differences (and much random variation) in leisure participation rates. These differences for young workers must indeed reflect the impact of childhood background or personality, but they are barely statistically significant. Workers with over 30 years of working experience show substantial differences in leisure participation: four times the difference for workers just beginning their careers. After the full occupational career, workers with 'active' jobs have over twice the probability of participation in active leisure pastimes as workers with 'passive' jobs." (Karasek, 1978: 15–16)

It may be assumed that behind this extensive change in the behaviour repertoire there lies a gradual change of personality in, if it is a question of low qualified, pacifying jobs, a negative direction with respect to breadth and depth of capacity for action. We can speak of socialization in the direction of a limitation of the possibilities of life. This should mean, given a certain amount of endurance, that the individual's conditions and interest in self-actualization and development become extremely limited. The lack of the latter can thus be easily explained by continuous socialization resulting in the individual becoming more and more concentrated on passive and relatively unskilled occupations.

If we combine this with the results from Chapter 2, which indicate that a large proportion of industrial jobs are associated with low qualification requirements – Korpi (1978) reports, for example, that two-thirds of the metal workers considered that "just about anyone" could perform their work – we can conclude that a large number of individuals are being developed in a direction *away from* the utilization and development of their capacities.

The socialization which ensues from working conditions does not fully account for the largely destructive and far from complete adjustment of individuals to monotonous, divided and unfree working conditions. As Salaman (1981) points out, the social and cultural context must also be brought into the picture. This is of importance because in different ways it prepares the individual for the deprivation of work. Salaman formulates the question how it can happen that individuals develop "minimum and self-destructive conceptions and expectations" faced by work and answers it by saying that, amongst other things, in capitalism much emphasis is laid on consumerism and materialism and that an instrumental attitude to work is encouraged by this for the groups which have little possibility of securing the good and interesting jobs. He also points to the work ideologies which exist and which emphasize the moral duty of working (see further Anthony, 1977) and the importance of the class society for the conceptions and expectations of those who are at the bottom of the hierarchy:

"The damages of work within class society have a psychological dimension. One important aspect of the problem is this: in class society different jobs are not only evaluated and rewarded differently, but they are allocated or seen in terms of merit, moral character, intelligence and ability. The implications of this, for the mass of the population, are very clear: workers deserve to be workers; their repetitive, low-skilled work reflects their personal ability and worth." (Salaman, 1981: 103)

Furthermore, Salaman discusses women and immigrant groups in terms of discrimination and the preparation for the worst jobs for which these groups are trained in various ways, and – as I have tried to explain above – the massive socialization which takes place in consequence of the design and organization of the work.

These points of view indicate that the attitudes of individuals to their jobs are expressions of complicated patterns of social and cultural conditions and that socialization processes at and away from work just as much as the qualities of the job in terms of corresponding to the needs, interests and conditions of individuals. As was made clear in the previous chapter, it is far from certain that a job has good mental consequences for an individual merely because the person in question, in answer to a questionnaire states that he or she is content. The views described also indicate that light must be shed on the phenomena treated in this and the preceding chapter from a broad spectrum of perspectives: from the psychological to the cultural and sociological.

On the basis of what has been said in this and the preceding chapter I should like to pose the questions: how much of the individual's potential is destroyed by current industrial life? Not merely through the direct influence on workers but also indirectly: we know that parental background is of decisive importance to a child's capacity and interest in many forms of learning. If, instead, working life really placed demands on skill and utilized and developed the capacities of individuals: what would this mean for the quality of the lives of individuals? For interest in education, creative capacity, etc.? It is reasonable to assume that the social genesis of individuals could be radically different from what it is today, if working life tended to develop instead of to deform the capacities of individuals.

4.6 Summary

The material treated in Chapters 2–4 will be introduced into a comprehensive context in Chapter 9. Here I shall only give a preliminary very brief summary of the contents of this and the two previous chapters.

The development which, according to Braverman and others, has left its mark on working life during the Twentieth Century stands out in sharp contrast to the central mental needs and interests of the individual. The consequences of unskilled and often unfree working conditions are mental and psychosomatic problems, the pacification of leisure time and life situation. Even using positivist methods, which are otherwise very unsuitable for capturing phenomena such as repression and alienation, results have been obtained which clearly demonstrate the negative mental and social consequences of the division of labour and dequalification (Chapter

3). (An exception here is a number of measurements of attitudes and job satisfaction, which tend rather to conceal these.)

Here it can be appropriate to link up briefly with the Frankfurt School. In an essay written forty years ago Marcuse writes:

"Human behavior is outfitted with the rationality of the machine process, and this rationality has a definite social content. The machine process operates according to the laws of physical science, but it likewise operates according to the laws of mass production. Expediency in terms of technological reason is, at the same time, expediency in terms of profitable efficiency, and rationalization is, at the same time, monopolistic standardization and concentration. The more rationally the individual behaves and the more lovingly he attends to his rationalized work, the more he succumbs to the frustrating aspects of this rationality." (Marcuse, 1941: 420)

This quotation may be said to be something of a Frankfurtian summary of the results reported and the discussions held in this study. Admittedly the quotation does not express some of the essential findings of working life research mainly during the 1960's and 1970's, although at the same time as Marcuse has some points over and above these results. In my view Marcuse succeeds in compressing into a few lines the central aspects of the individual's situation in working life.

The contents of Chapters 2–4 are based on the individual's (the employee's) perspective, or, rather, on research which attempts to capture how the individual is affected by various working conditions. Thus it is a question of a humanist or, to use the Frankfurt School concept, a practical interest in knowledge which constitutes the terms of reference. (Whether the empirical-analytical research results are suitable to attain to this interest in knowledge can be subsequently discussed. Cf. Chapter 1.)

In the following chapters I shall change perspective and try to see matters from the management perspective. I shall apply this to aspects corresponding to those dealt with in the preceding chapters. The management perspective can be said to be something of a concretized expression or a "special case" of technological rationality. To the management perspective also belong interest in social control and the adoption of an attitude favouring the interest of capital owners. This means that the management perspective is not a pure expression of technological rationality.

The purpose of my analysis in what follows is to study what possible incitements may exist in technological rationality for the development of working conditions in a direction different from that described in Chapter 2. It is not the case that a purification of this rationality leads to an extremely inhumane working life. In technological rationality there is naturally to be found the consideration of problems like job satisfaction, motivation and other social-psychologically related conditions which are of importance to efficiency. The following chapters deal with this.

5. Job Satisfaction, Motivation and Meaning of Work

The well-being and job satisfaction of personnel are not *in themselves* of major interest from the management perspective. Job satisfaction, however, is regarded as being closely related to motivation. Since the problem of motivation is of the greatest interest to executives these must, at least indirectly, take account of the well-being of their personnel. In order to understand why working life assumes the form it does and why employees feel as they do, the attitude of companies (management) to job satisfaction and motivation poses an interesting problem.

The management-orientated organization theoretical literature often ascribes greater interest to motivation than to job satisfaction. In this chapter I shall also focus on the motivation problem, job satisfaction being treated more implicitly.

I wish to emphasize that in this chapter I examine the aspects of motivation above all as they are relevant from the point of view of management perspective. Most of the literature I have studied is based on this perspective. Amongst other things this fact has certain implications for the concepts which are applied. Normally I prefer to use words such as engagement or intentionality rather than motivation when describing the interest of individuals in taking action. In management-orientated motivation theory these expressions are not frequently used. If it is a question of motivation (engagement, intentionality) in connection with an acting/behaving concerning tasks which are narrowly defined and controlled by a management function, motivation is perhaps a more accurate expression than engagement, for example. The former concept is associated with instrumental reason, while engagement refers to the negation of this reason (see Ch. 1).

Sievers (1984), whose point of departure is rather the latter concept, in a paper with the striking title "Motivation as a Surrogate for Meaning", regards the entire organization-psychological theory of motivation as an expression of the lack of meaning in fragmentized jobs and organizations in modern working life. I sympathize with this approach and will to some extent incorporate it into this chapter, but my main task here is to deal with conventional motivation theories of management interest with the aim of identifying the driving forces behind the design of work.

In this chapter the presentation is based on a survey of some assumptions of a central character with respect to the theory of motivation and a relating of these to the development described by Braverman. An important aim of this chapter is to find out to what extent job satisfaction and motivation-problems contain incitements for management to draw up working conditions so that they corresponds to the needs of the individual, i.e. that they are free, varied and qualified (cf. Chapters 3 and 4).

5.1   The Relationship between Job Satisfaction and Motivation

As far as an organization, and particularly its management, is concerned, the problem of motivation is mainly of importance

- To recruit and retain suitable personnel.
- To induce personnel to perform a reliable job in accordance with the requirements and aims of the organization (management)
- To stimulate personnel to creativity and thereby to contribute to the development of the organization.[1])

To some extent these requirements may be assumed to agree with the individual employee's interest for a satisfactory job, since a satisfied employee may be expected to stick to his job, be reliable, etc. As may be seen in what follows, however, it is open to question how much these requirements overlap each other.

Schwab and Cummings (1970) have made a summary of theories on the relationship between individuals' satisfaction and their performance. That there exists a certain link between job satisfaction and work contribution appears likely, but the question is in what way they are related. Schwab and Cummings speak of three points of view:

- Job satisfaction $\longrightarrow$ Working performance
- Job satisfaction $\longrightarrow$? $\longrightarrow$ Working performance
- Working performance $\longrightarrow$ Job satisfaction

According to the first point of view performance is dependent on satisfaction, according to the third the contrary is true, and according to the second there is no clear causal relationship between satisfaction and performance.

Thus Schwab and Cummings do not explicitly take up the aspect of motivation, but see in this an aspect of job satisfaction. This means partly a

---

[1]) This aspect is treated in rough outline only in the remainder of the study. The emphasis is laid on problems of absence, personnel turnover and (particularly) performance.

lack of nuance in the presentation, partly the disregarding of motivation which is not related to satisfaction, i.e. such as is based on avoiding negative consequences.

Schwab and Cummings refer to some studies which indicate that the connection between job satisfaction and performance is weak and ambiguous. Lawler (1973) and Locke (1975) are of the same opinion. Lawler (1973) writes that most psychologist believe that satisfaction influences absence and personnel turnover, but not work performance. Lawler finds it hard to understand why many people believe that a high degree of satisfaction leads to high standards of performance: there is scarcely anything in the literature on the subject which points to a causal relation of this kind.

This means that working conditions need not in themselves be particuarly satisfying in order to result in good performance. If this is true, it means, the management of a company should find it possible to disregard the job satisfaction of its personnel without that having, to any great extent, a negative influence on their work performance.

What significance has this for the problem of motivation? Motivation, at least "instrumental" motivation (in which the reward for activity in the form of wages, etc. is the essential thing, not the activity in itself[2]), assumes that an action results in some form of satisfaction.[3] This can be formulated like this: motivation ——➤ performance ——➤ satisfaction.[4] If the activity itself is motivating, there is a tendency for motivation, performance and satisfaction to happen at one and the same time. If the relationship between performance and satisfaction in working life is generally speaking weak (as Schwab and Cumming's survey suggests), the connection between motivation and performance would also be weak. It is difficult to believe that employees in the main would be truly motivated to carry out a good performance which was not accompanied by some job satisfaction.

The above discussion indicates that in organizations there are other ways of creating good performance in accord with the organization's (the management's) demands without making motivation and job satisfaction the basis. Severe control and checking of work can force the employees to maintain work performance for which motivation is of little importance. E.g. when the rhythm of work is entirely subject to machinery and conveyor belts and the job consists of only a few simple manual acts (and when the qualitative aspect is irrelevant or of subordinage importance). Cf.:

---

[2]) Motivation can naturally also be of "negative type", i.e. aim at avoiding suffering of any kind. I disregard that type of motivation in this study.
[3]) This assumption corresponds to the third point of view in Schwab and Cumming's survey.
[4]) This naturally provided that we have knowledge of the satisfaction that the performance brings about.

"For many jobs there is no room for high performance. The assembly-line worker can only do an adequate or a poor job, not a good one, for he does not control the pace of the work or make any decisions that might increase productivity. He may fail to make an adequate weld, but making one that indicates great skill and craftsmanship will bring him no recognition. In fact, it may bring a reprimand for wasting energy and metal when only an adequate weld is required. I suspect that many managerial and white-collar workers are in the same position. An adequate level of productivity is determined by the volume of input received and the volume of output absorbed. These depend upon other units of the organization. A worker or a manager and his staff may not receive an increase in inputs, or other groups may not be able to handle an increase in outputs. If so, an increase in productivity is impossible, and superior quality is likely to be wasted. The so-called 'pride of craftsmanship' is systematically excluded from as many jobs as possible because it is difficult for management to control this variable. Productivity, it is safe to say, depends much more upon such things as technological changes or economies of scale than upon human effort." (Perrow, 1979: 100–101)

We may therefore assume that in some types of jobs a fairly "good" job performance can be attained without motivation being of central importance for the purpose. This applies above all to jobs which to a large degree can be supervised and controlled by planning, control and checking systems, technical equipment and organization or "input-output" requirements in general. This type of control is thus exercised by means of the technological design and works in an entirely different way than control by means of motivation-encouraging measures other than pay incentives.

The importance of motivation to results of work is perhaps of least significance in jobs which leave no scope for self-determination, personal judgment, personal proficiency in craftsmanship and creativity – i.e. jobs at lower levels of the organization hierarchy. These jobs usually are accorded the greatest attention from the point of view of motivation because the difficulties in getting people to do what the management wants are often greatest in the case of these types of jobs. That the motivation problem is most clearly expressed here and that managements as well as motivation research experts and consultants devote explicit interest to them does not mean, however, that they are prepared to make major efforts to solve the problems. The fact that this is the case is indicated by the way organization hierarchies are built up and working processes are so designed that these problems have become commonplace.

When it is a matter of jobs where the scope for the employees' own influence is greater, motivation probably acquires more central importance. This may above all be assumed to be the case with jobs in which such qualitative characteristics as technical proficiency, creativity and powers of initiative are essential. Jobs of this kind are difficult to control in detail. In this type of job there is often no strong reason for top management to take an explicit interest in the motivation question since it partly solves itself: people have interesting and stimulating tasks which provide their own motivation.

Schwab and Cummings do not differentiate between different types of tasks in their comparison of the different ways of regarding the relation between satisfaction and performance. (The only draw attention to the difficulties entailed in measuring performance in different types of jobs.) I believe that an understanding of the motivation problem requires that it be linked to type of job content and working process. This is also Perrow's (1979) view.

Motivation does not only affect work performance. It is also, as mentioned above, of great importance to personnel turnover/absence. Low motivation reduces the probability that one goes to work and stays there (see e.g. Lawler, 1973). High personnel turnover and absence due to sickness are problems above all in the case of industry and other organizations with monotonous, unfree jobs. Control by technological means may be able to maintain productivity in industry, but with regard to factors such as frequency of absence, poor motivation may make itself felt. This is a problem which paradoxically enough can be tackled by the division of labour, specialization and dequalification being driven still further:

"Absence and personnel turnover in this way become easier to deal with the simpler the jobs are – at the cost of still higher rates of absence and personnel turnover." (Sandberg, 1978: 40)

This strategy assumed that the costs for every employee who leaves diminish so much that an increase in personnel turnover in spite of everything does not imply heavier total personnel costs.

This strategy is of course not a patent solution which always solves personnel turnover and absence problems, but it does indicate that after all these personnel problems do not necessarily constitute an incitement for changes which are in accord with the needs of personnel and which generate motivation for personnel to come to work and stay there. The extent of recruiting, absence and personnel turnover problems is probably correlated to a considerable degree with the labour market situation: problems may be assumed to be much more extensive when business is booming involving low or very little unemployment than in times of depression with high unemployment. This probably means that the willingness of corporate management to invest in the working environment is greatest during periods of business prosperity. At such times the problem of motivation can be important.

To attempt an overall judgment of the significance of various aspects of motivation as economic incitements for the designing of working conditions calculated to generate job satisfaction is, naturally, a difficult task. I believe that it is doubtful whether the importance of these incitements is particularly great. Problems of recruiting, absence and personnel turnover are in themselves problems which cannot be ignored and in which in some situations can be of great importance, but as pointed out above it is not certain that the problems constitute the incitement for allocating priority to increased job satisfaction.[5]) The most usual method of stimulating motivation is to apply economic means (which possibly leads to satisfaction with wages but scarcely with the job itself). Another well-tried method is to appeal to the employee's working morale, possibly stimulated by attempts to encourage "the we-ourselves spirit", "corporate culture", or other human resources management or personnel administrative measures to integrate the individual in the activities and secure a rather well adjusted type of behaviour (see further future chapters). These methods do not mean that the satisfaction with the work content is affected to any extent worth mentioning. In the other hand satisfaction *from* work or the attitude to the company can be influenced in a positive direction. However, this has in itself no direct consequences for the way the work content affects the individual, nor can it compensate for possibly existing working conditions which have negative mental consequences for the individual (cf. Ch. 6.6). When it is a matter of motivation in relation to performance, it seems as though this aspect does not constitute a central business economic motivation for the emphasizing of satisfaction in work for categories of employees whose working situation is largely determined by organizational and technological factors, even if management must of course to take the satisfaction aspects into some account.

5.2   Humanistic and Behaviouristic Motivation Psychology

In motivation psychology based on organization theory there are two main schools of thought. One of these is derived from humanist psychology and has been influenced by Maslow's theory of motivation, the so-called hierarchy of needs (Maslow, 1943; 1954). This direction might be refered to as content theory, need theory or *humanistic motivation psychology*. Briefly Maslow's theory is based on the ideal that the needs of the individual are hierarchically arranged from primary physical needs via needs for security, fellowship and status to the need for self-actualization, which is the highest and most exclusive need. Before a higher need comes to the fore and acts as a motivation for the individual, the immediately subordinate need must have been relatively well provided for: an individual who is starving is not

---

[5]) Possibly this kind of problem is becoming somewhat more pronounced, which would mean that they might become more important as economic incentives (Davis, 1980).

so very much troubled about possible dangers in the future, if a person's needs for fellowship and status are entirely unsatisfied, then he is not yet inclined to self-actualization.

A theory of motivation having striking similarities to Maslow's, but which is probably more advanced and which in any case has received better empirical confirmation is Alderfer's so-called ERG theory (Alderfer, 1969). The basic ideas are similar, but there are fewer needs than in Maslow's model. Alderfer speaks of Existence, Relatedness and Growth needs and these largely correspond to Maslow's physiological and security needs, fellowship and status needs and self-actualization need respectively. The difference between this theory and Maslow's is that Alderfer believes that all three needs are to a greater or lesser extent of current interest at one and the same time and that the individual can "regress" from having previously been occupied with one higher need to, if its realization is frustrated, compensate for this by further satisfaction of a lower need. Thus if an individual attempts to seek growth and success in his job, i.e. realize growth needs, but this proves a failure, social relations at and away from his place of employment or his consumption of material things (i.e. relatedness and existence needs respectively) can stand in the centre for his need for satisfaction. On the side of progression from the emphasis on lower needs to the emphasis on higher needs individuals can thus undergo a regressive development, i.e. proceed in the opposite direction.

One of the best known studies in this tradition within motivation psychology in working life is Herzberg's two factors theory (Herzberg et al., 1959). This theory declares that some factors in the job situation can give rise to dissatisfaction but *cannot* generate satisfaction and intrinsic motivation. At best they can they can cause an absence of dissatisfaction, i.e. some kind of neutral state with respect to satisfaction. Herzberg calls these factors "hygienic" or "dissatisfiers". Other factors, termed "motivational" or "satisfiers" can generate satisfaction and intrinsic motivation, but scarcely dissatisfaction. The former factors are thus to be found on the minus side, while the latter are found on the plus side, along the satisfaction dimension. The motivational factors are thus those which are concerned with the job content itself, such as success, acknowledgement of performance, the work itself, responsibility and personal growth, while the hygienic factors touch on conditions alongside the job itself such as company policy, the physical working environment, and wages. Thus the theory is based on the idea that, for example, work in itself (a motivational factor) can, if it is "positive", give rise to a high degree of satisfaction and intrinsic motivation but it can scarcely, even if it is "negative", generate dissatisfaction but only the absence of satisfaction. A good physical working environment or high wages, i.e. hygiene factors, cannot thus generate satisfaction and motivation at work but only the absence of dissatisfaction, whereas a bad working environment and bad wages can give rise to dissatisfaction and discontent.

The two factors theory harmonizes rather well with Maslow's hierarchy of needs, amongst other things as far as the motivational factors correspond to the higher needs in the hierarchy of needs (cf. Hunt and Hill, 1969). However, Herzberg's theory has now been subjected to severe criticism (see e.g. Lawler, 1973; Locke, 1975).

That job content should be of virtually no importance to the so to speak negative side of the dissatisfaction/satisfaction dimension is not reasonable. Thus there are doubtful elements in the two factors theory and one should not interpret it too strictly. Nevertheless I believe that there are some good points in Herzberg's presentation of the problem of motivation (see further p. 97).

The other principal school of thought, which is derived more or less directly from a *behaviourist tradition,* is the so-called expectancy theory. Behaviourism and expectancy thinking stress the rewards and punishments that follow behaviour as sources of motivation. A difference is that expectancy theory stresses the role of cognition, the expectations of what a specific action may bring about.

Willingness to perform a certain action is basically a function of a "force of motivation". This consists of the experienced evaluation of a certain goal (the desirability of the goal) in addition to an expectation of the probability that this goal will be achieved.

A certain performance and an estimation that a certain effort will bring about the performance required. One example: an individual who is interested in promotion. His motivation to try to achieve this through a certain effort (e.g. work hard 60 hours per week for a period in order to increase the results by 20%) will be a function of a) how he assesses the probability that the effort will bring about the performance/results, b) the assessed probability that the performance, if attained, will lead to the realization of the goal, and c) how much he experiences the value of the goal (promotion). If he judges that even a great effort is probably not enough to achieve the results, or that it is a low probability that the performance will lead to the goal, or if he does not regard the goal as important, the strength of his motivation will be low.

We can – if we wish to be critical – ask ourselves whether this line of thought is so advanced and interesting that as to justify the great popularity of this model. Criticism can also be directed at it for only taking account of motivation of instrumental type. An interesting and creative activity can be motivating *in itself* (if we are now to use the term motive to designate such activity). The expectancy theory puts emphasis on the instrumental aspects of motivation.

A large number of studies have attempted to elucidate which of the two schools is the better able to predict behaviour. Personally I do not think it is reasonable to make this type of comparison between theories with such different points of departure and approaches. Maslow/Herzberg take up and try to indicate the driving forces behind and the content of motivation, while Vroom/Porter and Lawler express a general type of relationship between motivation and performance withut defining what is the content of motivation (in the form of needs and such like). As a consequence of the difference in the approaches of the theories we cannot therefore say that they are mutually exclusive. Both may be right or wrong.

Which of the models/theories one may prefer is due not least to one's interest in knowledge. If this interest is mainly inclined to be able to predict and check productive behaviour, the expectancy theory has possibly a contribution to make.

If, on the other hand, interest in knowledge is mainly orientated towards mental health and personal growth, the humanist psychology of motivation might have more to offer. This, however, is not to say that this school is very theoretically advanced (cf. Sievers, 1984). It is, however, relevant to the questions posed in this study and has been sufficiently influential for me to continue to use it in the rest of this study.

The expectancy theory has little to say on the understanding of the influence of work on the individual, his mental health and the growth of his personality, at least not on the basis of the points of departure I have selected for this study. For that purpose this theory is lacking in content. It has nothing to say about what factors at work are related to motivation and job satisfaction. In fact all it says is that the individual tries to maximize his satisfaction, but nothing about what constitutes this.

"This is a theory based essentially upon what Locke has described as a 'a form of calculative, psychological hedonism in which the ultimate motive of every human act is asserted to be the maximisation of pleasure and/or the minimisation of pain. The individual always chooses that course of action which he expects will lead to the greatest degree of pleasure or which will produce the smallest degree of pain.' In effect, expectancy theory has given the kiss of life to objectivism in the waning years of the Hawthorne influences. It has generated a spate of empirical studies and now stands as the most popular approach to motivation among industrial researchers. Somewhat paradoxically, it turns the wheel of industrial psychology right back to the days of Taylorism, in that in place of rational economic man it seeks to substitute rational, calculative, hedonistic man." (Burrell and Morgan, 1979: 145)

The limited relevance of the expectancy theory to the problems which interest me means that I shall not go further into this type of theory. Instead, as mentioned above, I shall now deal with a couple of aspects taken from the human relations tradition theory of motivation.

5.3   On the Importance of Self-Actualization

A study of working life psychological literature indicates that there are above all two aspects which are of central importance to job satisfaction, mental health, etc. One of these is self-determination/influence on the personal working situation, while the other is the dimension of qualification or "self-actualization", i.e. job content. These two aspects are also of importance to understanding engagement and "intrinsic" (non-instrumental) motivation in work. The importance of the self-determination/ influence aspect seems to have been for along time neglected as a result of the concentration of the classical human relations school on good social relations. The human relations school's experimental results from the Hawthorne study, which concluded in findings on the importance of group relations and the emotional aspects of leadership, have long afterwards been reinterpreted to deal instead with self-determination and participation (Blumberg, 1968; Kahn, 1975).

Here I shall not deal further with the self-determination/participation aspects, but instead I shall examine some points of view on self-actualization in work, so that in the following section I may be able to try to integrate these with the self-determination dimension in relation to the problem of motivation.

In work psychology and organization theory the concept of self-actualization began to be introduced in earnest at the end of the 1950's. Herzberg et al. (1959), McGregor (1960) and Argyris (1964a), who are usually considered to belong to the modern variant of the human relations school (the neohuman relations or the human resources school), have been of great importance in this connection. All of them have been strongly influenced by Maslow's needs theory. All the motivational factors identified by Herzberg can be wholly or partly subordinated to the "self-actualizing" dimension (Herzberg et al., 1959). McGregor emphasizes "the capacity to make use of the imagination, inventiveness and independent creativeness" (see Chapter 6.2). Amongst other things Argyris stresses the more profound interests and capacity of the individual (see Chapter 4.5).

With effect from the mid-1960's the idea of the "self-actualizing" man became popular and began to replace Mayo's, and the classical human relations school's, concept of "social man". As becomes evident in Chapter

6.2, how powerfully the idea of self-actualization is expressed may be open to question, but it is important to note in this context that it is this type of aspect of human action that is regarded as being of central importance in organization research.

Much empirical material confirms the assumption that self-actualization and qualifications are of considerable importance to many people. Argyris (1973) refers to a large number of studies which support this view. Rim (1977) found that the persons investigated in his study of eight "work functions" regarded "self-actualization" as most important. One problem in studies of this type, however, is concerned ith the possibilities of distinctly capturing and of separating self-actualization from other aspects. In Rim's study the respondents were, in addition to "self-actualization", also required to grade "intrinsic work satisfaction", amongst other things. It is possible that his respondents found it as difficult as I did to understand how these aspects can be separated from each other.

From the studies on the relationship between working conditions and mental health which were referred to and discussed in Chapter 3 we can also draw some conclusions as to the importance of self-actualization and the level of qualification. Bolinder and Ohlström (1971) found, for example, that amongst employees who replied "Yes, very" to the question about stimulating work, 24% had no, while 12% had considerable, psychosomatic symptoms. Of those who replied "No, not at all", 7% had no psychosomatic symptoms, while 30% had severe symptoms. Kornhauser (1965) found that the workers' feelings with regard to the utilization of their proficiency at work was the factor which correlated most strongly with mental health.

In a theoretical analysis Björkman and Lundqvist (1981) reached a corresponding conclusion, to which we can also link the self-determination aspect:

"Our study of the process of development and socialization as well as of the basic structure of human action has clearly indicated that qualification is the most important aspect of human activity and the indispensable condition for intellectual growth. Indissolubly united to qualification is self-determination: included in qualified activities is the setting up of a plan of action to achieve the aim." (p. 208)

Thus there are grounds to support the conclusion that the "self-actualizing", i.e. above all the qualification and self-determination aspects are of central importance to job satisfaction and also, as becomes evident in the following to motivation.[6])

---

6) Björkman and Lundqvist (1981) take up the employee's social relations as an important aspect beside self-determination/influence and level of qualification. They believe that little self-determination and a low degree of skill at work can hamper social relations. This view receives empirical support from the Hawthorne experiments as they are interpreted by

5.4   An Integrated Theory of Motivation

Hackman et al. (1975) have developed a theory of motivation which integrates several of the theories and points of departure which have been treated in this chapter. It looks like this:

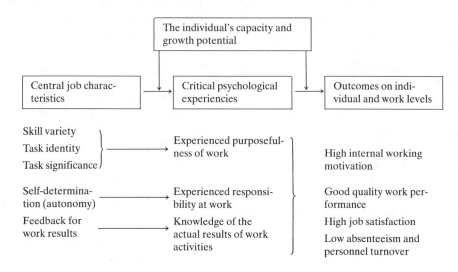

Hackman et al. assume that five dimensions in work are of central importance to the creation of high job satisfaction and high internal motivation:

– It shall be possible for different kinds of skills (skill variety) to be utilized
– Work shall be designed as an entire unit (task identity)
– It shall be socially purposeful in the sense that it has a substantial and identifiable influence on the lives of other people (task significance)
– Work shall make possible a higher degree of autonomy
– There shall be a feedback for the results of the work.

These dimensions in work form the basis for certain central psychological experiences and states. The first three affect purposefulness, independence influences the feeling of responsibility and the feedback determines the knowledge of the result achieved by the work. These psychological states subsequently influence the individual's results and the results of work (e.g. work satisfaction, absenteeism and internal motivation).

Blumberg and Gardell and Svensson's study (1981). In both cases an increase in the collective influence of the working group led to an improvment of the social contacts.

Individual variations with respect to capacity as well as growth potential influence the social relation between working conditions and the psychological reactions to work as the relation between the latter and Hackman and others' terminal variables (high internal work motivation, good quality of work performance, etc.).

On the basis of their theory Hackman et al. believe that a job which is to yield high motivation must score high on at least one, but preferably more, of the three dimensions which result in experienced purposefulness in work as well as on autonomy and feedback.

The theory is largely based on the results of the study presented by Hackman and Lawler (1971) and is linked to Herzberg's theory of motivation. One difference with respect to Herzberg is that Hackman and others also take some account of personality factors. They believe that the model as a basis for practical work does not apply to people who are not interested in developing themselves (why some individuals should not be interested in this possibility is not discussed by Hackman).

Hackman and others' theory harmonizes well with the factors in the job situation which I discussed in the previous section and claimed were of central importance to mental health, job satisfaction and internal motivation: self-determination and self-actualization (high level of qualification). Job contents characterized by variation of requirements for skills and the experience of purpose in work related to these correspond closely to what has been previously referred to as the qualification aspect.

The third central dimension according to Hackman and others, feedback, is subordinated, as far as I can understand, indirectly under self-determination and self-actualization. This is the case in that feedback must be regarded as having at least partly the character of a support for responsibility and purpose for work. If anyone is to be able to make a complete decision and know that the job is meaningful, knowledge of the results is essential.

Empirical support for the model is presented in Oldham and Hackman (1981). In relation to the attempts to create motivation on the basis of the classics of the human relations school, Hackman and others' model appears to me to be more advanced, although it basically expresses common sense in a well structured way. Possibly it is also more difficult to apply. It focuses on job content, the central dimension in the working situation. To change the content of work in the direction of the characteristics which Hackman regards as necessary means, of course, something quite different from attempting to generate satisfaction and motivation on the part of personnel by, for example, investing in information via personnel journals or better social relations as a result of training managers in sensitivity.[7]) Hackman, however, makes it clear that it is impossible to ignore job content when it is a matter of questions of motivation. At the same time it appears to be difficult to force the necessary changes from the point of view of motivation (according to Hackman's model) in the direction of technological requirements, for example. If motivation is to be markedly improved, far-reaching changes in the three dimensions must take place, i.e. the working conditions which give rise to purposefulness, experienced responsibility and knowledge of the results of work. This places extensive demands on the changing of the technical working conditions (which are largely determined by machines and other production equipment). Certainly *minor* modifications of the central dimensions can often be implemented, but the improvements in motivation will probably only be marginal.

The *technically affected* division of labour, i.e. splitting up/specialization of tasks in accordance with the demands of the technical system, does not constitute the sole obstacle to the enrichment of work as set forth in Hackman's model. A *social* division of labour, with its origins partly in demands for efficiency and partly in power factors (mainly the company management's desire to control personnel and the supervisors' wish to retain their job conditions) and which is not necessary from the point of view of the technological conditions, also renders difficult a development along the three dimensions defined by Hackman.[8])

How the implementation of job enrichment can be made more difficult due to problems in connection with the hierarchical dimension is illustrated by Lawler et al. (1973), amongst others. In this example, job enrichment of the the employees' (telephone operators') working conditions led to a certain impoverishment of the foremen's working conditions.

---

[7]) Hackman (1975) describes the attitude of the human relations school to job content as follows:
"The human relations movement, the design of piece rate and other incentive systems and experimentation with various supervisory styles were all more or less aimed at compensating for or overcoming the 'natural' pulling apart between the worker and his work. It can be argued that the failure of behavioral scientists to have more impact on organizations has largely to do with their acceptence of the assumption (shared with management, to be sure) that the work itself was inviolate, that the role of behavioral scientists was simply to help organizations select and motivate people within that terribly significant premise." (p. 100). This criticism also strikes at considerable parts of research on organizational culture, which is treated in Chapters 6.5 and 8.

[8]) The distinction between technical and socially influenced division of labour originates with Edqvist (1977). As Edqvist remarks, the boundary between these two types of division of labour is in practice often diffuse and difficult to define, but of course this does not prevent the division from having a heuristic value.

Thus it seems as though job enrichment is a difficult strategy. Hackman (1975) has observed that "job enrichment has failed just as often as it has succeeded."

Hackman does not seem to entertain any hopes that job enrichment should be able to revolutionize working life (even if he believes that it should be possible to make some progress). As has been said, the problem is linked up to production-technical aspects. It is probably also difficult to change working conditions by exclusively keeping to a level which only includes the job content of the individual and does not relate to the design of the work and conversion to the more general aspects of the organization.

In the main the entire branch of activity dealing with job enrichment, job design, sociotechnics, etc. is an expression for the fact that workplaces and companies are structured in a way that the basic tendency for the impoverishment of job content for various employees must be meagrely counteracted with the aid of a special expertise. As Sievers (1984) writes:

"This approach expresses and admits what work has been reduced and fragmented to in our organizations very well."

"What constitutes the working field for job redesign experts very often seems to be what has been left over from work after all managerial and satisfying aspects have been taken away and what often enough has lost the taste of the crumb from the rich man's table, so that it finally – via motivation – has to be enriched and flavoured artificially." (Sievers, 1984: 19)

Many authors regard the existence of job enrichment as an expression of the development of working life in the direction of an increasing endeavour in higher and higher degree to find the answer to human needs. Braverman's critics sometimes point to measures of this kind as evidence that traditional scientific management-inspired division of labour and controlled strategies for the organization of work have at least to some extent been forced to give way to modern principles. We can, however, also accept the contrary interpretation and see the efforts to raise the level of motivation by the enrichment of tasks as an expression of the fact that the latter are basically impoverished. Job enlargement and enrichment assume in a way that the jobs, by virtue of their nature are deskilled and impoverished.

5.5   The Impoverishment of Working Life and Problems of Motivation

Here I shall endeavour to relate the above discussion of motivation to Braverman's presentation. Superficially Braverman's argument can be refuted on the basis of the following: in order that a company should be efficient and able to survive, it must take account of its resources, not least those represented by its personnel. Companies which do not do so, and whose personnel feel no job satisfaction or motivation, are ousted from the market or are compelled to transform the organizational conditions and work design so that the employees are content and maintain a good standard of working performance. Good job conditions, in other words, go hand in hand with efficiency and profitability.

This thesis is expressed in many books on organization theory/psychology, e.g. by Schein (1980):

"... it is possible to maintain both ... the perspective of the individual attempting to use organizations for the fulfillment of his or her needs, and the perspective of the manager attempting to use human resources optimally to fulfill organizational needs." (p. 22)

This line of thought can largeley be derived from Maslow, whose theory on needs and motivation is often the point of departure for notions as to how human needs go hand in hand with business economical ideals of efficiency. This ideal is applied, as I shall show in greater detail in the following chapters (above all in Chapter 7), often in an ideological manner. As a simple illustration it may be mentioned here that a disciple of Maslow's ideas gives the following crude and naive interpretation as to how controversies and conflicts can easily be overcome:

"Business efficiency and the recognition of 'higher ceilings of human nature' are not incompatible; on the contrary, the highest levels of efficiency can *only* be obtained by taking full account of the need for self-actualization that is present in every human being." (Wilson, 1972: 198)

"It is hardly necessary to point out that the consequence of these ideas – in our strike-disrupted society – could be enormous. They may be regarded as a Hegelian synthesis of what is best about communism and capitalism, the end of the notion of class war in which *either* the workers or the bosses are 'top dogs': Maslow has pointed out that, if the full potentialities of human nature are taken into account, the freedom of one need not encroach upon the freedom of the other: there is plenty enough freedom to go round." (p. 188)

Whereas Wilson's ideas can probably be dismissed as slightly ridiculous, I shall make some brief comments on Schein's formulation, although it is only a more subtle presentation of an idea which is basically the same as Wilson's. Schein's thesis is only reasonable within certain (narrow) limits. Even if the individual's and the company management's interests are congruent in some respects, this scarcely applies without extensive restrictions.

From my survey of the theory of motivation it follows that an enduring intrinsic motivation demands much of the job situation. Much more than the opportunity to earn money or good relations between employees and management, on which Taylorism and the classical human relations school had concentrated. (The former largely disregarded motivation, assuming that the economic incitements were the only factors of decisive importance with respect to interest in working.) As has already been said, it has become increasingly clear in the course of time that work content constitutes the vital dimension for well-being, satisfaction and the conditions for motivation in working.

Hackman and others' model for motivation seems to be much more advanced and well structured than the earlier naive lines of thought associated with Mayo and the early human relations tradition. It is reasonable to use Hackman et al. as a starting point for understanding what job conditions can form the basis of intrinsic motivation (engagement in work). If we relate these to the survey in Chapter 2 we find, however, that the development of working life has rather implied to a considerable extent a departure *from* job conditions of this type. The impression of the collected studies of work processes – which in themselves yield a contradictory picture – is that the working conditions have been transformed into divided and unskilled processes, at least just as often as they have been changed into more unified and qualified processes. According to Hackman et al., intrinsic motivation requires job content of the latter type of characteristics. *The fact that development has partly taken a path towards working conditions which make difficult/impossible intrinsic motivation indicates that the aspect of motivation is of relatively slight importance and does not constitute a sufficiently powerful incitement seriously to counterbalance the impoverishment of work content which often follows from the technological and other interest which are evidently the driving forces for the development of working life. In any case it does not seem as if the psychological forces in this situation have a decisive impact as to how working conditions are devised* (cf. Chapters 2 and 6).

A high degree of personnel turnover, absenteeism and other (expressions of) psychosocial problems lead to problems of efficiency and can prove costly, especially in times of favourable economic cycles and low unemployment. Here we may find incitements for emphasizing the importance of having satisfactory working conditions for personnel. It must, however, be observed that the costs involved in replacing unskilled personnel are very much less than is the case with skilled personnel, and a possible strategy to reduce the economic importance of these problems is to force the division of labour and dequalification – and thereby the replaceability of personnel – still further.

One consequence of the standardization of working tasks at low levels in organizations is that the people working there are quite simple and cheap to replace. Lawler (1973) estimates the cost of personnel turnover at middle-management level as 5 to 25 times greater than that involved in replacing employees with unskilled working tasks.

That problems generated by unsatisfactory working conditions in the form of a high rate of personnel turnover need not necessarily constitute problems but in the case of some companies can even turn out to be an asset is illustrated by Goldman and Van Houten (1980):

"... industries that have simple production processes and depend on unskilled labor do benefit from high turnover. McDonald's, which pays minimum wages to teenage workers, avoids paying fringe benefits and salary increases by encouraging high turnover." (p. 59)

In normal cases, however, high rates of personnel turnover involve consequences for companies and motivate measures to keep the figures down.

It appears likely that fairly reasonable efficiency can often be generated by external control, coercion and instrumental corporate and work ideologies based on creating loyalty to management and norms for 'a fair day's work', so that the lack of motivation need scarcely mean that production must suffer to an excessive degree. The scope for allowing intrinsic motivation to express itself in skilled performance, for example, seems in any case to be limited for many employees.

According to this argument there certainly exists a clear contrast between what we can call the "social-psychological side" of economic efficiency and the job conditions which Braverman and others regard as the prevalent conditions, but the social-psychological efficiency aspects do not appear to be regarded as particularly important incentives. Naturally they are far from negligible seen from the management perspective, but in the case of personnel at lower qualification levels these aspects do not seem to be accorded any decisive importance. Consequently the problems of motivation which ensue from the development described by Braverman and others are unable to provide sufficiently powerful incentives, *effectively* to counteract the tendency towards dequalification and impoverishment of the job content.

In recent years, when unsatisfactory conditions at work began to be more clearly noted in the form of recruiting difficulties, a high rate of absenteeism and of personnel turnover, the incentives for company management to modify job conditions has somewhat increased. Some investments in more psycho-socially attractive job conditions have been made. The Kalmar factory of the Volvo Company is often mentioned as a striking example of far-reaching reform of the work organization in a humanistic direction. This factory is frequently mentioned in international literature to illustrate the humanistic organization principles (with which I shall deal in the next chapter). However, the factory only cost about 10% more in the way of investment than a "normal" factory, which shows that not even at places of employment where, according to the propaganda, exceptional regard has been paid to mastering absentee and personnel turnover problems, has this involved any major financial investment.

We may interpret this as meaning that not even business managements which are regarded as specially far-sighted consider that the satisfying of the employees' motivation and job satisfaction necessary motivates largescale economic surplus investment. (I shall revert to the Volvo factory at Kalmar in Chapter 6.5.)

With this I am not trying to claim that the problem of motivation can be ignored by organizations, but am rather expressing scepticism towards the view of Schein and many others on the possibility, given motivation as the point of mediation, of integrating at one and the same time management interest in highly productive behaviour on the part of personnel and the interest of personnel in job conditions providing optimal satisfaction of needs. For certain groups of employees interest and engagement may be assumed to be of decisive importance.

This applies above all to employees with marked "qualitative" tasks demanding good judgment, planning, thought and initiative. Here good performance cannot be generated only by control and checking. A lack of motivation can also result in considerable economic consequences. In jobs involving such tasks motivation is seldom a problem, however. Various individuals with jobs of this kind are managers or are employed in staff capacities, for whom this problem mainly consists of dealing with lack of motivation on the part of others. (This ist not to say that lack of commitment cannot also arise in the case of people in high positions.) There is a certain contradiction in the manager's task in the institutionalized idea that managers shall, amongst other things, take care of the motivation of others, since it is precisely this point which is at the root of problems of motivation. Modern work places are split up between managers and workers, between people who are presumed to manage and motivate (even if business leaders, quite contrary to management ideology, deal with many other things apart from managing) and people who work, are managed and, with the aid of good managers and specialists, may be presumed to be motivated. This means that there is an uneven division of the tasks and functions which can create interest and commitment at work. What remains for those who, according to the management ideology, require leaders in order to be motivated are the fragmented and impoverished parts of the entire jobs which the planning and management function divides up into the far-reaching vertical and hierarchical division of labour characteristic of modern companies and management thinking.

5.6 Reflections

The above discussion illustrates the slight overlapping to be found between, on the one hand, job satisfaction and motivation, in so far as these are of relevance from the point of view of management, and on the other hand purposefulness and positive effects of work which are of decisive interest to the employee. Two basic conditions speak against the interests being anything like identical. In the first place the "objective" worker interest in connection to work content is not limited to comprising only experienced or reported job satisfaction – as was evident in Chapter 3, a series of important functions are affected to a greater or less extent by the job content and situation without necessarily being involved in the individual's experience of or attitude to work. And these mental functions and ways of reacting, e.g. pacification of leisure time, are of not the slightest interest from the point of view of management. And secondly, motivation and job satisfaction are not the same thing – as long as extrinsic rewards (wages, prospects of promotion, etc.) and working morale maintain an acceptable level of motivation, satisfaction with job content is of little interest from the management point of view.

Of decisive importance to this large gap between interest in psychologically stimulating jobs and "instrumentally rational" jobs (as defined by company managements) is the fact that the individuals' interest in terms of experienced or manifested needs comprise only to a limited extent the former aspects. The object of work is a low priority value. The late capitalistic society and its dominant technological rationality bring about a streamlined socialization aimed at the allocation of priorities for material rewards and mass consumption. This constitutes the motivational psychological foundation, in turn based on needs or at least wishes, for "the instrumentalist ideology of work", in which strains and lack of purpose in work are ignored while the importance of wages and leisure time is emphasized with regard to expectations and evaluations. This is one important aspect of the way values and engagement in work have been allowed to be reduced to a question of "motivation". Cf. the following way of regarding the background to the interest in this issue:

"Here, *the hypothesis* I would like to offer and explicate is: that motivation only became an issue – for the social sciences as well as for the organization of work itself – when meaning either disappeared or was lost from work; that the loss of meaning of work is immediately connected with the increasing amount of differentiation and fragmentation, with the way work has been, and still is organized in the majority of our Western enterprises. As a consequence motivation theories have become surrogates for the search of meaning." (Sievers, 1984: 3)

One important aspect of the decline of purposeful work has been, and is, that an increasing proportion of total production does not correspond to any important needs – in fact a great deal can be said to imply the opposite to the satisfying of needs. This is discussed by Bosquet (1977), amongst others, who asks: "What meaning is there in a job whose products are meaningless?« (p. 379) This question should be regarded as particularly significant to the theory of motivation, but is conspicuous by its absence from the theory. To some extent an exception is the aspect of "task significance" in Hackman and others' model, but this aspect only demands that tasks should have some identifiable importance to someone, not that they should lead to any meaningful (= satisfying of needs) result.

The interest of organizational psychology in motivation and its lack of interest in the meaning of work illustrates its technocratic orientation. The objects of study are small well-defined questions, the answers to which form the basis of piecemeal social engineering intended to counteract tendencies for the division of labour and the impoverishment of jobs, as well as the horizontal division into people with management and planning tasks and those with tasks of implementation to lead to consequences which disturb production and the realization and continued domination of instrumental rationality. The lack of interest in the contextual aspects is striking. Motivation is regarded as an exclusively individual phenomenon which exists in an historical and social vacuum, apart from the fact that the social and material environment can encourage or hinder needs and motives from being realized or bring about various rewards/penalties. This applies, for example, to practically all research explicitly concentrated on motivation and satisfaction. Some organization theoretical/psychological research has been devoted to studying the importance of the organization for the norms of relevance to motivation. For example, organization cultural research goes so far as to take up the organization environment and the values expressed by this as a potential motivation factor (see further Chapters 6.5 and 8). In a recent summary article dealing with a large number of theories of motivation in organizational psychology by Thierry and Koopman-Iwema (1984) not one word is said about the importance of social or cultural conditions to motivation.

The historical-social context of the psychology of human motivation must be regarded as being of decisive importance. It is difficult to conceive of any "law of motivation" other than an exceptionally general and abstract one would characterize Mankind throughout different cultures and historical epochs. Nevertheless the majority regard theories of motivation, and especially in the field of organization theory, not in the social and cultural contexts. (To some extent Maccoby, 1981, is an exception.) The structure of motivation which distinguishes an individual is strongly influenced by the socialization to which he is subjected, before, during and away from work, by the ideologies, the systematic form of control of needs and pseudo-needs and the (lack of) awareness of these characteristic of a particular society. According to critical theory the task of research is to facilitate for the individual the determination of his "real interests" by revealing the conditions and mechanisms which generate false and self-destructive needs and wishes or which place unimportant or compensatory needs in the foreground, while basic needs are neglected. (The determination behind this is normally that the former allow themselves to be most easily satisfied, while the latter can be subversive, for example in our times the need of a good environment.) Motivation research is focused on almost the opposite. It tends to reveal a distorted picture of human motivation by concentrating on a very restricted part of the complex (social, cultural, psychological, material) contexts, namely those on the individual or micro level and that might be affected by management, and on this basis to present theories and results which are claimed to explain the phenomenon of motivation and the way motivation functions in practice. It also removes from the agenda essential but controversial questions concerning the meaningfulness of work and production – although these are probably of importance to engagement and interest in work.

A broader analysis of needs and driving forces in connection with work indicates that there is a systematic social influence (by company managements, trade unions and the various agencies of "consumption capitalism") to allocate priorities to wages, leisure time and consumption as values. At the same time the quality of work as a value tends to be given a lower priority than is motivated, on the basis of its importance and consequences (of which many individuals are unaware). We may observe that this leads to a systematic distortion of the needs which will appear as desirable motives and wishes. The "real" or "important" needs might be concealed and less important wishes (in terms of psychological well-being etc.) appear as crucial needs.[9] The latter express only to a limited degree the former. The theory of motivation, however, completely disregards this distortion and is based on warped result as a natural fact – and it gives the impression of expressing itself about "natural" rather than about systematically and socially-controlled driving forces and aims. (It is, of course, difficult to take into consideration all the relevant circumstances and aspects in complicated phenomena of the type human motivation. The criticism I express should perhaps be interpreted more mildly if this is borne in mind. Researchers

---

[9] To determine what are "real" needs is extraordinarily difficult and there may be good reason to disregard this concept (cf. Leiss, 1978). However, I believe that the individual "needs" job conditions which do not generate negative mental consequences. Jobs having the characteristics Gardell refers to on p. 59 may be said to embody the antithesis of "real" needs.

who choose to concentrate on one or a few aspects should, however pay regard to and express awareness of the problems which are indicated here.)

To sum up we may say that the theory of motivation largely presents a restricted and misleading picture of motivation conditions. Its results may possibly be of value to social engineering of workplaces. Its contribution may be said to be of a "technocratic-scientific" character, i.e., knowledge is subordinated to the interests of a controlling élite in taking measures to tackle certain problems. This is not, of course, to say that it is incapable of solving or reducing problems, even for wider groups. When it is a matter of job enrichment, for example, this is certainly often the case. From the "critical-scientific" point of view, however, this research leaves much to be desired. It fails to give a balanced picture of the way interaction between various social forces, needs, pseudo-needs and motives form the basis of the individual's motivation in relation to work. By presenting a distorted and virtually false picture of the latter, it counteracts rather than encourages a critical understanding of the individual's needs, interests and motivation in relation to work.

6. Theories of Organization and Work Conditions

The development trend and conditions which work psychology describes according to Chapter 2 do not appear to harmonize well with the lines of development of a "humanist" nature which are generally considered characteristic of modern working life: the delegation of decision-making, industrial democracy, etc. Important lines of organizational theory such as human relations and organizational development, OD (which is dealt with in this chapter) have hardly been of no significance to the development of working life. The result in the form of democratic labour management, investment in personnel-administrative measures, etc. have won general acceptance at places of employment (how "powerfully" this has taken place I shall discuss later on).

How, then, do human relations theories such as McGregor's Y Theory (McGregor, 1960) and group-orientated management and decision-making (Likert 1961; Likert and Likert 1976) harmonize with the trend towards division of labour and dequalification of work?

The basic philosophy to which the human relations tradition and similar schools give expression accord ill with the facts cited and the discussions held in this book. Contemporary working life and its conditions can scarcely in the main be referred to as humanistic.

In order to understand this inconsistent state of affairs it is necessary to scrutinize the various organizational theories and to clarify on which phenomena and on which conditions they are based. To make this possible it is required that the theories should be subjected to a critical examination, which is the aim of the following study of some of the most important organizational schools from the point of view of work organization. Here, too, I shift the emphasis from the level of the individual to that of the organization.

The following study is, in some respects, of a summary character and deals with only some of the aspects of the schools under review. Thus the scientific management movement is discussed on an overall level, while the human relations school is treated by my comments on a work representative and influential for that school. My account is to some extent historically structured in so far as I deal with the schools in the order they came into being: thus I start with scientific management and end with organizational culturel research.

6.1 Scientific Management

The so-called scientific management movement (also known as Taylorism) arose in the USA towards the end of the Nineteenth Century and was dissolved as an "official" school during the 1930's. However, we cannot deduce from this that the principles and influence of this school are no longer to be reckoned with on this account. However, some of the literature does give the impression that the scientific management movement is something of a relic which has long been out of date. Bruzelius and Skärvad (1975) write, for example, in a textbook that the negative influence of scientific management on employees

". . . enforced the need for new organizational principles and forms. This process began as early as the 1920's."

As we see from the following, however, this presentation is misleading.

The basic thought behind scientific management can be summarized as follows:

"The overall assumption behind the scientific management theory was that by simplifying work the job could be carried out more efficiently, less qualified workers could be employed, the company management's control of production could be increased and, finally, the profits of the organization could rise." (Hackman and Lawler, 1971: 215)

Hackman and Lawler express themselves still more concisely when they write that the aim of scientific management was to find means by which work could be simplified, specialized, standardized and subjected to routines.

According to Braverman (1974) it is just these particular job conditions which are characteristic of modern working life. In Braverman's view Taylorism has by no means lost its influence, but on the contrary is of the greatest importance to the forming of the modern work organization:

"It is impossible to overestimate the importance of the scientific management movement in the shaping of the modern corporation and indeed all institutions of capitalist society which carry on labor processes. The popular notion that Taylorism has been 'superseded' by later schools of industrial psychology or 'human relations', that it 'failed' – because of Taylor's amateurish and naive views of human motivation or because it brought about a storm of labor opposition or because Taylor and various successors antagonized workers and sometimes management as well – or that it is "outmoded" because certain Taylorian specifics like functional foremanship or his incentive-pay schemes have been discarded for more sophisticated methods: all these represent a woeful misreading of the actual dynamics of the development of management." (p. 86–7)

A survey of the literature concerned with the importance of Taylorism to contemporary working life reveals that most writers are of an opinion similar to that of Braverman on this point (see Chapter 2).

According to Edwards (1979), Taylor's own ideas on the formation of the working organization exercised little influence. Taylor himself failed to implement these when he had the opportunity to test them in practice. Edwards' view that the Taylorist principles had but slight powers of penetration stands in sharp contrast to the views of the majority of research scholars in the field of working life and the community. The explanation for Edwards' point of view does not seem to be lack of agreement with regard to the facts so much as another application of the concept "Taylorism" and scientific management. As a rule the terms are not used to define Taylor's specifically own ideas but to designate general organizational principles of which Taylor was an advocate. Even if Taylor himself was undeniably the most notable, he was nevertheless only *one* – and perhaps not even a particularly successful – representative of a broad trend in the field of industrial organization. To speak of Taylorism or regard the scientific management movement as a dominating organizational theory in practice is perhaps conceptually misleading. In common with current conceptual usage I speak of Taylorism, as do the authors to whom I refer with regard to Taylorism and scientific management, in a general and possibly rather loose sense. For a further discussion of narrow and broad definitions of Taylorism and scientific management, see Thompson (1983: 126–132).

Björkman (1978) believes that the principles of this school have exercised a greater influence on the formation of Sweden's industrial work places than any other production organization model. He writes that the way the physical working environment is formed is still primarily determined by the rationalization movement.

Lichtman and Hunt (1971) also refer to the importance of the scientific management tradition outside the production sector:

"... the scientific management movement is hardly dead, even if it appears more often now in the form of computer-oriented management science exercises in model building, operations research, cost-benefit analysis, etc. Moreover, it often disguises itself today in a more dynamic 'systems' terminology and posture, sometimes leaving behind many of its earlier oversimplifications." (p. 329)

This probably means that even if strict applications of the traditional scientific management type have become less common, the basic line of thought is still widespread.

The management author Drucker writes that

"The concept that underlies the actual management of work in American industry... is Scientific Management. Scientific Management focuses on the work. Its
core is the organised study of work, the analysis of work into its simplest elements
and the systematic improvement of the workers' performance of each of these
elements... And it has no difficulty proving the contribution it makes; its results in
the form of higher output are visible and readily measurable. (quoted in Braverman,
1974: 88)

Thus it would seem that the scientific management tradition is by no means
dead and buried. The short review I have made harmonizes well with
Braverman's assessment of the importance of Taylorism to modern working
life. There are reasons for agreeing with Braverman when he writes:

"If Taylorism does not exist as a separate school today, that is because apart from
the bad odor of the name, it is no longer the property of a faction, since its
fundamental teachings have become the bedrock of all work design." (Braverman,
1974: 87)

However, as is made clear in Chapters 2 and 6.4, there are tendencies that
Taylorist principles are not used so much and work organisational forms
with different points of departure have come into use. The following point
of view seems to constitute a suitable summing-up of what work process
research has concluded in recent times (cf. Thompson 1983):

"most present technology was born and developed in a strictly Taylorist spirit...
Only, in general, when a new technology has been developed, and is put into
production, is there any recognition of the social problems embodied in it. At that
stage, the techniques of the social sciences can be applied: job enrichment, job
enlargement, or the use of semi-autonomous work groups." (Rosenbrock, 1979: 2)

The Taylorist work organization doctrine has thus gradually during the
Twentieth Century become a regular feature of the organization of production, but in recent time it has been supplemented by other organizational measures which follow an at least partly different form of logic
(aiming at stimulation and motivation of the employees and increased
flexibility) such as, e.g. suggestions, MBO (Management by Objectives),
personnel-administrative techniques (e.g. quality circles) and socio-technical solutions (Sandkull, 1981: 19–20).

6.2   Modern Human Relations

As I pointed out in the beginning of the chapter, it is not my intention to
give any kind of overall survey of the various organization theoretical
schools. In this section I shall deal with a work from the human relations
tradition, one of its "flagships", McGregor's standard work "The Human
Side of Enterprise" (1960). This is probably the work in modern human

relations (human resources) book (no change) to which reference is most frequently made. This book will serve to illustrate the human relations tradition in its modern variant as contrasted with the classical variant from the 1930's (Mayo et al.).

McGregor formulates two basic theories on human nature, which for reasons of neutrality he calls X and Y. These are well known, but I shall quote them (in McGregor's own words).

Theory X assumes that:

- "The average human being has an inherent dislike of work and will avoid it if he can."
- "Because of this human characteristic of dislike of work, most people mus be coerced, controlled, directed, threatened with punishment to get them to put forth adequate effort toward the achievement of organizational objectives."
- "The average human being prefers to be directed, wishes to avoid responsibility, has relatively little ambition, wants security above all."

(Ibid. pp. 33–34)

Theory Y, which is the negation of X, instead assumes that

- "The expenditure of physical and mental effort in work is as natural as play or rest."
- "Man will exercise self-direction and self-control in the service of objectives to which he is committed."
- "The average human learns, under proper conditions, not only to accept but to seek responsibility."
- "The capacity to exercise a relatively high degree of imagination, ingenuity, and creativity in the solution of organizational problems is widely, not narrowly, distributed in the population."

(Ibid. pp. 47–48)

McGregor himself supports (naturally) Theory Y and asserts that:

"If employees are lazy, indifferent, unwilling to take responsibility, intransigent, uncreative, uncooperative, Theory Y implies that the causes lies in management's methods of organization and control." (p. 48)

McGregor's X and Y theories stand out as rather simple, rough-and-ready stereotype assumptions. There is more than a little of the theories of "Good" and "Bad" about them.

Thanks to its simplicity, McGregor's theory has a certain amount of force. His dichotomy can probably be applied as the starting point for a certain understanding of the view of humanity on which various organizational conditions and structures are based. The value of the theory is perhaps greater on the practical and pragmatic rather than on the theoretical level.

Since Theory Y has the character of a slogan it may be important to grasp what McGregor means in practice. His attempts at concretizations and exemplifications of the Y ideal in practice leave a remarkable impression.

Among McGregor's examples it may be noted that the Y view expresses criticism that the individual has nothing to say with regard to his promotion and placing. McGregor considers that this view "... requires active and responsible participation of the individual in decisions affecting his career (ibid. p. 103). This means that

At very least, data which he can provide concerning his interests, goals, and qualifications can be utilized to permit him to become an active candidate for promotional opportunities under most circumstances." (Ibid. p. 106)

Thus McGregor means here that the employee should not be promoted against his will (or without being consulted). Otherwise McGregor exemplifies Theory Y thinking with the Scanlon Plan (a proposal and profit sharing system) and discusses the influence of the employees on decisions: opportunities should be created

"... under suitable conditions for people to influence decisions affecting them." (p. 126)

Thus McGregor draws only very limited conclusions about what "Theory Y in practice" ought to lead to. It is difficult to see the connection between the positive view of man to which Theory Y gives expression and the cautious implications which McGregor sees it leading to.

McGregor's definition of Theory Y can therefore be regarded as rhetoric, a setting up of non-binding theses to which, as a result of McGregor's exemplifications, virtually anyone can subscribe. With a more incisive formulation it could be said that McGregor's Theory Y gives the business leader a) a basis for expressing on the ideological level an attractive view of man and b) an alibi for not being required in practice to follow up this view of man except to a very limited degree. Perhaps this is one important reason for the great deal of attention which has been devoted to McGregor's ideas.

Another central defect in his presentation, which is in part associated with the inability to draw far-reaching conclusions as to what is implied by Theory Y, is that he does not touch on the technical systems of organizations (i.e. production equipment and the way of organizing work) and their decisive importance to the way in which the view of man can be expressed. For example, McGregor says nothing about whether the conveyor belt as work organization and the Y view can be combined. This is otherwise typical of considerable parts of the human relations tradition, which has neglected the technical system (as well as to a large extent the administrative control system) and the decisive importance of these in many respects if Theory Y and similar ideas on man are to acquire any real force in practice.

What conclusions may we draw from this discussion about human relations compared with the Taylorist influence on job conditions and against the background of the working conditions which, according to Braverman and others, prevail in working life? Naturally it is hardly the case that these job conditions harmonize with the ideas of the human relations school. This can be illustrated by McGregor (1960) who writes that people today have grown used to being controlled, manipulated and checked up on in their organizations and to finding their satisfaction and self-realization away from their jobs.

McGregor (in common with others of the modern human relations tradition) is thus dissatisfied with the appearance of the working conditions. And yet the tradition which he serves has hardly consistently and powerfully followed the humanistic basic view which, for example, Theory Y, according to McGregor's definition even if not according to his examples, is (or could be) an expression of.

The aspects of the job situation which the human relations school representatives have concentrated on have sometimes been peripheral, like the examples referred to in McGregor's book. No direct contradiction between human relations ideas and the impoverishment of job content needs perhaps necessarily exist: a proposal and profit-sharing system can exist parallel to a conveyor belt.

We must be careful when making generalizations on the entire human relations tradition on the basis of McGregor's book. Nevertheless I consider that a study of McGregor's book can provide a good illustration of large parts of the modern (as opposed to the classical) human relations school.[1]) Few books on the theory of organization have been referred to so often as that work.

6.3   Organizational Development (OD)

OD is largely based on the human relations school. I shall therefore treat it only briefly. Rohlin's anthology (1974), like Friedlander and Brown's survey (1974), indicates that OD can be defined in many different way. Friedlander and Brown also include job design and sociotechnics in their OD concept. They speak of two types of OD studies: the human-processual

---

[1]) It is perhaps misleading to refer McGregor's book to the "modern" human relations school. It is slightly more than twenty years old. The important point in this context is in any case to distinguish McGregor and other representatives for the neo-tradition of the 1960's and 1970's from Mayo and others who represented the school in the 1930's and 1940's.

approach and the techno-structural approach. To take up even the latter study is to give the OD concept much too broad a content. In this section I speak of OD only in the sense of application of a behavioural scientific theory and method aimed at influencing attitudes and manner of relationship at the individual and organizational level with regard to work, relations and organizational climate. In the next section I shall deal with studies which are also devoted to the technical aspects.

Whereas the majority of OD authors stress the humanistic side of their work, French and Bell (1973) express the aims of OD in a loosely bound, scarcely humanist, manner:

»OD problem-solving interventions tend to focus on real organization problems that are central to the need of the organizations rather than on hypothetical, abstract problems that may or may not fit the members needs."

This formulation motivates the query: are the needs of an organization more real than those of its members? A common criticism levelled against OD is concerned with its manipulative element. Abrahamsson (1978) considers that OD interventions are focused on a limited conflict consciousness through the emotions of participants in OD activities being released in the direction of interpersonnel relations, bureaucracy and hierarchy. The perspective is thus shifted from the basic conflicts, conditions of power and the aim of the organization.

Abrahamsson sums up his criticism of OD:

"Its aim is mainly ideological; its methods manipulative; its final result a person who believes he has become more open, aware and sensitive to changes, but whose sensitivity is exploited by aims outside his control."

Possibly Abrahamsson is a little too categorical in his judgment. OD can probably be applied in different ways: from psychologizing away problems of power and goals in companies to supplementing economic thinking with humanist points of view. The latter should be regarded as the normal intention. It should, however, be observed that the risks of OD being applied manipulatively are considerable:

"OD as a field runs the risk of encouraging and implementing subtle but pursuasive forms of exploitation, curtailment of freedom, control of personality, violation of dignity, intrusion of privacy – all in the name of science and of economic and technological efficiency. Within the hierarchical fabric of everyday organizational power struggles, OD researcher/consultants typically represent the control needs of management." (Friedlander and Brown, 1974: 335)

Whether or not OD is liberative or manipulative, its influence on the job conditions of production workers and office workers seems to have been rather limited. Without explicitly discussing which categories OD works with, Argyris (1964 b) mentions top executives and French and Bell (1973) speak of middle management and top management. Friedlander and Brown write that OD interventions (of a human-processual nature) have mainly been performed with management groups, while few efforts of this kind have been made with and for workers. These authors consider that

"The needs of those lower in the organization for a higher quality of life, for an expanded range of occupational and life choices may seldom be known or acted upon by the consultant." (Friedlander and Brown, 1974: 335)

To some extent OD work does affect personnel categories at lower levels. OD interventions and programmes focused on higher organizational levels also indirectly influence personnel groups at other levels within the organization. OD has therefore primarily been a theory of organization for business leaders and professional employees at somewhat higher levels and its influence on job conditions for production workers and office workers has probably been rather limited. This may be due to the fact that OD, like human relations, does not really evince much interest in technical conditions.

To devote resources to increasing sensitivity and interpersonnel competence among workers whose tasks, due to noise and other physical restriction, do not permit social interaction with the environment (except during breaks) does not seem to be specially motivated from the point of view of efficiency.

During recent times, however, there has possibly been a tendency for OD to pay more attention to sociotechnical aspects and to come closer to job enrichment, sociotechnics and similar efforts (Faucheux et al., 1982). This could naturally imply that OD efforts could have affected the job conditions of production workers. However, the influence of OD on the development of job conditions for personnel at the lower organizational levels, particularly that of manual workers, may for the most part be assumed to be of rather small significance.

6.4   Sociotechnics

The Taylorist work organization has led to a series of problems for companies (company management), e.g. absence, turnover of personnel and recruiting problems. Organizational principles based on human relations thinking do not seem to have been seriously able to deal with these problems, possibly in the main because this tradition neglects, amongst other things, the importance of the technical conditions.

There are, however, other ways to deal with the abovementioned problems than those offered by the human relations school. Sandberg (1978) gives a survey of attempts by employers to tackle the problems. Amongst other things he mentions four different ways:

1. To find people who are willing to accept the job conditions such as they are, e.g. by locating activities in depopulated areas or abroad or by exploiting immigrant workers.
2. By driving labour management and planning control still further, so that personnel turnover and absence may be more easily dealt with.
3. By modifying the tasks by means of extending and varying the work.
4. By changing the production-technical plant from functional to flow orientation and/or basing the organization of the work not on isolated tasks and isolated individuals, but on larger production sections and entire working groups.

In this section we shall mainly be concerned with the last point. The first point lies somewhat outside the scope of this book, even if it is important to bear in mind in order to understand the employers' possibilities for dealing with a dissatisfied work force. If dissatisfactions are expressed too strongly, employers can reply by moving production. I dealt with Point 2 in the preceding chapter. The third point is dealt with partly in connection with the fourth, which is usually known as sociotechnical systems (sociotechnics). Job enlargement and job enrichment are examples of methods often applied within the framework of the sociotechnical system. Since the end of the 1960's sociotechnics has attracted much attention on the part of research into working life. Here I shall refer to some views on the conditions for changing, on the basis of sociotechnical theories and methods, those working conditions which the principles of scientific management orientated production and organization have led to.

Within the framework of the company or division regarded as an entirety sociotechnical research workers and consultants draw a clear distinction between the technical and social systems. They emphasize that these affect each other.

"Study of a productive system therefore requires detailed attention to both the technological and the social components. It is not possible to understand these systems in terms of some arbitrarily selected single aspect of the technology such as the repetitive nature of the work, the coerciveness of the assembly conveyor or the piecemeal nature of the task." (Emery and Trist, 1960: 284)

The sociotechnical method is to shape or modify the work organization by paying regard to the technological and social conditions simultaneously, thereby facilitating the attainment of maximum efficiency of the total production system. In other words sociotechnics endeavours to find methods by which the technical and social "components" of the organization can best be integrated. (Davis, 1979).

Group and work relations are structured so as to support the technological system at the same time as the degrees of freedom in the latter are utilized in such a way that the formation of the technology is made as far as possible compatible with the demands of the social structure. Sociotechnics is mainly concentrated on conditions at working group level. Thus it deals more with the tasks of the group than with those of the individual.

A notable series of experiments involving sociotechnical changes of industrial work places in Norway is reported in Thorsrud and Emery (1969). These experiments resulted in some successes, even if the authors in at least one of the cases in the conclusion and in the summary seem to have given a somewhat too positive picture of the results compared with what appears to be justified on the basis of the report of the progress of the experiments. How, then, should the influence and possibilities of sociotechnics be judged in relation to scientific management principles for the organization and development of work, as described in Chapter 2?

Ahlmann (1978) sees sociotechnics as something of a synthesis of scientific management (thesis) and human relations (antithesis). He believes that while the scientific management school paid too little attention to the social side of the job, the human relations representatives for their part were insufficiently concerned with the technical conditions (and therefore had only a limited influence in practice). Sociotechnics, on the other hand, offers a reasonable compromise between these two sides of the work situation, states Ahlmann.

Naturally it is of the utmost importance that the social sides of the work situation are not presented as something separable from the technical working conditions, which is what the human relations school did. The "humanistic" element in sociotechnics is indeed less striking than in human relations and OD. In so far as sociotechnics pays explicit attention to the technical/physical frameworks in a fixed mechanically controlled job situation, it grants different – and possibly better – conditions for improving working conditions than the human relations schools seems to have had, for example. At least this can be regarded as true in the case of employees with a job content which is largely determined by production-technological conditions and demands.

The Volvo factory at Kalmar is one of the best known examples of a factory constructed in accordance with sociotechnical principles. This factory has aroused international interest and is cited as an example of the way "humanistic" ideas can assume concrete form for the changing of conveyor belt production (see e.g. Schein, 1980). The design of the factory has amongst other things enabled the workers to do their work in teams, vary their tasks and to some extent influence their own job situations.

According to Agurén et al. (1976) the majority of the employees are rather positive to these working conditions. They point out that absence and personnel turnover are lower at the Kalmar factory than at Volvo's conventional factory at Torslanda. The differences are relatively small, however: 14% as compared with 19.2% with respect to absence and 16.3% as compared with 20.8% with respect to personnel turnover. It is also likely that at least part of these differences can be accounted for by the fact that the Kalmar factory is new and much smaller than the factory at Torslanda.

The advanced control system required for the type of production in use at the Kalmar works may be assumed to make difficult the employees' possibilities of influencing those working conditions which lie outside the immediate job situation. The Swedish TUC newspaper LO Tidningen No. 41, 1979 describes the control of the working teams as follows:

"It is thanks to the computers, and the fact that they can be used to control and check production in detail, that the assembly line has become unnecessary. The computers give the company management a complete picture of the production situation. Everything is checked and errors are stored in the computer. Possibilities of detecting scapegoats at Volvo are applicable only in the case of entire working groups – not individuals.

The marketing division at Gothenburg decides, on the basis of information from the sales side, the daily production, model and colour. The working teams at Kalmar receive their orders via the computer."

Thus sociotechnics does not have to mean that the employer loses his possibilities of controlling and checking. This fact has been pointed out by several authors:

"The Swedish Employers' Confederation's new factories may be regarded as embodying an effort, mainly in the manufacturing industry, to organize production so as to ensure strict control over the workers' 'self-management'." (Helgeson, 1978: 52)

The critics also point to the relationship between sociotechnical analysis and the overall influence on the company. Some authors believe that the sociotechnical division of working groups into small autonomous units, as in the case of Volvo at Kalmar, splits up the unity of the workers and reduces their union strength (see e.g. Perby, 1978).

Another form of criticism also questions the "novelties" of sociotechnics on the micro-level. Kronlund (1975) writes that the content of sociotechnics consists of techniques which have long been in use, rotation of work, broadening of work, partly autonomous groups, target guidance in collaboration, production groups and consultations.

There are, of course, also research workers who express more positive and optimistic views on the possibilities of sociotechnics. Two of the best known are Davis (1979; 1980) and Walton (1979; 1985). Davis considers that production engineers have concentrated on optimizing the efficiency of the technical system while neglecting the social aspects. Since the total efficiency of a factory or a company must take account of both technical and social aspects, there are scope and economic incentives for increased investment in the social aspects. Davis (1980) points to a number of changes outside the organization, e.g. increased education, higher standards of living and changed sex role patterns (where the husband's duty as family provider is no longer as central as in the past) which mean that more regard must be paid to the social conditions within the organizations in order to achieve optimum sociotechnical efficiency. Walton (1985) substitutes for the traditional Taylorist strategy for the organization of work a strategy which emphasizes commitment and which is based on sociotechnical thinking. He believes that the earlier strategy is no longer effective in a period of growing international competition.

"Especially in a high-wage country like the United States, market success depends on a superior level of performance, a level that, in turn requires the deep commitment, not merely the obedience – if you could obtain it – of workers. And as painful experience shows, this commitment cannot flourish in a workplace dominated by the familiar model of control." (p. 79)

Walton states that more and more American companies are abandoning job design principles that deskill and fragment work and separate doing and thinking in favour of a commitment strategy which, among other things, means the reduction of hierarchy, group organization, the performance of entire work tasks and the combination of doing and thinking.

In comparison with the human relations school, which hardly took account of the importance of the technological conditions, the sociotechnical approach has greater possibilities of humanizing working life in so far as it embodies ambitions to modify the technical conditions surrounding the work content.

An important problem in this context is to what extent the technical conditions can be modified:

"Thus in existing production systems there do not exist the degrees of freedom in relation to technique which would make possible the organization of work in accordance with social requirements. An important condition for sociotechnical change is thus lacking. Current production technique has not been developed separately from organization principles. The production system is constructed with the expressed aim of being as predictable and closed as possible. If we are to succeed in bringing about changes which would really satisfy social requirements, then we must try to change the entire production system. Then we cannot, as the sociotechnicians have hitherto done, limit ourselves to the 'operative system'." (Björkman and Lundqvist, 1981: 339).

Over and above this type of discussion we can naturally try to judge sociotechnics on its actual results. It is a little more than a decade since the fairly extensive experiments in Sweden and Norway involving autonomous groups and sociotechnics had so to say the chance to prove what it was worth.

"Experimental activities involving 'autonomous groups in both Norway and Sweden only became parentheses, although the evaluation results were positive. They led to no lasting changes. The original ideas of sociotechnics have become increasingly superficial and nowadays people only talk about 'group organization' or 'production groups'. In the manufacturing industry the individual tasks are being increasingly simplified at the same time as group-stressed production organization is being brought into line with efforts at rationalization." (Björkman and Lundqvist, 1981: 339)

A similar view is expressed by De Geer and Giertz (1980). Kern and Schumann (1984, referred by Broady and Helgeson, 1985), however, found that a production concept in harmony with sociotechnical thinking has been rather common among West German corporations during the end of the 1970's. My impression is also that elements of this type of thought have some impact on parts of Swedish industry. In USA there is some optimistic literature on the subject of implemented changes and – especially – on changes which are in the course of being brought about. Walton (1985) states, for example, that there are thousands of American companies which are revising their principles for work organization on the basis of sociotechnical principles. This judgment certainly has a certain foundation, but the question is whether it is a case of exaggerated optimism. Criticism of Walton for allowing scientific accuracy to weigh lightly as against the ambition to inspire changes has been expressed by York and Whitsett (1985). These authors take up a famous example General Food's production plant at Topeka, Kansas, which has been widely publicized as a prototype of the plant of the future (especially by Walton), emphasizing worker participation and the quality of working life. However, York and Whitsett state that

"when examined more closely, the plant appears to be unusual but less radical and more difficult to operate and manage than often described." (p. 22)

York and Whitsett consider that it is the ambition of Walton and of many other humanistically inclined organization research workers to stimulate changes in companies which can mean that data will be reported and presented in a selective manner. This means that caution must be exercised when judging their results.

It is important that sociotechnics should not be permitted to function as some kind of alibi for working life in its entirety. Sociotechnical experiments, such as the Volvo works at Kalmar, have been used for propaganda purposes and are referred to almost as a routine in international literature as examples of how far-reaching changes are possible within the framework of the existing system and its objectives. Mendner (1975) takes up this aspect, pointing at the interest of capital owners to

".... launch an extensive propaganda campaign for the 'humanizing' of work, to cultivate the illusion that a basic restructuring of the work process, especially the abandoning of the Taylorist principle of division of labour and separation of planning and implementation, is also possible under capitalistic production conditions and can also be brought about gradually on a wider basis. Furthermore, the few examples of application of work enrichment and autonomous group work which have passed out of the experimental stage also serve this purpose." (p. 154)

As a final and summary comment on this brief review of sociotechnics the following may be said: it is still not clear whether sociotechnics can achieve any extensive qualitative improvements of the individual's job content and work situation. The contribution of sociotechnics on a broad scale to such a change remains to be seen even if occurence of sociotechnical thinking and principles for organizations indicates that a long tradition of far driven division of labour was partly broken or at least reduced in the 1970's.

6.5   Organizational Culture

As distinct from the organizational schools hitherto discussed in this chapter, the broad current in research on organization which is usually known as organizational culture is not only, or even mainly, orientated towards organization of work or quality of working life. Research on organizational culture includes numerous diverging lines, perspectives and focal points of interest, including customer relations, strategic planning and the symbolic operations (rites, ceremonies, etc.) which distinguish an organization and which are of little direct relevance to the sets of problems dealt with in this book.

Here I shall not attempt to give any survey of the various theoretical lines and fields of study treated in organizational culture research. (Good surveys and introductions have been produced by Allaire and Firsirotu, 1984, Morgan, Frost and Pondy, 1983 and Smircich, 1983 a.) My brief presentation will be limited to some points of view directly relevant as far as organization of work and quality of work are concerned. I shall also later in this chapter have something to say about the organizational symbolism theory, which partly comes under culture research.

The concept of culture is defined in various ways in organizational research. Some authors look on organizations in their entirety as cultures, which means that the cultural dimension in all conditions and phenomena in an organization are observed, while other authors regard culture as "the organization's expressive and affective dimensions in a system of shared and meaningful symbolds manifested in myths, ideology and values" (Allaire and Firsirotu, 1984: 213). In the latter sense thus the concept of culture is separate from formal structures, technologies, power and control conditions, organization of work, etc.

Irrespective of which specific definition is accepted, the representatives of this line do not often go into the latter conditions (Alvesson, 1985 c). A corporate culture can, however, have implications for these. By no means seldom a "strong corporate culture", i.e. an organization with clear values and powerful symbols which support these and where the system of values and the symbols characterize the entire organization, is sometimes regarded as a replacer or even standing in a state of opposition to narrow and direct control which checking of the employees.

This has been most forcefully expressed by Peters and Waterman (1982) in their bestseller "In Search of Excellence". On the basis of a study of extremely innovative and successful American companies they found that the following assumptions and principles amongst others, paved the way for high efficiency.

– Accent on action and experimentation rather than (too much) analysis and planning.
– Encouragement of independence, enterprise and practical risk taking among employees.
– The primary source of productivity is a motivated employee. Respect shall be shown to the individual and every employee should be regarded as a source of ideas.
– Co-workers are motivated by, amongst other things, the participation of corporate leaders themselves. The basic philosophy of the company is of great importance to motivation and this is inspired by corporate leaders in concrete practice in the form of frequent visits to the shop floor or as a customer in a service company.

A company culture built up on these ideas is regarded as efficient, amongst other things because it corresponds to people's needs and preconditions. At least outwardly it stands in opposition to Taylorist and bureaucratic principles of organization. The point about a good corporate culture is that it is the strong, clear-cut values, understood by all the employees, and the rules as to what is good, which are important for peoole's behaviour. The formal supervision and control of the business management and a hierarchical control apparatus are considered to be less crucial.

A partly different aspect of corporate culture is based on the idea that a "strong" culture in itself is good for the personnel (and for long-term efficiency). This claim is made by Deal and Kennedy (1982), for example, who go on to say that a strong culture increases people's satisfaction with what they are doing, which in turn probably leads to increased work investment. The corporate culture gives people identity in their work by connecting up their individual tasks more strongly to the collective unit which the company is assumed to be. Through the culture we understand better how our own work, possibly limited in scope, is associated with the company's comprehensive aim (the business idea), so that this is felt to be more purposeful.

In their book Deal and Kennedy oscillate between regarding cultures as something which places the individual in the centre and which are in accord with a "humanist" rather than a technical-bureaucratic point of view and on the other hand regarding business cultures as being capable of assuming entirely different forms, even of a purely bureaucratic character. (They speak of the latter as "process culture".) Nevertheless they seem to consider all cultures as being good in themselves (except when they go wrong in relation to marketing and business objectives, which can happen for example when the company's strategic situation is changed), because of the fact that the culture spreads purpose and social integration in relation to the fundamental aims of the company.

Some authors in the organization research field are restrictive about talking about or in any case about carrying out research on organization cultures in their entirety. The object of research can easily become too extensive and studies will then lack precision (cf. Pettigrew, 1979). The problem is then that an entire culture comprises an enormous quantity of different aspects. Culture can, for example, be defined as

"the integrated pattern of human behavior that includes thought speech, action, and artifacts and depends on man's capacity for learning and transmitting knowledge to succeeding generations."

(Webster's New Collegiate Dictionary, ref. in Deal and Kennedy, 1982: 4). To take on the study of culture in organizations without making extensive restrictions is in such cases a gigantic task. Criticism can also be levelled at various stuides of corporate culture in which the concept of culture is in practice reduced to being made equivalent to a few central evaluations of instrumental significance to the company's objectives (Alvesson, 1985 d).

Instead of taking on the entire culture many research workers on organizational culture concentrate on some important aspect of the culture, e.g. ideology, sets of values, myths, rituals, ceremonies or stories in the organization. These phenomena express in symbolical form essential characteristics of the culture. With regard to these penomena, organizational cultural research overlaps the symbolical perspective of organizations (organizational symbolism research). A symbol can be defined as a sign which expresses more than its manifest content. They are representations which contain a wider meaning system. They refer to subjective meaning. Culture and symbolism research share, apart from a largely common field of research, interest in the informal, expressive-affective side of organization, in symbols, linguistic usage, etc. One difference is that symbolism research does not necessarily relate its perspective to an overall cultural unit or to conditions specific to an organization but assumes that symbolic aspects can be applied to, in principle, all types of actions, occurrences, structures and material objects. The basic assumption for the perspective of organizational symbolism is that.

"... organizations are human systems manifesting complex patterns of cultural activity ... Members of an organization are able to use language, can exhibit insight, produce and interpret metaphors, are able to vest meaning in events, behavior; and objects, seeking meaning in their lifes – in short, can act symbolically." (Morgan, Frost and Pondy, 1983: 4)

A central thought in this perspective, as in cultural research, is that people do not (nor in organizational contexts) only function "rationally-instrumentally" but also on the expressive-affective level.

As typical organization symbols we may mention the size and design of managing-director's offices, the architecture of an organization, jargon, jokes and stories which shed light on some specific feature of company activities, 50 year jubilees and the company logotype. Also a number of phenomena which should not perhaps primarily be regarded as symbolic can yet have an important symbolic function: thus, for example, the setting up of a committee with a certain task indicates that the organization takes a particular problem seriously (at least seriously enough to invest much time and resources to make it appear that the organization is really trying to do something about the problem) or the formulation of a new business strategy can symbolize the wish of the management or the collective to revitalize or bring about a new birth of the activities (cf. Pfeffer, 1981a; Berg, 1985).

The symbol perspective does not convey anything directly new in the form of ideas about "substantial" changes of work organization or quality of working life. A number of suggestions about new features at work places which could be conceived to enrich job conditions are, however, to be found in this type of literature.

Dandridge (1984), for example, takes up the ceremony as an instrument through which work and play can be integrated. He discusses what is characteristic of work and play respectively and argues the desirability of introducing more play as a legitimate activity in work.

The ceremony can be defined as a ritualized act which is planned to take place at a particular time and place and is accepted and desired by some particular group which participates in it. Dandridge includes a great many from the daily coffee break to the annual party of the firm and one-time ceremonies such as the "birthday celebration" of a company product.

Dandridge cites the following advantages of ceremonies in organizations:

1. Participants can experience and reinforce competence of relevance to their usual work.
2. Individuals can transcend their job roles and form links to the organization in its entirety, experience the product or the company in its entirety.
3. Social needs such as fellowship can be satisfied.
4. Values, roles and objectives for the organization can be passed on in that the ceremony expresses the company's image.
5. New lines of communication are formed or possibilities of communication which are normally unavailable or are not utilized become available and are utilized. This applies, we may imagine, with regard to both the content of the communication as well as to those who take part in the communication. Vertical communication is made possible (temporarily) during the ceremony.

Through the introduction of several pre-planned (rather than spontaneous) ceremonies the basic structure of the place of employment is not affected, but it is rather a question of a peripheral addition in relation to the work process and the hierarchy of the organization. The effect of the ceremony on the employees' working conditions will probably be at least partly dependent on the basic structure of the work place. If this is in accord with the attributes of the ceremony, it can probably bring about something of what has been mentioned above, whereas it is difficult to imagine that this would have any notable consequence at a workplace characterised by hierarchy, direct control and far-reaching division of labour. In the latter case it is likely that the ceremony is only an odd and peripheral feature of the organization, which for the moment permits a little play and relaxation rather than a source of influence on day-to-day practice and of integration of work and play. (Spontaneous cases of phenomena similar to what Dandridge calls ceremonies can also take place in activities having the latter type of characteristics, e.g. cf. Burawoy, 1979, who speaks of games in a workplace culture in connection with the attitude of the workers to fulfilling a contract. However, this is an activity which arises spontaneously in a workers' collective and scarcely something that can be introduced as planned activity. Nor does it to any great extent affect the relationship outside the work group.)

In so far as organizational culture and symbolism theory contain a great many diverging lines and completed studies it is difficult to express a general judgement. Many studies also lack direct relevance to the working life perspective, which means that the scope of the following comments is limited as regards research on culture and symbolism in its entirety. With these reservations I maintain that the following judgments are valid for "typical" research in this field.

Organizational culture and symbolism research to a great extent takes up the same theme as the early human relations school did more than half a century ago. It is the informal side of the organization, the social relations, group norms and the company as source for the satisfying of social needs which stand in the centre. Peters and Waterman refer with approval to Mayo's old ideas "that it is *attention to employees,* not work conditions per se that has the dominant impact on productivity" (p. 6) and "that the simple act of paying positive attention to people has a great deal to do with productivity" (p. 94). Even if the majority of research workers concerned with culture and symbolism do not care to borrow freely from Mayo's old larder and other sources associated with the infancy of the human relations school, there are obvious similiarities between these and current research on "Social Man" as the basic concept for organizational understanding and management. This despite lengthy and very severe criticism of this tradition (see e.g. Blumberg, 1968, Perrow, 1979 and Yorks and Whitsett, 1985). Amongst other things the critics maintain that Mayo and others interpreted the results incorrectly, wildly exaggerating the importance of social needs to both satisfaction and productivity and they proposed manipulation. Motivation research in recent decades has instead, as has been made clear in Chapter 5, emphasized the central importance of working conditions and job content, regarding interest and attention as well as other attempts to satisfy social needs on the part of management as rather peripheral. And it is precisely the labour process and job content which culture and symbolism research tends to ignore, exactly like the old and even, to a considerable extent, modern human relations (cf. Alvesson, 1985 c).

Nevertheless, still regarded from the point of view of working life, culture and symbolism research has made an important contribution by bringing to light the affective-expressive needs in people and this side of organizational activity. Here current research is very much more advanced than human relations in the 1930's. The culture and symbolism perspectives give important reminders with respect to theories stressing the significance of the work organization and industrial democracy to the satisfying of human needs, meaning and development in work. This has been achieved by bringing to light the significance of the "cultural context" which the organization constitutes around the work, amongst other things for the experience of meaning, involvement and fellowship at work. Furthermore, these perspectives have emphasized (and unfortunately sometimes also overemphasized) that not only the "objective" (manifest) attributes of socio-structural and material conditions are important to people but also that all conditions also possess a symbolic content, which is of significance to the consequences these have for people.

To sum up we may say that whereas the culture and symbolism perspectives deal with conditions in organizations which are of relatively peripheral importance from the point of view of working life, "substantial" conditions such as the labour process, technology, power and hierarchy are scarcely touched upon, neither in theoretical analysis nor in suggestions for revised organizational and management principles. As working life research stresses, these conditions should be regarded as central from the point of view of working life. A full understanding of the labour process, job content and industrial democracy should, however, take into account cultural and symbolical aspects, for both the construction of theories and for reform strategies for the humanizing of working life. Unfortunately, with a few exceptions (e.g. Burawoy, 1979), such studies are lacking.

In the remainder of this chapter I shall not go explicitly into culture/ symbolism research, but let the comments with respect to the human relations tradition also cover this type of theory. This is justifiable, bearing in mind the similarities of these schools with regard to *work organization* and the inspiration which the human relations tradition has passed on to culture research. In Chapter 8 I shall revert to this form of research, mainly then from the ideological point of view.

6.6   An Apparent Contradiction

I shall now take up the relation between two outwardly contradictory development tendencies in working life: continued and possibly increased checking, control and dequalification on the one hand, and on the other increased participation (consultation, information, etc.), democratic work management, emphasis on the social, informal side of organizations, personnel-administrative investments, etc.

The increasing interest in organizational cultural aspects is contained to some extend in the latter line of development and will not be treated explicitly here. Even if the majority of authors are agreed that a certain change has taken place with regard to general company policy towards personnel, as expressed in increased interest in human resources management, the question is how extensive the change is. In their study of human resources management functions, Jain and Murray (1984) state that these have often failed to implement practices which are optimal from the point of view of personnel development. As a rule rather than the exception, job analysis, participation management styles and training programmes only exist on paper, have been tried and afterwards discontinued or exist only in weak forms and/or have low priority. Thus there is reason for doubt not only with regard to the importance of human relations thinking for the design of work but also for company policy towards employees in general, at least in the USA and Canada (which Jain and Murray's study comprises). Nevertheless I shall assume here that human relations thinking has exercised a certain amount of influence on company attitudes towards personnel.

The arguments in the preceding sections emphasize that while the human relations tradition for example can be thought to exercise influence when technical factors are of less organizational importance, the state of affairs is practically the opposite for the scientific management school; its influence has been and still is greatest in the production sector, even if its influence is hardly limited to this. The human relations traditions has nevertheless to some extent been of significance to the production worker, but only to a slight degree for the job content itself – the most central factor in the work situation. This way of regarding the human relations tradition is in agreement with Braverman's presentation (even if he is dealing with the early human relations school):

"Work itself is organized according to Taylorian principles, while personnel departments and academics have busied themselves with the selection, training, manipulation, pacification, and adjustment of "manpower" to suit the work processes so organized. Taylorism dominates the world of production; the practitioners of "human relations" and "industrial psychology" are the maintenance crew for the human machinery." (Braverman, 1974: 87)

Also according to working life research workers such as Gardell and Dahlström (1966) and Kornhauser (1965) measures in the human relations spirit have been unable to compensate for deficiencies in the job content itself:

"Various measures aimed at increasing the participation of the individual in decision-making, such as company committees, proposal activities and individual-centered management have not proved capable of replacing the psychological disadvantages of a working organization which means in principle the separation of planning and implementation, a routinization of the executive work and a chopping up of various elements into such small details that the context is lost." (Gardell and Dahlström, 1966: 150)

"We find that attitudes toward supervisors, closeness of supervision, feelings in regard to fellow workers, the company and its treatment of employees, all make extremely little difference as between upper- and lower-level jobs. They account in only very moderate degree for the better and poorer mental health that characterizes the several occupational groups in our study." (Kornhauser, 1965: 130)

We can roughly speak of lines of development in working life: *a humanizing* of the "peripheral" conditions and *a continued harder control* and structuring of the central features in the job situation, even if sociotechnical and human relations ideas have brought about a few changes in the work organization. This reflects something of the dilemma of management tactics and the theory of organization: the problem of being able both to control/ check the conduct of the members of the organization and offer them working conditions which are so reasonable ("free") that they are motivated to remain at their work and carry out their tasks.

The relationship between the principles of different theories of organization can be illustrated against the background of changed management conditions in organization. The development of the labour management and administrative systems indicates how social and administrative-technical changes at different levels can cooperate and give rise to an apparently contradictory development.

There is a tendency for the authoritarian "boss" to be succeeded by the seemingly democratic individual-centered "chummy" manager and for the company's general policy to become more participation-minded. But this does not necessarily mean that the control of the employee by managers and management has lessened and that the employee has acquired greater freedom, more influence on his own situation and organizational conditions as a whole. Control and checking are not implemented only in the form of the manager's direct work supervision but also by impersonal means of control. Brunander (1979) considers that the power problem has changed character, but that this has not necessarily brought about any improvements for the employee:

"Weber spoke openly about legitimate power in the form of compulsory control. Since Weber the discussion about power has gradually been replaced by theories of decision-making systems. The authoritarian leader has been succeeded by the decision-maker. Power has been diluted of its individual-emotional content and pumped into channels of information and other control systems. But power still remains and therefore powerlessness." (p. 81)

Brunander believes that "authoritarian control has turned into system control". On these grounds we may ask if a possible democratization or "softening-up" of management style can only be explained by the results of leadership research or by the spreading of humane values. Perhaps changes of management style are closely linked to the development of other forms of leadership and control than the "direct" interpersonnel work management. To this belong, amongst other things, administrative planning, control and checking systems. In recent decades these have been developed and refined to a high degree. This, naturally, is closely associated with the development of computer technology. The availability of advanced control systems can be thought to imply that business management to a higher degree now than formerly can control and check personnel by administrative-technical means.[2]

---

[2] According to Whisler (1970), the introduction of computer systems tends to mean that

A manager can thus be individual and group-minded, practice a democratic leader style and in other ways try to satisfy the social needs of the personnel in the best human relations spirit without management control having to be reduced for the purpose. This control can be maintained by various kinds of system design.

The change of management style in a democratic direction has probably contributed to the employees' job satisfaction and motivation to some extent. According to the point of view I have outlined, parallel to this development the technical-administrative systems' build-up and refinement have probably contributed to establishing the limits for the employees' possibilities of autonomy and influence. If a development towards an increased element of democracy in the interpersonnel works management has run parallel to increased control via administrative channels, it is uncertain how the total "aggregate" of management and control forms has been developed in relation to the job satisfaction of the employees. We should be careful not to draw too far-reaching conclusions about what a (possible) democratization of management style and the spread of theory Y view of people, the stressing of values common to the company, etc. bring about. A democratization of this alone need not imply any major changes.

In itself it is very possible and probable that a democratic management style by itself, i.e. irrespective of the nature of the technical-administrative control possibilities, in many cases is more efficient than traditional authoritarian management. The question is whether the business-economic efficiency of different interpersonnel management styles can be regarded as unconnected to the designs of other forms of management. It is likely that business managements would be less inclined to apply participative management if the risk of diminished control and checking which can be associated therewith could be compensated by other, and possibly more efficient, forms of control.

These views are seldom expressed by research workers who proceed from the management perspective, however. From that quarter the management question is sometimes presented as if it was unconnected to the appearance of other forms of management than the interpersonnel one. The material aspects of the activity is forgotten. By focusing solely on the interpersonnel factors in the management problem, on views on people and values, and there showing how the humanistic forms are superior to the authoritarian, an exaggeratedly positive and therefore false picture is obtained. I consider that it is more reasonable, in common with Brunander, to shed light on

---

decisions are referred upwards in the organization hierarchy. For a study of the influence of computer systems on job conditions, see Bradley (1977) and Sandberg (1979).

management – subordination on the basis of the totality which constitutes this relation, instead of regarding the interpersonnel management style as an individual isolated aspect, unconnected to the control and checking question in its entirety.

An essential aspect in this context is that companies and other organizations have become increasingly complex – companies have become larger and have been swallowed up in international and multinational constellations, they have become more complex technically and administratively. In their jobs many employees have only a limited view of the labour process and the organization in its entirety. All this can have meant that the possibilities of the employees in certain respects to assert their point of view on a "real" level have been reduced. Perhaps we may say that modern large-scale, technologically advanced production in itself constitutes an obvious restriction on the way employees can utilize the possibility of future participation which modern business management principles sometimes put on view. This is because the complexity and inertia of the material conditions make them difficult to survey, understand and influence from the side of the personnel. This can mean that business management principles of the human relations, OD and organizational culture type in their attempts to stress the importance of satisfying the social and psychological needs of the personnel will come more to constitute a kind of semi-humanist structure contrasted with the base constituted by technology, large-scale organization and the labour process. Certainly the latter can also be influenced by these business management principles and by sociotechnical systems, but it appears that at least so far this has only taken place to a limited extent.

6.7   Different Organization Theories for Different Jobs and Different Functions[3])

Ideas and recommendations from the human relations school (or from other schools) cannot be seen as disassociated from a context in which other organization principles are of great importance (e.g. a production organization built up around the scientific management idea). This was an important point in the preceeding section. Here I shall develop this idea further and shed light on the importance of the organization principles on the basis of the nature of the job conditions. I shall start with a couple of examples. The first is concerned with Theory Y.

---

[3]) The aspects taken up in this and the following section are dealt with in greater detail in Alvesson (1982).

McGregor (1960) states that a Theory Y view is generally superior to its opposite. The majority of organization theorists who express themselves on this question adopt the same standpoint. The great problem is that people in working life are socialized in an "X" spirit and have adjusted themselves to being controlled, manipulated and checked in the industrial organizations. This means that it will take time for Theory Y to come into effect, but McGregor has good hopes that this will come about.

Morse and Lorsch (1970) are of another opinion. These authors base their standpoint on the contingency theory.

Very briefly we may say that the contingency theory is opposed to the assumption that there is a generally applicable "best" organization model. Instead it is held that management and internal organizational structure are dependent conditions of the type of aim, size, technology and external environment of the organization. If the organization is to be efficient, these "internal" characteristics, e.g. style of management, must be in harmony with factors such as technology and market structure.

Morse and Lorsch compared two different organizations with respect to the X and Y points of view. They concluded that organization conditions built up in accordance with the X view yield the most efficient results for one type of organization included in the study, a company which manufactured containers with highly standardized technology. A company with a similar technology, but which was organized according to the Y view, was less efficient. They also compared two research laboratories, one based on X principles, the other on Y, and concluded that the Y organization was more efficient. Morse and Lorsch therefore believe that the Y view is superior in organizations with a technology and a business idea which are characterized by uncertainty, require creativity and a long-term perspective. An X view is suitable for activities characterized by standardized well structured operations.

Thus Morse and Lorsch believe that it is particularly the organization's overall task which decides the formal structures and the social climate which is most "suitable". The question is, however, whether it is not rather positions in the hierarchical structure which have the greatest influence on where theory Y and theory X, on the basis of the criterion optimal efficiency, should come into expression.[4]

---

[4] In itself it is possible that theory Y is generally superior to theory X. Schein (1975) believes that the contingency theory and the Y theory harmonize well because the Y theory, unlike X, is flexible and permits scope for different modes of operation. I do not react to Morse and Lorsch's statement on the economic suitability of the X theory in certain forms of organization. My aim is to demonstrate some absurdities in their analysis.

It is difficult to imagine that working conditions for research and development personnel and managers of standardized manufacturing industries should be structured according to the X view in order to be efficient, while holders of corresponding positions in research organizations should have Y conditions. Or that Morse and Lorsch should mean that caretakers and typists in research companies work best in a working organization based on theory Y,while their opposite numbers in the production industry are more efficient in a working environment based on the X view.

From some aspects it can naturally be motivated to regard organizations, organizational structures and organization climate as entities, but in large complex organizations there is often scope for social structures and working processes of various kinds. To describe organization conditions in relation to the employees' job situation without differentiating between levels and sub-systems in the controlling organization should only be attempted when there is a certain homogeneity between various working processes and the work organization in the company. If this is not the case, we may assume that different organization principles prevail in different parts of the organization. To stop only at the overall description level will be misleading, as in the case of Morse and Lorsch (1970), for example.

In most cases I believe that descriptions of both the actual as well as the optimal from an X/Y dimension should be based on the type of job and position in the hierarchy rather than on the overall field of activity of the organization. The latter is mainly of indirect interest in the context.

A similar example of inability to differentiation between different organizational levels is based on a discussion on wage systems. Lawler (1971) discusses the organization's wages policy and the possibility of using this to attain the organization's objectives.

Lawler state that

"... a pay plan must fit the characteristics of an organization if it is to be effective; it must be individualized in terms of organization size, management style etc."

Above all Lawler discusses the relationship between the characteristics of the organization and the wages system. Only in some forms of organization, of a large number listed, does he touch on the differentiation between the various categories of employees. He then points out that workers and managers ought to have different kinds of pay plans. Otherwise Lawler seems to believe that there is no great need to pay regard to different conditions within the organization.

This is truly remarkable. In most organizations there is a very wide spectrum with regard to the amount of salaries, the form of salaries, possibilities and ways of evaluating employees' work results (e.g. through piecework rates, bonuses and increases in salaries). A manager with a high salary and whose work effort can only possibly be evaluated in the long term differs greatly with regard to salary characteristics from a routine worker with only a fraction of such a high salary and with tasks which can be measured after every working day. It does not seem very likely that a wages plan which "is individualized in terms of the size of the organization, style of company management" can suit both the manager and the worker.

It is not primarily between different organizations that a wages system is adjusted, but between different types of jobs and positions in the organization.

These examples indicate the unwillingness or incapability of organization theorists to differentiate between different jobs and/or positions. Instead various categories of employees are regarded as a single, often enough entirely artificial, aggregate, whose common denominator is that they belong to the same organization. The examples above demonstrate how unreasonable such assumptions can appear.

The remarkable idea of conceiving of organizations as coherent units without any major degree of internal differentiation is also expressed in large areas of organization culture research. Here it is normally assumed that we can look upon organizations as *one* culture or claim that organizations have a culture, i.e. we assume that for all members of the organization there are values, basic assumptions, methods of conduct, linguistic usage, customs and symbolic operations. Shared beliefs, values and meanings are regarded as key words. It is improbable that the greater part of all organizations are homogeneous in these respects. An organization can certainly to a greater or lesser degree exercise a cultural influence on the employees and to some extent regiment them. However, it is difficult to believe that this regimentation is so powerful other than in extremely exceptional cases that the cultural attributes resulting from social background, class membership, profession, age, job situation and hierarchical position should be reduced to any extent worth mentioning. A more reasonable point of view would be to consider organizations either as reflections of the prevailing community, with its elements of cultural homogeneity and heterogeneity or else as consisting of several different cultures, on the basis of different social groups, professions and classes which exist within the organization and display clear cultural differences (Alvesson, 1984 b; 1985 e and Van Maanen and Barley, 1984).

There are, of course, organizations which are comparatively homogeneous in terms of working tasks and personnel and in such cases it is reasonable to speak of a dominating principle for the organization of work and sometimes even of a type of culture specific for the company in question. And it may sometimes be justifiable to oversimplify to some extent and not delve into more differentiated analyses in order to come to the point more rapidly. It is, however, problematical when organizational theoreticians often present a picture of organizations as largely homogeneous in various respects when in fact they normally contain a high degree of differentiation in terms of job conditions and organization principles as well as of the cultural dimensions of the individuals and groups contained in the organizations.

Literature on organizational theory concerned with analyses and discussions frequently favours the aggregate view of organizations. I believe this aspect is important for the understanding of the relationship between organizational theories and the development of work.

6.8   The Design of Work Organization and the Organizational Hierarchy

That many humanist organization theorists with a social-psychological orientation have a tendency to express themselves generally or on the basis of the overall characteristics of organizations such as technology, business idea, marketing conditions, etc., is in a way deserving of praise. Undoubtedly it would be rather undesirable to read normative assertions to the effect that managers, for example, should be treated with Y assumptions, while unskilled workers should be directed by X principles. Nevertheless the unwillingness (or inability) of organization theorists to differentiate their assumptions with regard to job content and hierarchical position gives rise to certain problems. Amongst other things, this leads to a misleading view of the scope of the humanist organization principles, and a false notion that everyone in a company is treated according to the same principles. Light should therefore be shed on the significance of the organization hierarchy to the organization principles which are applied.

In today's organizations it is apparently believed that adequate performance by employees at lower levels can be generated without it being necessary, to any considerable extent, to be obliged to design job content and work organization so as to create conditions for satisfaction, intrinsic motivation and personal growth among the employees. To perform routine duties pleasurably does not demand a high degree of involvement. Organizational problems in consequence of expressions of discontent in the form of absence and personnel turnover or recruiting difficulties can raise problems for the company management, but the question is whether these are of a critical nature other than in exceptional cases. It is not, after all, particularly expensive to replace people in routine work who only require a brief period of training (cf. Chapter 5). The same can hardly be said of personnel at higher levels. The problem of motivation is here of central importance (at least for organizations of hierarchical type).

From this it follows that the business economic incentives to achieve good social psychological efficiency differ between different hierarchical levels. At the same time the job content is qualitatively different, which probably also contributes to the fact that organization principles aimed at social psychological efficiency assume different expressions at different levels of the organization.

In accord with what has been said here is Jain and Murray's (1984) study of the human resource management function. They found that only a small proportion of the employees in American companies underwent any formal training of any kind under company auspices during a period of several years. The exceptions were primarily managers.

It is, as has already been pointed out, rare that organization theorists explicitly indicate that, and in such cases how, the organization hierarchy influences how organization principles are applied. Occasionally, however, this does happen:

"The higher the level in the organization, the more important it is to be oriented attitudinally toward people and to be interpersonally competent, and the less important it is to be oriented to task problems and to be task competent, provided task orientation and competence remain at some reasonably high level." (Schein, 1980: 131)[5])

In other words: at high levels it is important for heads to focus on social psychological problems, whereas at lower levels it is important to see to what is to be done (to be competent with respect to tasks and work orientated).

In accord with this there is a tendency for job satisfaction to run parallel to organization hierarchy to the extent that the higher the position, the greater the job satisfaction (Berger and Cummings, 1979). This indicates that the social psychologically inclined principles of organization aimed at efficiency through job and needs satisfaction have greater influence at higher levels in the organizations.

It is reasonable to ask ourselves whether the organization hierarchy is not central in order to understand the influence of various organization theories and principles. It seems as though the social psychologically dominated organization theories have mainly exercised influence at the higher levels of

---

[5]) This quotation is located in a part of Schein's book on "task versus people orientation". In the book in its whole, Schein does hardly touch upon the significance of hierarchical differences for the organizational principles which determines he work situation of the employees. I will treat Schein further in Ch. 7.

companies, while the job situations of the lower categories have been formed on the basis of technical-administrative principles. This appears to have meant that for a large number of employees at lower levels Neo-Tayloristic ideas have largely characterized the job content, while the influence of the psycho-social aspects has been both limited and has mainly affected peripheral aspects of the work situation and not the job content itself. Thus there would appear to be two different theories (organization principles) which are simultaneously applied to the forming of job conditions – a "humanistic" one concentrated on management and managers and a technically inspired one for workers and other unpromoted personnel. This assumption concerning two theories for the organization can only with difficulty be deduced from the literature on the subject, and then only if it is studied critically.

Literature often presents a different picture of reality. Amongst other things many organization theoretical authors express the notion that efficiency in the long term demands contentment and growth on the part of personnel – meaning all personnel – and in this way the problems of dissatisfaction, etc. at work which exist in the long term could be solved by efficiency criteria as the guiding star.

In order to understand how organization theorists deal with these questions I believe it is important to examine the ideological function of the organization theories. I shall therefore devote the following chapter to this subject.

6.9   Resistance to the Humanization of Work

The tendency for organization theoretical principles to be differentiated for reasons of efficiency on the basis of job content and hierarchy is scarcely the only reason why there seem to be obstacles to the humanizing of working life. Another important reason seems to be resistance or at least restricted interest on the part of company management. This aspect is presented by both "bourgeois" as well as Marxist authors, e.g. Marrow (1975), Menninger (1975), Dunnette (1975), Lorsch (1975), Kling and Stymne (1982) and Robbins (1983) as well as Zimbalist (1975), Goldman and Van Houten (1977) and Noble (1979).

"There is ample evidence that, once given a taste of control over their work, workers go after more. If this occurs, the capitalist's control over the program is lost and his/her control over the entire production process becomes threatened." (Zimbalist, 1975: 56)

According to Zimbalist this has meant that many programmes for the humanizing of work have been discontinued because they proved too "successful".

An interesting and important question is to what extent the control interest of company management is permitted to extend to efficiency aspects. Some working life theorists seem to think that modern working life appears to be the way it is not mainly because it should be maximally efficient from the technical point of view, but because it satisfies the interest of managers and capitalists in social control. Braverman, for example, adopts this line. I believe, however, that even if there is much to be said for this aspect, it should not be pressed too far. Pressure from marketing often leaves little scope for allocating priorities other than efficiency maximization (for a more detailed discussion see Friedman, 1977, cf. however Galbraith, 1967). Many business leaders also wish, given the granting of priority to the economic targets, to bring about as satisfactory working conditions as possible. There are also examples of company managements which have permitted and even encouraged far-reaching autonomy on the part of the workers without this leading to any threats to their position (Gardell and Svensson, 1981: for a more detailed discussion on the forming of working life in relation to company management/capitalists' interest in social control, see Alvesson, 1986 and Berggren, 1980).

6.10 Summary

I have shown that the contradictions which prevail between on the one hand the dequalification trend and on the other the social psychologically orientated organization principles such as McGregor's Y Theory gives expression to, are largely apparent. A certain humanization in the human relations spirit seems to have left its mark on the interpersonnel forms of management, but at the same time other forms of control have been developed: authoritarian control has to some extent been replaced by system control (Brunander, 1979).

The decisive point seems to be, however, that the job content itself has been affected by the humanistic organization theory only to a limited degree.

On the basis of the discussions in this and the preceding chapter I wish to emphasize the importance of job content and of the hierarchical position to the organizational design principles which are maximally efficient and will be applied in practice. Now, job content is partly a function of organization thinking, and if this does not take account of technological conditions, as McGregor's and several others' ideas fail to do, the importance of the social psychological principles of organization for job content will be negligible.

The modern human relations tradition therefore lacks the possibility to function as a theoretical-normative starting point for solving the extensive mental and social problems in working life. This can be illustrated by possibly the most noted work of this tradition. McGregor's book, which is discussed above, seems to be much more powerful and influential on the rhetorical rather than on the level of implementation. Its influence on the majority of (in any case on American) companies seems to be less than that often exercised by textbooks. An organization theory which takes no account of technological (or administrative) conditions, is largely forced to regard job content as given and, in cases where the employees are largely controlled by technological/administrative demands, will only exercise a peripheral influence on the job situation. Another phenomenon I have emphasized is the importance of the hierarchy to the principles of organization design which are applied are often left out of account in the management-orientated theory of organization. The hierarchical structure leads to different theories for the organization of work being evidently applied to management and workers. Not to pay regard to this is associated with certain ideological points.

7. Organization Theory and Ideology

In this chapter I shall build further on the analysis made in the previous chapter. I do this by presenting problems on the basis of the arguments contained in these, and also by linking them with the level of interpretation of the critique of ideology (see Ch. 1.4). With the point of departure in the analysis in Chapter 6, I wish to formulate the following question: if the humanistic organization principles are mainly applied to high qualification and organization levels and only to a limited (or at least to a far-less) extent to lower levels, why is this fact not explicitly stated in literature?[1]) Can the answer possibly be that from the ideological point of view it is more advantageous if modern human relations thinking is presented as something of a universally applicable solution to the problem of the impoverishment and dequalification of work? If its practical influence appears to have been negligible, it accords poorly with the concept with which it has been disseminated. Ideas and organization principles concerning self-realization, participation and such-like in the modern human relations spirit have on the whole been of limited importance in practice. The interest or capacity of receptivity of the corporate executives has turned out to be of little account when it has been a matter of putting the ideas into practice at lower levels of the organization. At the same time these ideas, theories and recommendations have been spread very extensively by means of books, articles, courses, lectures, etc. Keyword such as "intrinsic motivation", "satisfaction of needs", "self-realization", "participation", "group orientation", "democratic leadership", "theory Y" and "system 4T" should be familiar to many managers.

We may therefore ask ourselves whether the, at least superficially, great popularity of the theories and recommendations, in combination with their limited importance in practice, indicates that there are also other motives behind the popularity than the practical value and influence of the theories. One possible motive could then be of an ideological nature.

This argument motivates a discussion of the legitimizing and ideological functions of organization theories. Certainly not all organization theories fulfil such functions. (At least not to such an extent as would make it

---

[1]) "Humanistic organization theory" refers to modern human relation and authors close to that tradition, e.g. McGregor, Likert, Argyris, Schein etc.

worthwhile to examine them.) It is, however, difficult to make a clear distinction between "ideologically charged" organization theories and those which deal with sets of problems in a manner which does not legitimize prevailing values and social conditions.

The type of organization theory mainly delt with in this chapter is concerned with the individual – organization relationship in a broad sense from the perspective of management. I believe that we can speak of a dominating organization theory in which we can distinguish more or less obvious ideological elements (cf. Burrell and Morgan, 1979; Zey-Ferrell, 1982). Here in the introduction I refrain from making any formal demarcation and assume that the object of my criticism will become apparent from the chapter in its entirety.[2])

In this chapter I shall begin by discussing the ideological concept on a more general level and then take up the ideologies of business managements, which legitimize the practices of heads of businesses as well as the conditions and rationality which dominate companies and working life. Much of the chapter will be devoted to discussing the importance of organization theories in this context and to indicate how ideologies assume concrete form in organization theory literature.

7.1 Ideology

Few concepts, such as ideology, have been treated by such an endless number of authors in a number of different ways. Within organizational research it seems as if the concept has attained a rapidly increased interest during the last few years (cf. Beyer, 1981; Hartley, 1983). This is parallel to and to a large extent intertwined with the fact that questions concerning culture, values, symbolism and legitimacy have come to be viewed as highly significant for the understanding of organizations. In Chapter 8 I shall make some comments on the societal base for this rather sudden interest in the cultural issue and similar topics.

The various views on ideology appearing in social science texts are normally divided by review writers into two or three categories. Hartley (1983), for example, talks about two basic views, with different philosophical assump-

---

[2]) Burrell and Morgan (1979) and Zey-Ferrell (1982) attempt to limit and define a predominant type of organization theory that is fairly well in agreement with the objective of my discussion of critical ideology. Because of space considerations, however, I shall refrain from referring to their discussions and also from trying to determine the predominant organization theory myself. A review of organization theories that break with this is presented in Burrell and Morgan (1979) and Zey-Ferrell and Aiken (1981).

tions and value connotations. One sees ideology as consisting of false beliefs and the person holding an ideology as being the victim of delusions. Ideology and irrationality go together, according to this view. The other view conceptualizes ideology as a set of assumptions and values about the world. Here the term has a "neutral" meaning and stands for a frame of reference. All people and groups are supposed to have one. The first mentioned view indicates that ideology might either have a personal or a social origin. When the origin is of a social nature it is social relationships and conditions, especially related to the interests of powerful classes or groups, that comprise the base for the misleading beliefs. Where ideology is understood as a personal phenomena, distortions located within the individual, cognitive processes, possibly affected by emotional factors or mental disorders are viewed as the cause. Geertz (1973), in addition to the "neutral" meaning of ideology, discusses (and criticizes) two other ways of looking at ideology: "the interest theory" and "the strain theory". According to the first view, ideology is explained by a groups search for power, in the second view, ideology is a means to reduce anxiety.

In recent times, most authors seem to argue for the "neutral" or analytical conceptions of ideology, rejecting it as a critical or pejorative term and seeing it as "a frame of reference, a set of assumptions, or a world view" (Hartley, 1983: 13) or something similar. See, for example, the definitions by Allaire and Firsirotu (1984), Beyer (1981), Brunsson (1982 a) and Therborn (1981). The popularity of the analytical, non-pejorative definition is to some extent a result of an extended awareness of the problems with an "objectivistic" approach to social science. The ideal of a value-free study of social phenomena, a clear separation between science and ideology, between "truth" and false beliefs is viewed by more and more scholars as totally unrealistic. Also Marxist authors, like Therborn (1981), argue now against earlier conceptualizations of ideology as false, unscientific beliefs to be confronted by objective, Marxist science and a proletarian consciousness.

In addition to the arguments made from the recognizing of the inevitability of values in all statements about the social world, the usefulness of an "noncritical" conceptualization of ideology in management and organizational theory and the application of this in practical settings, might be seen as a force behind the present interest in and definitions of ideology.

I totally agree with the notion of the impossibility of making clearcut separations between science, objective truth, "real interests" etc. on the one hand and ideology, illusions or "false interests" on the other. This, however, does not necessarily lead to the conclusion that the critical evaluative concept of ideology is inappropriate. There are a large number of different views concerning how to use the ideology concept in a critical sense, and far from all of these fall into the positivism trap of objectivism. What Burrell and Morgan (1979) refer to as "the radical humanist paradigm" contains a large number of exceptions. When the critical-evaluative view on ideology is discussed, this "paradigm" is not seldom neglected and crude Marxist and positivistic opinions become targets easy to hit (see, e.g. Geertz, 1973; Hartley, 1983). This leads to a too easy dismissal of the critical conceptualization of ideology.

In a book primarily orientated toward examining the concept ideology as used by Habermas (and the Frankfurt School), Geuss (1981) finds three main senses in which the concept are used. These cover to a large extent the categorizations mentioned above and present also the more advanced evaluative, critical conceptualization of the Frankfurt School which is being neglected by these authors as well as the large majority of organization theorists discussing ideology (cf. Beyer, 1981).

Geuss talks about ideology in the descriptive, the pejorative and the positive sense. In the first sense, the concept is defined as follows:

"... the ideology typically will include such things as the beliefs the members of the group hold, the concepts they use, the attitudes and psychological dispositions they exhibit, their motives, desires, values, predilections, works of art, religious rituals, gestures, etc." (Geuss, 1981: 5)

The definition is very broad and overlaps many definitions of culture. Geuss is, however, very open also to more narrow definitions of the term in its descriptive sense. The important point is that the concept stands for a world-view and this is studied in a purely descriptive way, i.e. without reference to critical, evaluative comments or to the need fulfillment of people holding or mastering the ideology, The opinion of the matter by Hartley (1983) roughly corresponds to this view, as does Beyer's (1981), which might be seen as an example of a rather strict definition of the concept:

"Ideologies can be defined as relatively coherent sets of beliefs that bind some people together and that explain their worlds in terms of cause-and-effect relations." (Beyer, 1981: 166)

The second sense is the pejorative, negative or critical one. Ideology is viewed as beliefs and forms of consciousness that are misleading, false or distorted. The distortion is of a systematic kind and rooted in social conditions. It has nothing to do with lack of information, coincidental mistakes or misunderstandings or with individual "private" pecularities. The critical theory of the Frankfurt tradition, of course, uses the concept of ideology in this sense. Ideology is viewed as an obstruction for the rational discussion of how the unrepressed social life could be organized. It is the task of critical theory to investigate ideology in order to increase the possibilities of individuals to emancipate themselves against the constraining forms of beliefs, induced by present social arrangements and the dominating class and groups.

This view of ideology does not place ideology in a kind of state of opposition to science or objective truth. Ideology is rather placed in relation to the way sectional interests tend to dominate social conditions. Ideology does not so much cover falsehoods, mistakes, prejudices or irrationality (even though such attributes can also be related to the ideology) as much as the way some interests tend to dominate and others to be pushed aside. In common with the representatives of the Frankfurt tradition, Giddens (1979) looks on the question of the relation between valid knowledge and invalid knowledge as problematical (even if he believes that the social sciences can deliver objectively valid knowledge). He continues:

"We can break with the whole orientation just referred to *by treating the sectional interests/ideology polarity as basic to the theory of ideology,* rather than the opposition of ideology and science. ... For to locate the theory of ideology primarily in terms of the sectional interests/ideology differentiation is to insist that the chief usefulness of the concept of ideology concerns the critique of domination." (Giddens, 1979: 187)

As examples of the forms which ideologies in the above senses can assume we may mention the following (according to Geuss, 1981; Giddens, 1979; Held, 1980):

– A form of consciousness is ideological if it contains 'an objectification mistake', i.e. if a socially produced phenomena is assumed to be a natural one. This means that the products of a particular society or a group of individuals which potentially could be controlled and changed by the participants, are seen as natural phenomena, governed by processes outside their control.

– If a form of consciousness falsely assumes that the particular interest of a subgroup in a society or an organization is the general interest of the group as a whole it can be referred to as ideological.

– The glorification of social conditions as harmonious when they are, in fact, conflict-ridden and the denial or transmutation of contradictions might be seen as ideological forms of thought.

The third way in which the ideology concept is used stresses the need of ideology. Here it has a positive content, quite unlike the way the critical theory applies the concept. With this content ideology corresponds to human beings' existential need of meaning in life and or social needs of fellowship, social solidarity, communication and capacity for productive cooperation. Ideologies specific to religion, vocations, class or organizations might thus be understood on the basis of the wishes and needs of individuals.

This classification of different ways of defining ideology should in my opinion be regarded as analytical in the sense that it clarifies some typical approaches which are not necessarily fully accounted for in factual studies. In reality it is difficult to carry out analysis of ideology which consistently apply the concept in a strictly descriptive, critical or positive sense. Studies aimed at achieving a certain depth of interpretation usually touch on two of these definitions of the concept. This can be illustrated by Hartley's definition, which contains the following characteristic features:

"The essential characteristics of ideology are, first, that it consists of values and beliefs or ideas about the state of the world and what it should be. Second, these cognitive and affective elements form a framework. In other words, ideology is not simply a summation of a set of attitudes, but consists of some kind of relatively systematic structuring (though the structuring may be psychological rather than logical). Third, ideologies concern social groups and social arrangements – in other words, politics in its widest sense of being concerned with the distribution and ordering of resources. Fourth, an ideology is developed and maintained by social groups, and thus is a socially derived link between the individual and the group (in contrast to the concept of attitude, which is generally seen as an individual attribute). Fifth, ideology proveds a justification for behavior." (Hartley, 1983: 26–27)

The author believes this definition to be analytical, descriptive rather than critical, pejorative. In my opinion the same definition can be applied in the latter sense and that some elements from a standpoint critical towards ideology must of necessity be included in primarily good quality studies of ideology. (The opposite also applies.)

With regard to the attributes of ideology, for example, social arrangements, politics in the widest sense as well as the distribution and ordering of resources, it is difficult to conclude otherwise than that ideology often works (is used by different groups) in a way that results in ideas that are systematically oversimplified, misleading, mystifying or false, having a tendency to exert influence on politics and the distribution of resources. This is virtually, per definition, to the advantage of certain, usually powerful, groups possessing considerable resources, while other groups are discriminated. Even the first and fifth attributes, beliefs or ideas about the state of the world and a justification of behaviour, respectively, in the case of the ideologies of many groups probably contain numerous elements which even to a scholar who defines ideology in a "neutral" way appear to be contradictory, gross and oversimplified, misleading with regard to a reasonably balanced and undistorted view of reality or which are quite simply false. And even a research worker, who is primarily not interested in ideology in the critical sense of the concept, often finds it difficult in his presentation to avoid conveying nuances of evaluation/criticism or in any case of giving the reader the opportunity of drawing the evaluative/critical conclusions himself. This, at least, should apply to "good research", which is distinguished by a reasonably balanced presentation of the phenomena studied, which should also include the presentation of material, if any, (observations, reports, secondary analytical reflections) which speaks against (implies the falsification of) the beliefs or ideas about the world held by a group and its justification of behaviour.

One example of how a study primarily concerned with ideology in the descriptive, analytical sense, but which in various ways also deals with "the critical dimension" is Anthony (1977). Amongst other things he writes about the ideologies expressed by the elites of business organizations. He speaks of "business ideology" and "management ideology". The former is involved with the free market, the sovereignity of the consumer, the importance of private ownership and free enterprise as well as the value of business contracting. The latter ideology stresses instead "the death of the capitalist", the predominance of professional business management, rational planning, the acknowledgement of pluralistic interests and the importance which should be ascribed to satisfying the needs of employees. This ideology therefore emphasizes the "post-capitalistic" element in the way a company functions. Anthony does not tell us directly whether the ideologies are "true" or "false", but presents the ideologies one after the other and mentions that they are applied by the same group (i.e. the contemporary business elite) during the same epoch but in different contexts and for different purposes: "business ideology" is invoked against criticism and any intervention by political or government quarters of a negative nature from the point of view of business leaders, while "management ideology" is utilized to legitimize business managements in the eyes of employees and trade unions. In his presentation Anthony goes into the critical aspects of these ideologies and hows how oversimplified, selective and "partially false" these ideologies are. A more benevolent view would be to regard them as "partially true". Possibly one of them is "entirely false" – but in any case it is logically impossible for both of them to give a just view of reality when they are used to describe and legitimize the same set of circumstances.

However some research has now been undertaken which carefully avoids dealing with the critical aspects of ideology. Amongst other things I am referring to some of the research on organization theoretical ideology which also includes much of what is commonly known as organization culture theory (see further Chapter 8).

In common with numerous primarily descriptive, analytical studies, the critical theory does not confine itself to a strictly defined concept of ideology in accordance with the brief classifications of the use of the concept described above. In his study of critical theory Held (1980: 186) emphasizes that the Frankfurt School regards ideologies as forms of thought which, due to dominance factors in society, express a limited and distorted view on reality, but ideologies cannot be reduced to being regarded only as false ideas:

"Ideologies are not however, merely illusions. They are embodied and manifested in social relations. The ahistorical and asocial character of certain kinds of interpretation of social life may itself be a reflection of the transformation of social relations into impersonal and reified forms. Ideologies can express 'modes of existence'. Therefore, ideologies are often also packages of symbols, ideas, images and theories through which people experience their relation to each other and the world. The degree to which ideologies mystify social relations or adequately reflect distorted social relations (but thereby mystify the possibility of non-distorted social relations) is a question for inquiry in particular cases and contexts." (Held, 1980: 186)

When Marcuse speaks of one-dimensional thinking (and when other representatives of the Frankfurt tradition take up similar themes), the problem about this is not that it is "false" in itself but that the form of rationality of advanced industrial society tends to monopolize all thinking in accordance with its own 'logic', characterized by mass production and mass consumption on the basis of standardized needs. (See further Chapter 9.3). What distinguishes the critical theory is that even if we operate with ideology in a critical sense, it is not a question of simply placing ideology on an equal footing with false forms of thinking. The ambition is rather to study how social conditions (primarily under late capitalism) influence ideas, political discussions, forms of rationality and needs, as well as to what extent and in what way the rational considerations of individuals with regard to needs, the satisfaction of needs and liberation from "unnecessary" repression are disturbed by the social conditions.

This discussion of the relationship between ideology in the descriptive and critical senses thus leads us to the conclusion that in reality they have difficulty in avoiding overlapping each other (at any rate when it is a matter of "good research"). When it is a matter of the gross objectivistic statements which distinguish clearly between "science" and "ideology" or between "what is real" and "what is ideological", these are of course clearly distinguished from ideology in the descriptive sense (as Geertz, Hartley and others, representatives of the above-mentioned non-evaluative ideology tradition, assert). Also studies which are of a descriptive nature which carefully avoid all forms of critical treatment of the ideology of a social group can be clearly distinguished from a critique of ideology concept.

When it is a matter of the relationship between ideology in the critical sense and in the positive sense there is probably less overlapping than in the two senses mentioned above (i.e. descriptive and critical). However, the distinction is not quite as clear as it would seem at a first glance. Certainly we can point out that a given ideology may fulfil a positive function for a particular, e.g. dominating, group, whereas ideology for another group can result in the establishment of a condition of dominance. This is by no means uncommon. We can point to management, professional, upper-class and racial ideologies as both typical as well as widely spread (and dissimilar) examples. Normally, however, studies concerned with the repressive aspects of this type of ideology deal very little with the positive content, subordinating the interest which lies behind the relations of dominance (over employees, clients, an oppressed minority, etc.). Thus ideology in the positive sense is very seldom elaborated in studies of this type. Research based on a positive concept of ideology can, however, like the descriptive, come into contact with circumstances which reveal that the ideology, at least in some respect (in some situation, for some group, etc.), is unreasonable or problematical in relation to self-knowledge and capacity for the satisfaction of legitimate needs. An ideology which can mainly be regarded as positive on the basis of the needs of a group or organization, can also partially, have the opposite effect.

One example in the literature mainly concerned with ideology in a positive sense but which also takes account of critical points of view is Abravanel (1984). He speaks of organizational ideology "when a set of representational ideas and their operational consequences are linked together into a dominant belief system which serves to define and maintain the organization" (p. 15). Ideology is, Abravanel believes, positive and perhaps even necessary for the functioning of the organization. However, ideology has a dualistic character: it both contains the purely moral principles (representational concerns) and it must also enable the solution of immediate practical tasks, i.e. it must take account of operational concerns. Abravanel points out that "inevitable contradictions emerge and re-emerge between representational and operational concerns" (p. 15). By drawing attention to the contradictions within an ideology or between this as a moral and legitimizing superstructure and concrete practice, the border between ideology in the positive and critical senses is transgressed. And because contradictions of this type are probably common in ideological practice, it is difficult to undertake serious studies of ideology in the positive sense without straying into a border region between the two senses of ideology (I speak here of "serious" because there are numerous inadequate studies which take no account of possible existing contradictions. See further Chapter 8.)

It remains to compare ideology in the descriptive and positive senses. Here, too, we find overlapping, perhaps to a greater extent than in the case of ideology in descriptive-critical and positive-critical sense. It is often difficult to make descriptive analyses of ideology without at least implicitly assuming that the ideology corresponds to some kind of need. In the same way studies of ideology in the positive sense must in all likelihood contain descriptions of ideologies as value and belief systems in a manner similar to the analytical, descriptive studies.

As examples of studies concerned with ideology in both the descriptive and the positive senses attention may be drawn to much of the research on organizational culture. This is dealt with from the point of view of ideology in Chapter 8.

What has been said in this section can be summed up in the following figure:

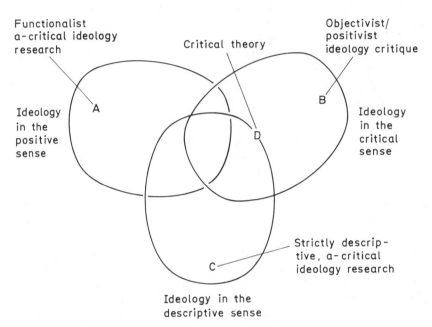

Figure 7.1: The Relationship Between Different Meanings of the Ideology Concept

Positions A, B and C are based on strict definitions of ideology in each of its three meanings discussed here. I believe that in various ways these are problematical. Position A, like C, implies that the possibility

This point of view implies that ideologies cannot be studied without paying regard to the elements of dominance and repressiveness at the same time as these elements are not regarded a priori as characteristic of the ideology. We can conceive of ideologies which are relatively neutral in terms of distortions, which do not mix up ideals and reality and in which the value component is reasonably separated from the concept of existing conditions (including inadequacies in these) and where dominance is negligible. This is an extreme case. Another extreme case is that of ideologies painting a highly idealized picture of actual conditions, where ideals (values) and reality (state of conditions) are mixed together, where the ideology is obviously to the advantage of one group and to the disadvantage of another, where the conditions for rational dialogues on how social life should be organized are impoverished due to the influence of the ideology on the forms of consciousness (Cf. Alvesson, 1985 a, pp. 4–5).

My view as to how the ideology concept should be applied is thus that we must take into account the precise nature of a specific ideology before it can be judged more precisely than I have done above. From the point of view of critique of ideology it is important to observe the elements in ideologies which make it difficult to reflect on actual conditions and on emancipation from repressive conditions. Normally there are at least minor elements of this kind in ideologies – which is one aspect of the way these impose limits on the picture of the world and on the understanding of reality. From the point of view of critique of ideology the only ideologies which are of interest are those which systematically and strongly oppose

"that the basic institutions of society and the basic political institutions would meet with the unforced agreement of all those involved, if they could participate as free and equal, in discursive will-formation." (Habermas, 1979: 186).

7.2 Ideology and Theory

In connection with the discussion on ideology in texts with some claim to be scientific, it is justifiable to express some modifying and supplementary views on the concept of ideology in relation to what has been said above.

One vital aspect of ideology is whether it is in any respect erroneous, i.e. an aberration separated from objective, neutral knowledge (e.g. science), or whether it is ineluctable in all its forms of presentation. In the first case we can distinguish between science and ideology; and in the second science is just one form of ideology among others – although possibly truer, more consistent, more cautious, better, etc.

The debate on social science has moved from the first-mentioned view to an admission of the difficulties in drawing a distinction between ideology and science. After some twenty years of debates on paradigms, the relativistic view of knowledge has won increased influence. (See Brante, 1980 and Elzinga and Jamison, 1984, for a survey of the sociology of research discussion in recent decades.) But there are still contributions to the debate which regard fidelity to the basic rules of method associated with science as a guarantee of the "scientific" as against the "ideological" (e.g. Yorks and Whitsett, 1985). This point of view seems in any case to predominate among many social scientists who have not become deeply involved in the discussion on the theory of science.

Social scientists who are interested in the philosophy of science and theory of science are normally less inclined to speak of any clear difference between research on the one hand and politics, ideology and values on the other.

A common view held by such social scientists is that all (social scientific) research and theory contains ideological (or anti-ideological) aspects in the sense that they contain explanatory systems with political implications, which form the basis for adopting an attitude for or against the prevailing social order. Such a standpoint seems to be shared by the large majority of social scientists who have taken an interest in the question of the "neutrality" of social science (e.g. Mills, 1959; Myrdal, 1968; Israel, 1972; Wilson, 1983). Mills has this to say on the relationship between social science and ideology:

"In fact the ideological relevance of social science is inherent in its very existence as social fact. Every society holds images of its own nature – in particular, images and slogans that justify its system of power and the ways of the powerful. The images and ideas produced by social scientists may or may not be consistent with these prevailing images, but they always carry implications for them." (Mills, 1959: 91–92)

I agree with this, but in an analysis based on the critique of ideology such a sweeping general assumption is of limited value. There is a difference between ideology and ideology. Ideological elements in social science can be more or less pronounced. The theory of social science can only in exceptional cases be reduced to dealing exclusively with ideology. We can speak of some or relative theoretical autonomy, which means that science possesses a certain amount of independence with respect to social ideology. As has already been said, the element of ideology in research may be greater or less and stand normally in inverse proportion to the degree of theoretical autonomy in the research in question, i.e. the more independent a researcher is to power constellations in a society – in the question of economic and other forms of dependencies – the less obvious the ideological element tends to be in the research. In my view it is justified to speak of and analyze ideology in social science only if the ideological elements are of a certain dimension. Then it is a question whether research approaches, the formulations of problems, descriptions and interpretations which reveal one-sidedness, cover problematical conditions, empirical/theoretical errors or in some other way defects in cogency and critical attitude in favour of results with obvious ideological points make it fruitful to speak of the latter. (According to this view critical research can also be ideological. Then it is not a question of covering up problematical conditions but rather of over-emphasizing them.)

In order that it should be fruitful to speak of ideology in a "scientific" text, there must thus in the first place be systematic errors or distortions, and in the second place these intellectual imperfections must be capable of being related to social ideologies held by powerful groups and to sectional interests. In other words, the critique of ideology is directed towards discourses which are expressed unindependently against dominating interests and ideologies, in which the intellectual independence of the theory against the ideology is slight and in which the discourse becomes more or less a diffusion of theory and ideology.[3])

Ideology in organization theory (as in other theories) differs to some extent from the general ideologies as defined in the previous section. Amongst other things this is because they are expressed in connection with a presentation which has at least some theoretical points. Only in exceptional cases can "ideologically-loaded" theory be reduced to being regarded as ideology only. Ideology must be derived or interpreted into being. A certain degree of definition of the use of the concept of ideology in this specific context can also be made. Ideology is regarded in relation to theoretical discourses as systematic descriptions, explanations and theories on social reality (here above all in organizations) which contribute to reproducing, legitimizing and reinforcing the prevailing social order and the rationality, aims and conditions of power on which this is based, by further developing, refining and reproducing the ideologies of the dominant groups.

Thus I speak only of ideologies which legitimize prevailing conditions. Admittedly research can allow itself to be influenced by other ideologies

---

[3]) It is admittedly very difficult and perhaps impossible to make a distinction in principle between theory and ideology. As various authors, e.g. Giddens (1979), point out, it is problematical

"... to *define* ideology as 'non-science': as necessarily involving 'invalid' claims to knowledge, or as distinct from science (natural and social) in some other clearly ascertainable way. No one who has taken this position has been able to defend it satisfactorily. The main reason for this is clear. To attempt to conceptualise ideology in such a way places too great a burden upon its proponents to separate science or 'valid knowledge' in a distinct and unchallangeable manner from the excuses and pretensions of ideology." (p. 185)

We can, like Althusser (discussed by Giddens), talk about science as "theoretical ideology". For my part I find both the reduction of theory of science to ideology as well as a clear marking of the boundary between theory and ideology unsatisfactory points of view. For at least on an analytical level to be able to distinguish between theory and ideology (or theoretical and ideological aspects of a discourse) I define theory as a research-based (academic) attempt at an explanation or an understanding of some phenomenon which is expressed as an independent (critical – remote) manner in relation to the dominance and sectional interests concerned.

aiming at the legitimizing of radical change. Criticism of this type of research can and naturally should also be made, e.g. when it is a matter of the denigration of prevailing conditions. However, it is not my task in the present work to express this type of critique of ideology and therefore I do not include this type of ideology in the above definition.

My use of the concept of ideology in the interpretation of research texts – in which obviously defective intellectual quality and legitimizing functions constitute criteria – does not mean that I defend the view that "non-ideological" research on the social and behavioural sciences should be characterized by the absence of the author's evaluations and points of view. All research and all discourses, naturally including my own, are characterized by being conveyors of conceptions of the world, values, interest of knowledge, and the "subjectivity" of the author. The present work obviously bears the stamp of my opinion on a number of questions to which, as a social scientist and researcher on organization and working life, one must assume attitudes, for example which aspects of people's work and the functional manner of organizations require elucidation and possibly change. I endeavour to be as explicit as possible in these respects in order thereby to reduce the risk of my values and attitudes being concealed, since a pseudo-objective manner of presentation increases the risk of the text becoming ideological. In studies of the critique of ideology, as maintained above, it is not fruitful solely on the basis of this to speak of ideology in the context. That discourses, theories, approaches to research and choice of concept are characterized by the author's values and attitudes does not thus necessarily imply that they are characterized by ideology (in the critical sense).

7.3   Management Ideology

Management ideology is concerned with the conducting of business and management. These ideologies are held primarily by heads of businesses, other managers (i.e. on the lower and intermediate levels) and by other groups which identify with this category and by the management perspective, e.g. many salaried employees, students of business administration, consultants, etc. Management ideologies are also to be found in the general ideological arena of society and in this way they influence the ideas, values and attitudes of politicians, officials, formers of opinions and the general public.

As is the case with many other ideologies, management ideologies can be related to the general set of problems made up of social order. To preserve and legitimize the prevailing social order is a central problem for every community and every organization – or more precisely for the individuals who profit from it, or for any other reason, e.g. rigidity, defective knowledge or awareness, who defend the order in question. In modern society, where violence and other kinds of open oppression are only in exceptional cases practised in order to combat opposition against the establishment, ideologies become of decisive importance for the maintenance of social order. The effect and influence of ideologies are emphasized by Gouldner:

"Domination is concealed when certain courses of conduct, definitions of the situation, or conceptions of what is real, are internalized by subordinates so that they give willing compliance to the expectations directed at them. For to internalize an ideology is to internalize a set of commands and reports. That being so, the struggle between social groups is now mediated by their struggle to shape the ideologies relevant for various situations and groups." (Gouldner, 1976: 203)

In common with other ideologies, management ideologies are of importance to the upholding of the social order. They legitimize prevailing power and privilege conditions like the general principles for the economic organization of society. In a narrower sense they have a direct supportive function for the people who identify themselves with this ideology. The ideology facilitates socialization and qualifications for certain positions. It can also fulfil therapeutical functions by giving support in a specific role against various stresses (e.g. various demands, criticism in mass media).

If we are to understand ideologies in a certain *practical social* context, it is probably more fruitful not to regard them as ready-made, demarcated and comprehensive texts or as mental possessions but rather as continuous social processes (King and Fitzgibbons, 1985; Therborn, 1981).

"For reasons of labelling or of analyzing, different ideologies can be demarcated with respect to origin, subject-matter, content and interpellated subject, but as continuous processes of interpellation and discourse they lack natural mutual boundaries between themselves. There are no natural criteria which distinguish one ideology from another or one element of an ideology from the entirety to which it belongs." (Therborn, 1981: 87)

This means that ideological "figures" tend to be continuously created and re-created in accordance with specific situations, with the way ideological elements converge and diverge, with the actors who enter and depart from the situation, the strategical actions they carry out, etc.

In this book my task is not, however, to take up in detail the way ideologies function in concrete contexts. Here, for "reasons of labelling and analyzing", I shall describe some central elements in management ideology. These elements have a marked plastic internal relationship to each other and form various configurations when they are expressed in various contexts. What I take up are elements, in or aspects of, a general ideology (or a set of ideologies), a kind of super-ideology which can then cooperate with different ideologies specific to companies which are more closely associated with concrete practice.

The basic elements in management ideologies can be divided into three kinds of aspects:

– The "foundation" or the overall rationality order on which the business activities are based
– The power organization or hierarchical structure on which the management function and business leaders as a class are based
– The social integration of various interests and forms for the satisfying of needs which the order is based on and permits.

The first aspect is thus concerned with basic rationality, the second with the legitimacy of the existing hierarchy (of the class structure) and the third with the satisfaction of needs. The three aspects are interlinked and are often expressed in combinations but for reasons of analysis can, with advantage, be distinguished in this study.

At the fundamental level (the basic rationality which distinguishes the economic order) there are, amongst other things, two types of ideologies or rather perhaps foundations for ideologies:

– technological rationality as (base for) ideology
– late capitalistic economy as (base for) ideology.

Technological rationality aims at the maximum exploitation of Nature. With the help of the most advanced and highly productive technology available an increasing flow of economic benefits is generated. Advanced technology is regarded as a good thing in itself. Political questions are re-defined as scientific and technological problems, for which expert systems, technology and science can be regarded as ideology (Habermas, 1971). In order that mass production shall continue uninterruptedly social control is a necessity: the labour force must be disciplined in accordance with the productivity ideal and needs must be subordinated to the principles of mass consumption. I touched on these ideas in Chapter 1 (pp. 9–12) and will take them up in greater detail in Chapter 9, for which reason I will not examine them further at this point.

Late capitalistic ideology expresses a certain ideal of the way the economic system functions. Normally this is not referred to as "capitalistic" since this word is considered to be charged with political values. Instead it is conceptualized as "postindustrial". The ideology is concerned with the good sides of phenomena such as free enterprise, the imperatives of the market, private ownership, etc. Late capitalistic or postindustrial ideology differs to some extent from traditional capitalistic ideology in that the "advantages" mentioned above are not stressed so heavily. This is because the state cooperates with companies and cooperation of this kind does not go hand in hand with traditional capitalistic ideology which lays stress on – in the relation to the state – "free enterprise" – and also because the latter version is also based on private ownership as the direct source of control over companies, something which does not really harmonize with the strong position and interests of professional business leaders.

As Anthony (1977) points out, capitalistic "business ideology" has at least in Europe in recent decades become less conspicuous and is applied for the most part against government interventions of a negative nature for a company and as a basis for legitimizing actions on the market. That the market at times brings about imperatives for companies in the form of compulsory rationalizations, the closing down of corporations, mergers, the dismissal of personnel, etc. still constitutes a dominant element in management ideology (and of course also in "reality").

The ideologies of technological rationality and late capitalism harmonize well – and to the extent they are accepted – they are the reason why the following values have become dominant and are hardly open to question:

– economic growth
– the allocation of priority to investment and the development of advanced technology
– the advantages of large-scale production
– mass production and mass consumption as primary sources for solving social problems
If this type of ideology means that the individual considers the dominance of these values as inevitable and feels compelled to comply with the laws of the prevailing economic system and to develop further and utilize increasingly advanced technologies due to the fact that they are highly productive, more or less in the same way as one is compelled to obey the laws of Nature, then – according to the Frankfurt School – it is a question of "false consciousness". Socially determined conditions are then regarded as an expression of those laid down by Nature.

When it is a matter of the ideological elements which are concerned with the legitimacy of the power structure and hierarchy in companies I believe we can speak of three, amongst others:

– technocratic ideology
– ideology of managerialism
– elitist ideology

These ideologies legitimize the position and privileges of management in companies and communities.

Technocratic ideology regards the running of companies as a neutral function. Modern scientifically-based rational technologies and social structures in companies and company environments generate clear imperatives which managements must follow up as best they can. Business management's actions and the results of these are regarded as determined by external circumstances and restrictions. Managers are looked upon as technical experts and have – provided they live up to their professional demands – limited influence and responsibility.

Ideology of managerialism lays very strong emphasis on the management function. This function is looked upon as clearly differentiated from organization work in general and is expressed as equally important or more important than the organization in its entirety, i.e. the work carried out by 95–99% of the personnel who do not belong to the management.

Interesting enough, management as a separate function was established in all seriousness with and by Taylorism. By separating thinking, planning and design of the work assignments, which came to be the preserve of the management function, from the implementation of tasks controlled from above, which was what remained for the workers, a separate management function was created (Littler and Salaman, 1982). With the installation of this form of organization, production would become impossible without the coordination and design functions of management.

Company management, as a special function of any great importance, is thus a phenomenon of relatively recent origin. This can be worth knowing when considering ideology of managerialism and the fact that the management function has become institutionalized. Today this ideology has become much more detailed than in the period immediately after the establishment of Taylorism. (At that time a technocratic ideology in accordance with the description above was more realistic.) Characteristic of ideology of managerialism is

"...major and critical claims to authority over the shop floor upon which the efficiency of the whole enterprise depends (except in times of recession or economic difficulty when external, uncontrollable factors are held responsible)." (Littler and Salaman, 1982: 259)

Compared with technocratic ideology, ideology of managerialism presents the importance and the scope of action of management as very much greater. According to this ideology, management is a difficult art, soaring far above the demands made by the technocratic function. This means, of course, a boosting of the profession at the same time as this ideology is exposed to a great deal of criticism because the area of responsibility of management is presented as being so large.

Elitist ideology stresses the rare qualities and qualifications which distinguish the good executive and the heavy demands which his tasks place upon him. It is the unique competence of the corporate leaders which legitimize their position, power, status and privileges. This competence can be of various kinds. Different ideas on what constitutes a good leader vary from time to time, in different states of the market and also in different branches and forms of organization. Qualifications which may be significant may be advanced education, further education and training in important positions which pave the way to a director's appointment. It may be said that experience from abroad and schooling at international institutes of management distinguish the management elite from people in general. Another type of qualification is of a psychological nature. Business leaders possess special personal qualities which make them more "holistic" in their thinking, strength of will, capable of bringing out "the best" in their subordinates or quite simply more "charismatic" than people who do not reach higher management positions in their careers, all according to the elitist ideology. As a rule it is positively formulated attributes which distinguish the efficient leader according to this ideology. We might also expect that efficient leaders could be described in more neutral terms than is currently so often the case and that possibly traits which can also be formulated "negatively", e.g. ruthlessness, thirst for power, the ability to exploit people, could be presented.

Naturally this elitist ideology is often presented simultaneously with the ideology of managerialism but the two are not necessarily linked together and can also be expressed independently of each other.

The third category of ideological elements in management ideology, which are concerned with interests and needs, contains the following ideologies:

– Harmony between the organization leadership and the psychology of the employees
– The ideology of the harmonious conflict
– The ideology of optimism concerning the future
– The organization as an instrument for the satisfaction of needs

The ideology of harmony between the demands of business management and the psychology of the employees is based on the idea that a complete integration of these is possible. Democratic leadership, personnel and group-orientated management, intrinsic motivation, involvement, personal development, self-realization, etc., are key concepts which focus on harmony between what the management and the employees set up in the way of demands for work and work performance. Several of the theories and arguments which I investigated in Chapters 5 and 6 are an expression of this ideology which tends to claim that all forms of alienation in activities controlled by modern progressive managers are disappearing or have at least started to disappear.

The ideology of the harmonious conflict asserts that the controverses and conflicts which not seldom occur in organizations are of a restricted character and are furthermore often constructive and fruitful. Against the background of a basic consensus on overall objectives and means, conflicts in companies, if properly managed, are potentially fruitful, because they can be stimulating, facilitate self-criticism and pave the way for innovations. In other words, conflicts are functional and should even by encouraged on the part of management. Both too little and too much conflict are a bad thing is the view of this ideology (see e.g. Robbins, 1983: 289 ff).

The ideology of optimism concerning the future reckons, as the name implies, that what is waiting around the corner always means, or, if the cards are played correctly, ought to mean, improvements. Development and change = improvement. The principles of modern business management are always wiser, more rational, advanced, psychologically correct or in some other way praiseworthy than methods previously practised. Employees are treated in accordance with psychological principles rather than "bossed around" and alienated by Tayloristic and bureaucratic managers. New technologies liberate employees from routine jobs, offering instead varied, exciting and challenging tasks. Increasingly rapid changes in the business world place demands on new flexible and decentralized forms of organization. Possible problematical conditions, which may also be open to criticism, with regard to company practise are regarded in this ideology as historical or temporary, soon to be left behind in a more promising future.

The organization as a source for the satisfaction of needs is what is expressed in slogans like "What is good for General Motors is good for the USA".[4]) The real objectives of the organization and the measures taken by the management and other leading actors are thus regarded automatically as instrumental in relation to the needs and wishes of some legitimate interest group. The principles on which the organization is structured and operates are assumed, in other words, to be based on a rationality, the guiding star of which is the needs of the community.

The four ideological elements described here are examples of (sub-) ideologies concerning interests and the satisfaction of needs in companies. They may preferably be regarded as aspects of a set of ideologies concerned with this extensive theme. It is difficult to find naturally demarcatable (sub-)ideologies on this theme.

With regard to concrete specific organization conditions and other social situations, it is – as pointed out previously – often more fruitful to regard ideologies as social processes rather than ready-made units which survive

---

[4]) This is a good example of ideology in the sense how sectional interests are presented as general interests. (Shrivastava, 1986 makes the same observation.)

for a time and return in different situations with the same or similar content. What I have attempted to report above are some overall ideological themes and different elements (sub-ideologies) in connection with these which in different forms and combinations tend to be derivable from various discourses, texts and debates. In different specific contexts they assume different shapes, have different meanings and lead to different consequences.

7.4 The Relationship between Organization Theory and Ideology

The time has now come to relate perspective, focusing and discourses in management-orientated organizational-theoretical research and texts to the concept of ideology stated above and to the management-orientated themes described in the previous section. (It is important to note that I do not express myself on all organization theory but only that part which is connected with the management perspective, and even there I concentrate rather on frequent than on constantly occurring phenomena. Caution should therefore be exercised against interpreting my presentation as an attempt at broad generalization.)

When observing the relationship between organization-theoretical research and management ideology it should be noted that the research worker's degree of independence with respect to the business leader is often limited. Both groups have some common socialization (academic basic training in management), very often a common contact surface, mutual dependence in the form of management training and consultant commission, sales and purchase of technical literature, etc. Research workers and management practitioners often share interests and common values. The latter offer an important market for the former.

Research workers are responsible for much of the official picture of companies and business management practice which is presented in the form of teaching, publications, etc.

As Rosen (1984) points out, management and organization theory are exposed to demands, influence and control by the business elite, especially in the USA. A basis of "reality", "usefulness" and "relevance" are demands on the part of commerce on business schools, concealing the fact that these are the values and interests of the dominant elite and shall be placed in the centre for research and instruction.

"'Relevance' as criticism is evoked not infrequently when a body of theory, rather than mirroring and reinforcing the dominant *Weltanschauung,* implicitly or explicitly challenges it. This is evident when the source of the resources supporting management theory and its theorists is considered. Support primarily derives from large corporations or individual capitalists, who 'donate' money to build office and class buildings, fund chairs, support research, support consulting and executive education fees, send some of their members to part and/or full time M. B. A. programmes, hire the bulk of undergraduate business school students, and so on." (Rosen, 1984: 319)

The interest of business management and capitalists in research and literature is by no means only of a technical nature. The ideological aspects are also of interest in the context. Astley (1984) even believes that

"...the ideas which dominate mainstream management science have very little payoff in a direct technical or engineering sense." (p. 269)

Instead, declares Astley, theory and terminology mainly exert an indirect influence, through ideologies which help to fuse organizations into a unitary body and thereby lubricate the process of change.

The company research workers' success with the business leader is probably in part determined by how well the former finds himself in agreement with the latter's ideological interests. Common ideological interests expressed in the research often facilitates the success. As we shall shortly see, there is a tendency for business management ideologies to be reproduced in a number of organization theory texts.

The latter are not, however, merely passive reproductions of the former. It is important to note that organization theory also plays an active part, as a source of influence on practice.

Unlike many other academic disciplines, organization theory is of great relevancy for practice in society, business and working life. University education, courses, seminar and books on organization theory are significant for the concepts and thinking on economy, working life and, ultimately, on the prevailing social order.

The theoretical management-orientated organization thinking can even be expected to have relatively great importance regarding ideologies that legitimize the management perspective and those values forming the basis of it. In this way one naturally influences even the prevailing order in companies and society.

This influence occurs primarily in the following way:

First, it fulfils a main function in the socialization of managers-to-be and other higher staff members of companies and, to a certain extent, even other job categories that in some way get in touch with business economics thinking, such as some white-collar workers, trade union officials and business administration students. Other categories of employees in companies are then influenced by these groups.

Secondly, it is instrumental in working life and society in bringing forward, creating and maintaining ideas about how organizations function and should function; it also diverts criticism from the prevailing economic and political order. The predominant organization theory is instrumental in helping managers to polish their arguments and bring forward subtle and tactical trains of thought in order to reach their goals in negotiations, general debates, etc. (Anthony, 1977). Theory also presents inspirations for changes in practice which facilitates social integration in the corporation.

Organization theory might be seen as performing ideological functions if the above mentioned management ideologies (or other kinds of ideologies) are uncritically reproduced in the theoretical discourse. These functions are carried out, partly by choosing a general suggestion, perspective and way of defining reality, and partly by treating problematic relationships in such a way that eliminates or reduces disruptive or potentially oppositional thinking. When ideas produced by theory lead to minor changes of a predominantly symbolic and ideological nature in relation to a specific conflict raising issue in a practical situation, and when the source of the conflict is not resolved in its substance, one can also talk of organization theory carrying out an ideological function. This is an important aspect of the theory/ideology relation. I am not, however, in this chapter treating practice but concentrating on he content of organization theory texts and not the (ideological) use of these texts in practical settings.

The first aspect of the ideological function in texts, i.e. the overall perspective/view on reality, concerns the general direction of organization theory and can, consequently, be discussed on a fairly general level while the latter aspect (the treatment of problematic topics) can be appropriately analyzed with the point of departure from concrete texts. I shall begin here by examining some general viewpoints and proceed in the next section to point out an ideological preponderance in some organization theory publications.

Zey-Ferrell (1982) criticizes the predominant organization theory (the comparative structural and contingency approaches) for one-sidedly assuming one form of organizational rationality, viz the technological and instrumental variant represented by the dominating publications. This is uncritically considered valid for, and to include, the total organization. In this way, the status quo is not questioned, nor is the power structure or the distribution or rewards within the organization. Zey-Ferrell emphasize that, on the contrary, various interests and rationalities exist in organizations and ask why many organization researchers for a long period have pushed the idea of one rationality she answers the question herself by pointing out the idea that an organizational rationality serves the managers' and administrators' interests of having the organizations appear as rational, adaptive, goal-rational systems of voluntary, well-treated workers and responsible managers. Dominance, force, manipulation and oppression of groups is seldom analyzed. Instead, it is stressed that organizations are free from conflicts and are striving for common goals and interests.

Pfeffer (1981 b) notes that power and politics, despite their crucial importance for what is going on in organizations, are neglected in organization theory, especially that being produced in U.S. business schools. He explains this by referring to the ideological component in theory and texts and to the fact that topics such as power and politics are basically incompatible with the ideology of managers, which stresses rationality, effectiveness and bureaucracy as characteristic of managerial work.

Lately, a number of organization theorists have modified this position and dissociate themselves from the idea of one rationality in organizations. Many of these proceed from a pluralist perspective which is supposed to be a type of criticism aimed at the predominant understanding of rationality and interests in organizations. It is maintained that several different interested parties exist within organizations and that these groups, depending on their diverse interests, act in accordance with various rationalities. The pluralist understanding of (limited) conflicts among different interested parties has lately become fairly common (see Ch. 7.6). Perhaps it is one the verge of replacing the idea of a unitary rationality, such as conventional wisdom, in organization analysis.

An important criticism of pluralism, when applied to the understanding of rationality, concerns the relationship between social structure and the predominant forms of conceptions characterized by the instrumental rationality, on one side, and, on the other, the organization and conflicts and the various rationalities that compete within it. The question is whether the latter are not often different variations *within* the predominant rationality in society. Many of the conflicts that the pluralists emphasize concern methods and resource allocations within organizations that aim to realize general goals (i.e., an advanced technological apparatus, maximal productivity, economic efficiency, and increase in size) and how privileges – that is, the fruits of this rationality – should be distributed. From this viewpoint, the various interested parties appear interesting and significant only in the light of the predominant rationality's being taken for granted (Alvesson, 1984 a).

The mentioned forms for criticizing the predominating view of rationality – which is defined in somewhat different ways depending on what the criticism implies – do not question the dominance of the instrumental rationality in organizational practice or in organization theory and everyday thinking. The criticism is often aimed at the various restricted definitions of rationality. By pointing out the different forms of rationality and even "irrationalities" and the limited social conflicts concerning the different ideals of rationalities, one avoids a far too restricted, technocratic view of the conditions required for the realization of the predominant rationality. By attempting to broaden the way of viewing rationality, organization researchers strive to incorporate a multiplicity of aspects in a more advanced management practice. Thus, the stated criticisms of rationality are sometimes normative-instrumental in character and are aimed at improving the predominant rationality – for example, by utilizing social conflicts "constructively" (Alvesson, 1984 a). Of course, this comment is not valid for all pluralists. Some of these are not instrumentally oriented in their approach (e.g. Crozier and Friedberg, 1977).

Even if pluralism expresses a different view of rationality, common interests and conflicts than the traditional view, it has still some features of the consensus perspective. As Carter and Jackson (1986) puts it ". . . pluralist theory rests upon the assumption that, either a consensus is always ultimately attainable, or that a resolution of forces will provide a modus vivendi." It is doubtful whether it stands for a radical new position with regard to the basic character of activities.

Zey-Ferrell's (1982) summary of the perspectives and basic assumptions in the dominant organization research, at least until the 1970's and possibly even until today, states that this is characterized by the following assumptions and direction:

– There is a consensus of goals among organizational members which unites them in a well-integrated system
– Organizations can be understood as a result of their pursuit of goals/need fulfillment
– Research questions are directed toward how efficiently and effectively the organization obtains its goals
– Researchers analyze questions and problems which are of concern to managers and dominant elite which in turn enables them to better realize their objectives of perpetuating control and dominance. The origin of power relationships is seldom among these questions.
– It is assumed that values and interests of management and workers are the same; they are neither contradictory nor antagonistic and therefore, not in conflict
– Due to this consensus data gathered from managers and/or respondents from the dominant coalition may be generalized to the organization as a whole.

It is scarcely possible to declare that all these characteristics of the dominant perspective in organization are ideologically dependent and therefore "false". On the other hand, at least in some contexts and situations, they are over-simplified, misleading and give a selective picture of organizations.

The perspective and the focus are structured in close agreement with the management ideologies described above. The questions posed and the results obtained by research therefore tend to agree with and support these ideologies rather than to uphold independence and potentially entering on to an opposite course to these ideologies, providing material for the critical evaluation of these (and the interests which lie behind the ideologies). Research thus means that primarily the interests, point of view and values of one specific category are upheld. These can agree or be in conflict with the interests and values of other groups.

Similar aspects are presented by Sjöstrand (1978). He points out that a clear-cut, "objectively correct" picture of the activity does not exist in companies and other organizations. Instead, there is continuous rivalry between individuals, groups and interests to establish a certain view of the organization as the correct and ruling one. The "winning" organizational view influences norms and behaviour. The organizational picture that normally becomes dominant is that which is embraced by management. They have the resources to push through their definition of the organizational reality. The theoretical organization research can be said to be a resource for management, enabling them to force through their picture of the organization. Business administration and organization theory build a great deal upon managers' approaches and experiences:

"Research, especially within business administration, has assisted, on the whole, in the systematizing and spreading of these experiences. Organization theory can largely be seen today as the codifying of certain (leading actors') experiences in organizations. It is those with strong resources (position, experience, knowledge, etc.) who have defined which problems are the most important... (Ibid., p. 36)

Even if Sjöstrand is more careful in his conclusions, his analysis supports Zey-Ferrell's criticism. Most organization theory considers the organizational reality from a certain perspective, viz management's. This biased view means that certain aspects, conditions and values are seen as significant and relevant for the guidance of practice while others are not treated at all, or are redefined to agree with management's perspective. Braverman illustrates the latter:

The problems addressed are the problems of management: dissatisfaction as expressed in high turnover rates, absenteeism, resistance to the prescribed work pace, indifference, neglect, cooperative group restrictions on output, and overt hostility to management. As it presents itself to most of the sociologists and psychologists concerned with the study of work and workers, the problem is not that of the degradation of men and women, but the difficulties raised by the reactions, conscious and unconscious, to that degradation. (Braverman, 1974: 141)

Thus parts of organization theory are instrumental in formulating man's alienation in work and organization as primarily a technical-administrative problem and not as the problem it actually is for the workers concerned. By biasedly representing the management perspective and, thereby, the managers' interests, and by neglecting the problematic conditions that are not in line with it, the preceeding rationality is presented as given, obvious and unproblematic by the dominating interested parties.[5])

This is a natural and perhaps unavoidable consequence of the majority of researchers and authors within the organization theory discipline addressing themselves primarily to managers, students, etc. who share, or are expected to agree with, the management perspective. It is important to subordinate one's attitudes under the basic management values if one wishes to attain new professional success and perhaps also a good income.

This question is also dealt with by Yorks and Whitsett (1985) who warn us that interest in research and interest in influencing practice become confused. The latter results all too easily in not keeping strictly to facts but giving presentation and conclusions a more definitive and clearcut form than what facts motivate in order to be better able to sell the idea or the research result to a non-academic public. According to these authors the problem is that a number of results and ideas lacking proper support in research begin to circulate. In their view the answer is that researchers should become more rigorous with regard to methods and above all more cautious when using or drawing conclusions from case studies. They should also more clearly differentiate between the researcher's role and that of the consultant and other activities with direct appeal to practitioners.

I agree entirely with the latter recommendation and can well believe that increased rigour would lead to less ideologically-infiltrated theory. However, Yorks and Whitsett miss a central point by formulating the point in

---

[5]) Naturally there is no fault in the management perspective itself or that this leaves its mark on the organization theoretical texts. The problem is that this perspective is presented in such a way that it makes the understanding of organizations and the work of individuals one-sided. A certain one-sidedness could follow if studies and texts which focused exclusively on job content, quality of work, problems of alienation etc., completely ignoring the economic aspects of organization and work were to dominate the field of research – and in time – the intellectual understanding of this. (Such one-sidedness can also leave its mark on individual texts and is certainly unsatisfactory but it will not be problematical until one-sidedness is characteristic of entire fields of research or knowledge. A definition removing the economic and instrumental conditions from the agenda would certainly give rise to similarly distorted consequences which technological rationality causes today for all-round understanding – and for conditions for rational dialogue and "communicative competence" about work and organization. The dominance of the management perspective in both companies and working life as well as in the academic world means that the risk of the economics aspects being banished to the periphery is virtually negligible. For this reason I have mainly refrained from taking up instrumental aspects on "equal conditions" with those who emanate from a negation of technological/instrumental rationality and do not offer an economically-based critique of the principal perspective and interests which are expressed in this book and of the critical tradition in the view of work.

positivistic terms, i.e. they regard conclusions which do not have full empirical support as the problem. To serve business leaders with well-founded research results is a praiseworthy and desirable aim in their opinion. They ignore the ideological interest on the part of business management and this type of link between management and research. Whether the research result is "true" and well-founded or not is scarcely of decisive importance to the consumers. Often it is just as important that they should be ideologically and/or pragmatically functional. (In some fields of management research, incidentally, the idea of making true reproductions of reality and establishing causal connections has been abandoned in favour or work on conceptual and perspective development, see e.g. Brunsson, 1982 b.) Research results of value to business leaders should not contain too many criteria on a firm scientific basis, but be open to political/ideological aspects of whatever may be considered to be of value. (As will be seen in the literature illustrations in this and the following chapter, much of what attracts the greatest appreciation on the part of the management market is in certain respects beneath all criticism from the intellectual point of view.)

It should also be noted that strictly positivistic research is not free of values and ideology. Such research can very well, under implicit assumptions concerning shared values and interest in companies, ideologically reproduce the dominant perspective, formulate descriptions, pose and answer questions which harmonize with management ideologies. This is to be found in Zey-Ferrell's abovementioned criticism, which is directed against studies carried out on a sound methodological basis.

The main problem in the relationship between management interests and ideology on the one hand and the attitude of the researchers to this on the other hand is that the latter shares the former, and that this is reflected much too clearly in research.

Of course, the acceptance and reproduction of management values does not warrant the conclusion that they are a type of "receiver of bribes". Similar to the great majority of occupational groups, organization theorists primarily share the prevailing norms in society, business and working life. Consequently, they are inclined to spread and support these values. What I am attempting to show in this study is, among other things, that one of the functions of organization theorists – next to the more "neutral" development of knowledge – is just to support and spread ideas and conceptions that reproduce the established order in society, companies and working life. This applies perhaps to the majority of developers of knowledge during most epochs and nothing else is really to be expected. But this does not reduce the importance of pointing out and illustrating the phenomenon.

7.5   Organization Theory and Ideology: Some Examples

I shall now proceed by giving some concrete illustrations of how ideological functions characterize many organization theory presentations. I shall start out mainly from three well-known and widespread books and one article written by some of the last decades' more prominent organization theorists/ psychologists: Herbert Simon, Peter Drucker, David McClelland and Edgar Schein. The main reason for my discussing these books articles is that the authors belong to the leading echelon within the organization theory of the last decades. They are also fairly dissimilar to one another.

Simon and Routinization

Simon (1965) treats the consequences of automation. I shall only briefly present one aspect here. (I make no attempt here to shed light on the whole of Simon's theme but wish only to select an illustrative point.)

Simon suggests that the development within organizations is proceeding in a direction towards more programming and routinization of work tasks. According to Simon, this concerns all levels, including management level. From working life psychological research results (see Chapter 3), one can conclude that low satisfaction, alienation, and other psychosocial problems accompany such a development. Nevertheless, Simon claims that the opposite is the case, in fact:

"Implicit in virtually all discussions of routine is the assumption that any increase in the routinization of work decreases work satisfaction and impairs the growth and self-realization of the worker. Not only is this assumption unbuttressed by empirical evidence, but casual observation of the world about us suggests that it is false . . . A completely unstructured situation . . . is, if prolonged, painful for most people. Routine is a welcome refuge from the trackless forests of unfamiliar problems." (Simon, 1965: 97)

Of course, Simon is right in as much as there certainly exists jobs where the lack of routine can present problems for the individual. This statement is trivial. However, generally speaking, the extent to which working conditions are severely routinized is the big problem in many people's work life. Simon envisions a strong, general tendency towards further routinization of work contents. It won't do to explain away the negative consequences of this development for the large majority of employees by pointing out that the complete lack of routine can also be a problem.

What is Simon's purpose with this argument? It is possible that he is trying to ward off the criticism of a development of man's working conditions; a development there is every reason to be critical of and about which a fair amount was known even in 1965. He thereby contributes to an idealization of reality that can be seen as an attempt to contribute to the prevailing social order.

Drucker and the Importance of Managements

In his book "Management: Task, Responsibilities, Practices" Drucker devotes a great deal of space to claim, without any real arguments, and to repeat time after time, a thesis on the tremendous importance and capacities of modern organizational managements. Some excerpts from the book may illustrate this:

"It is managers and management that make institutions perform. Performing, responsible management is the alternative to tyranny and our only protection against it." (Drucker, 1973: X)

"Management is fast becoming the central resource of the developed countries and the basic need of the developing ones." (p. 35)

"(Business management) has performed within its own sphere. It has provided economic goods and services to an extent that would have been unimaginable to the generation of 1900. And it has performed despite world wars, depressions, and dictatorships." (p. 9)

"All businesses have access to pretty much the same resources. Except for the rare monopoly situation, the only thing that differentiates one business from another in any given field is the quality of its management on all levels. The first measurement of this crucial factor is productivity..." (p. 111)

"But it is also clear that social responsibility cannot be evaded. It is not only that the public demands it. It is not only that society needs it. The fact remains that in modern society there is no other leadership group but managers. If the managers of our major institutions, and especially of business, do not take responsibility for the common good, no one else can or will." (p. 325)

Drucker here expresses the managerialism and elitist ideologies as described earlier in this chapter. Thus, Drucker emphasizes the importance of management very strongly. One of his main messages is that the alternative to

"...maintain management as autonomous, and indeed as 'private'... is the 'totalitarian' structure in which all activities, all individuals, and all organizations monolithically repeat the same pattern..." (p. 810)

To Drucker, this alternative "is grotesque" (p. 810).

Drucker's presentation can be considered extreme and strongly exaggerated. However, an uncritically disposed reader does not presumably understand the book in this way – it can be thought to appeal to managers and managers-to-be, in particular. It is hard to imagine a more flattering presentation for these categories.

But the book's obvious ideological points for the management perspective and its interests also contain certain problems. From Drucker's presentation, it should be possible to ask oneself if management doesn't have too much power? Doesn't a category of such importance – and which has effected so much – have significant power? Drucker denies this, however; and expresses instead a technocratical conception of management.

"Management has no power. Management has only responsibility. And it needs and must have the authority to discharge its responsibilities, but not one whit more." (Ibid, p. 300)

This is an impossible statement. Manager's altruism must be considered fairly limited. One does not need to be a Marxist or a cynic to count on management to use its position in promoting to at least some extent its own interests and goals (compare, for instance, Galbraith, 1967; Rhenman, 1974; Perrow, 1979; Robbins, 1983).

Power and Altruism

Drucker is not alone in describing the question of power and the interests of managers in the way shown above. In an article entitled "Power is the great motivator", McClelland and Burnham (1976) present similar ideas. These authors studied managers who had participated in so-called "management workshops" and came to the conclusion that good senior bosses have to have a great need of power, i.e. a strong desire to influence individuals. This power interest should be greater than the need to be liked. McClelland and Burnham claim that while 73–80% of the efficient bosses had a greater need of power than of being liked, only 10–22% of the less good bosses were more interested in power than in being liked, that is an inefficient boss lack the appropriate strong need for power.

An implication of this concept and approach, as expressed in the article, is illustrated by the following quotation:

"The manager with a high need for being liked is precisely the one who wants to stay on good terms with everybody, and, therefore, is the one most likely to make exceptions in terms of particular needs. If a male employee asks for time off to stay home with his sick wife to help look after her and the kids, the affiliative manager agrees almost without thinking, because, he feels sorry, for the man and agrees that his family needs him." (Ibid, p. 103)

This type of attitude, in considering the needs of the individual employee, thus characterizes the "bad" boss. Now McClelland and Burnham ask themselves, however, if their discovery is not just a bit alarming. Is it true that the good boss is the one how is striving for power and who is not at all interested in the needs of other poeple? one asks oneself. No, they answer because

"Above all, the good manager's power motivation is not oriented toward personal aggrandizement but toward the institution which he or she serves." (Ibid, p. 103)

McClelland and Burnham find that good bosses are well-controlled regarding narrow egotistical motives. They wish "to serve others" and practice an "altruistic" exercise of power. Thus, good managers are described as power-hungry altruists. Like Drucker, McClelland and Burnham express the leadership problem in a way that defends and supports elitist values. An effective leadership requires individuals who strive for power – individuals who altruistically strive for power – individuals who do not have this motivational orientation and opportunistically wanting to be well liked, are bad managers. The altruistic component makes the strong interest in power unproblematic, according to the cited article.

Of course, McClelland and Burnhams' discussion is not beyond objections. First of all, from the idea of altruism one can question the basic assumption that power is the great motivator. "The desire to serve others", rather than the possession of power in itself, should, from McClelland and Burnhams' discussion, be the general goal and source of motivation, while the power is more of an instrument with which to attain this.

Secondly, one questions the precise meaning of "to serve others" or "to serve the institution in question". Serving the institution should primarily represent the people associated with it. One could expect the clever bosses' altruistic striving to include their subordinates, above all, but such is not the case. The clever, power-orientated, altruistic bosses do not let themselves be especially influenced by the individual needs of their staff (compare with the above example of the man with a sick wife). Thus altruism – applies to other categories than the subordinates. It is then the higher stratum of the company, i.e. senior bosses, management and capital owners who remain?[6]) Is this perhaps the meaning of "serving the institution"? Since serving their interests probably also means that their own status, opportunities for advancement, etc. are strengthened, it seems a bit arbitrary to describe this direction of the clever bosses' power orientation as "altruistic", which is in fact what McClelland and Burnham do. The real signification of what authors describe in this way is a power direction which does not find expression in the form of despotism, downright oppression of others,

---

[6]) I disregard the possibility that the altruistic attitudes of the power-orientated bosses are intended for the company as a pure abstraction, i.e. disengaged from the individuals who have a type of interested party relationship to it. I do not want to deny, by this, that the loyalty directed at an abstraction such as a native country or a company, independent of the real people and groups who are an integral part of them, actually exists. Altruism and loyalty of such a kind must, however, be considered secondary to people of flesh and blood, at least at a time when religious and nationalist values are relatively insignificant.

sexual exploitation, etc., but works, instead, within institutionalized settings in socially accepted forms. One can also find a connection here between self-interests and the prevailing interest within the institution, making the power orientiation in question institutionally motivated and compatible with the institutionally dominated goals. Thus, McClelland and Burnhams' wording of the power orientation as "altruistic", i.e. directed at serving others, appears theoretically unmotivated and the conclusion, that the presentation of this point is dependent on ideological/legitimacy-oriented considerations rather than on strict, theoretical ones, appears reasonable. The idea of the strong power-orientated person with the interest to serve others is in line with the elitist conception of the efficient manager.

About Norms and Perspectives in Management Literature

The analysis of Drucker's and McClelland and Burnhams' texts show how modern management's work and the psychological motives behind it are presented in an idealized, almost glorified way. I think that this should be understood primarily from the ideological functions of the studies.

Even authors who, unlike myself, are not ideologically critical, note certain peculiarities in the literature on management and managers' work. Forsblad (1978), for example, characterizes the approach dominating the literature in the field in the following way:

"Descriptions of managers' working conditions are omitted to a great extent. The often abstract presentation, combined with edification features, strengthens the concentration on desirable conditions rather than on real ones. This results in the opportunities of the management position being over-emphasized while, at the same time, one disregards many of the work situation's limitations." (p. 162)

Laurent (1978) thinks that the organizational literature has, consequently, stressed the boss' perspective, emphasized leadership and the aspects of the superiors and neglected the perspectives of the subordinates. The literature is full of analyses, descriptions and instructions about how to be led and managed and how one, as a superior, should deal with subordinates. Laurent points out that education in management policy, organizational design and behavioral science biasedly addresses

"... to the grand architect having responsibilities in shaping the organizational life-space of others." (p. 224)

Laurent stresses that, not only are employees at lower organizational levels subordinate, but so are almost all the bosses. He means that even subordination demands serious consideration. Leadership would lose its meaning if the subordination aspect disappeared. Subordination has, however, normally been categorized and treated as a "dependent" variable. Laurent asks why such an imbalance between leadership and subordination exists in the study of management. He is of the opinion that the imbalance can be explained by the fact that leadership and dominance in our society are mostly associated with prestige and social status, while the position of subordinate is hardly associated with these attributes. Laurent summarizes his analysis with the statement that:

"...domination, under its socially acceptable from of leadership, is the prevalent cultural value among management practitioners, researchers and educators." (p. 227)

The organization theory literature expresses elitist values, thereby strengthening a practice built around elitism and dominance. It is echoing and strengthening the elitist ideology. How this occurs concretely is illustrated by the analysis of Drucker's and McClelland and Burnhams' texts.

This type of ideology counteracts organizational and working conditions built up a round humanistic and participative ideas. Dominance and elitism are closely related to an hierarchical organizational structure and a centralization of power and influence. Organizational literature thereby strengthens and legitimizes an organizational culture which is more compatible with bureaucratic-authoritatian forms of work organization than with bureaucratic-humanistic, participative organizational forms. Texts expressing concern with the latter from a strict management perspective contain a good ration of doubletalk.

Schein, Organizations and the Needs of the Employees

While the ideological and legitimating function of the prevailing social order is fairly clear and easy to identify in, for example, Drucker and Simon, it is not as clearly discernable in Schein (1980). From a humanistic point of view, this book appears sympathetic.

Nevertheless, a description of reality with clear ideological points appears distinctly in certain places. For example, he expresses himself in this way:

"...how can internal environments be created such that members of organizations will be enabled to grow in their unique capacities? The underlying assumption is that unless such personal growth takes place, the organization will not be prepared to cope effectively with an unpredictably changing external environment." (Schein, 1980: 7)

"...business and industry have become more complex and more dependent on high-quality performance from both managers and workers." (p. 57)

Here, Schein deals with managers and workers in the same way, in principle. He means that it is important for companies that both categories execute high-qualitative performances and implies that the trend is going in this direction. Organizations must attempt to stimulate the personal growth of all their employees. Schein indicates the conditions and a developmental trend that might, at least partially, be seen as an idealization of reality.[7]) (Schein's approach might be seen as an effort to contribute to the realization of such a positive reality. I can find that type of aim appealing. But this does not change the tendency in the text to give an ideologically biased account of present trends.)

Considering the relatively extensive empirical material that points in the direction of dequalification of work (see Chapter 2), it appears difficult for Schein to claim without argumentation that the general tendency should be that of organizations influencing their employees in the direction of personal growth stimulance and "high-qualitative" performance. Management's interest in and need of personal growth and high-qualitative performance are exceedingly different for staff at high levels and for employees with disjointed and de-qualified work content.

Schein does not present any data to prove his reasoning. He only states that this is the case – in a context that does not stimulate the reader to consider whether the statements really are reasonable.

The picture painted in Schein's book of today's organizations and the relationship between them and the individuals who are active in them is very positive. He gives the impression that the same positive trend towards high-quality performance characterizes, generally speaking, managers' as well as workers' work situation. According to Schein, the problems that can be found today are solvable without any interested party-conflicts about what is efficient in the long run:

"If the organization is genuinely concerned about building long-range effectiveness, must it not develop a system for hiting and socializing employees which makes them feel wanted, secure, meaningfully engaged in their jobs, and positively committed to organizational goals? Furthermore, must it not also build into its career development system a concern for creativity that may be required at some future time?" (Schein, 1980: 249)

Schein delivers his message in the form of questions. Strictly speaking, he does not state that the long-range efficiency means that people feel they have meaningful jobs and that they are positively engaged in the goals of

---

[7]) One can possibly think that Schein does not say anything about how things actually are, but only indulges in wishful thinking and poses questions. However, he also states something about the reality. For example, he says that companies have become more dependent on "high-qualitative" performance of the workers. His way of posing questions and presenting hypotheses results in the reader being led into thinking that, in the long run, companies do show great consideration for their staff's personal development.

the organization. However, the questions are rhetorical. Schein indicates that the efficiency of long-range business economics goes hand in hand with, and even demands, "the genuine psychological growth" of the staff.

In an article which is fifteen years older than Schein's book, Slater and Bennis (1964) formulate, in a less reserved way, a message similar to Schein's. "Democracy is inevitable" reads the title of the article, and this captures the article's message well. Democracy is inevitable if organizations are to survive, it is said. Schein's more guarded and careful presentation, compared to Slater and Bennis', intimates that the predecessor of the thesis on the inevitable democracy have been forced to back off somewhat in their view of the definite relationship between organizational efficiency and democracy. The "inevitable democracy" is thought, to a great extent, to be long in coming.

Commentary on the Discussed Texts

The books and articles are written by authors with very high status within management circles and have been read by a large number of people. After having read these and other books with similar contents, one can assume that the reader feels fortified in his assumptions about the prevailing order's wisdom and unproblematic character, and reassured about certain questions where he had perhaps entertained doubt.

If Simon, Drucker, McClelland and Schein succeed in this, they will have completed their ideological mission and have been instrumental in legitimizing the prevailing conditions and power relationships in companies and working life. This does not, of course, mean that I consider that the contributions of these researchers lack theoretical or intellectual value. My task in this book is to introduce a type av aspect – that of the critique of ideology and illustrate how ideology has impact on discourses – not to produce surveys of their authorship.

7.6   Pluralist Organization Theory

The completed analysis above of ideological features in organization theory has, above all, brought up studies with relatively clear ideological features. However, such is not thought to be unusual – according to Laurent (1978) and Zey-Ferrell (1982), it is the rule rather than the exception. However, recent pluralist conceptions about management and the functioning of organizations have influenced a certain organization theory. By pluralism is meant that several different groupings exist with partly conflicting interests. For a general review and critical discussion of pluralist ideas in organization theory, see, for example, Burrell and Morgan (1979: 202–217). The result of the pluralist perspective's influence has been a number of studies presenting a somewhat more shaded picture of the conflicts and problematic conditions in organizations.

It is, therefore, considerably more difficult to demonstrate ideological elements in large parts of the pluralist-inspired organization theory than in the elitist conflict-blind tradition discussed above. The ideological preponderance of this group is not obvious. However, I shall make an attempt to point out the ideological tendency of a specific organization theory text which, from a pluralist stand-point, takes up the conflict between humanistic values and efficiency thinking that I suggest constitutes a basic conflict.

Sjöstrand (1978) speaks in his article about two perspectives on organizations: "perspective from outside" and "perspective from inside". Sjöstrand defines the perspectives from the language. Usual concepts in the outside perspective are business idea, activity environment, participant, specific competition, strategy, product-market picture and technological development. This perspective is mediated principally by management and those associated groups. Sjöstrand does not name concepts such as staff turn-over and motivation problems, but these also belong, as far as I can see, to the from-outside perspective.

Lately, however, the traditional dominance of this perspective has been questioned to a greater extent in Sweden as the from-inside perspective begins to get more resource-strong mediators, especially in the form of trade unions. This perspective can be illustrated with the help of terms and concepts such as the value of work, power, work rights, collective, engagement, self-determination and the quality of work and life.

However, Sjöstrand does not place the two perspectives against each other. His view is the pluralist's, not the conflict theorist's. For him, the from-inside perspective is principally an amplification of the traditionally dominating perspective. The different perspectives and their mediators can agree in a pluralist context. I mean, however, that this method of presentation is problematic.

As far as I can see, a pluralist frame of conceptions about the relationship between different perspectives (interests) requires the fulfillment on the following two conditions:

– That the interests in question, through negotiations and compromises, can move at least a bit closer, without any of the interests (perspectives) being too unfairly treated. This means that the interests must have some equal influence.
– That there are more than two interests (perspectives).

If one can only speak of two interests (perspectives), one of which having only a slight influence, then it is hardly reasonable to use a pluralist frame of reference.

I would like to claim that the interests, described by Sjöstrand as the from-outside and from-inside perspectives, cannot be moved closer by some type of reasonable compromise within the framework of the capitalist economic system. It is difficult to imagine that aspects such as the meaning of work, the needs of people, the quality of life and self-determination can be as influential as aspects such as business idea and technological development in a working life characterized by competition and often by short-term profit maximization. Both the types of interests can, thereby, only be integrated to a limited extent. Companies which must show high efficiency in a market do not have more than marginal room to let the humanistic, staff-oriented, from-inside perspective encroach on the traditionally predo-minant marketing, technology, and efficiency-oriented perspective. The possible scope that can, nevertheless, be found for the integration of the perspectives is naturally the same one that the "humanistic" organization theory (McGregor, Schein, etc.) focuses on. The criticism I previously directed at this is naturally relevant even in judging Sjöstrand's presenta-tion.

The other assumption means that more than two central interests must be seen for the pluralist perspective to be valid. Characteristic of the pluralist theorists is that they try to find as many different social groups as possible to classify among a company's interest groups. The pluralist viewpoint can be seen as a special variant of consensus conception whose most important competitor in the intellectual arena is some (neo-)Marxist view of conflict. To show the absurdity of the theory of the basic, all-pervading conflict between work and capital, it is naturally valuable to be able to bring up more categories of interested parties than these two predominant ones, i.e. the workers and the capital owners/management. The credibility of plural-ism consequently lies, to a great extent, in whether one can demonstrate that conflicts dissension and problems are not merely, or even to a consider-able extent, a question of conflict between the work and the capital perspectives. Of course, one does not deny, however, that there can exist certain conflicts between them.

In Sjöstrand's presentation, however, one ends up extremely near a funda-mental conflict between these two interests or perspectives – i.e. which correspond to the concepts of technological rationality and its negation; that might be called humanistic or practical reason. These perspectives share important similiarities with capital and work interests, even if certain differences to exist (Björkman and Lundkvist, 1981, Ch. 3). However,

Sjöstrand attempts to maintain the pluralist approach by regarding the from-within perspective as a "supplementary" perspective preceeded by several categories. It is also unclear if the from inside perspective constitutes one or several perspectives – Sjöstrand speaks about supplementary perspective in the singular form (the perspective from inside), as well as in the plural (new perspectives). Since he does not make any distinctions to facilitate the separation of any different (part-) perspectives within the new ones, I interpret it as a question of one, connected perspective.

However, Sjöstrand explicitly claims that the perspective has several different types of exponents. According to him, the following interest groups are behind the presentation of the from-within perspective as a supplement or an alternative to the traditionally predominant perspective:

– trade unions seeking co-determination and responsibility
– business people advocating "decentralization", such as the introduction of divisions and profit centers.
– interested parties advocating group organization.

From these examples, Sjöstrand comes to the conclusion that "consequently, the exponents of these new perspectives have different roots" (Ibid, p. 39). But this conclusion does not really hold. I agree that trade unions have recently – at least for a period – begun to advocate a new perspective (even if they do not do so very strongly). But that business people advocating decentralization would stand behind the from-within perspective is hardly believable. Nor it is believable that these people, exemplified by Sjöstrand as members of SAF (Swedish Employers' Confederation), would really bring up perspectives embracing the value and meaning of work, the needs of people, etc. as ultimate goals to guide the practice of organizations. It is not their job.[8]) The advocates of various types of group organizations remain, then. These consist primarily of the trade unions, and researchers, to some extent. The extent to which the latter category contributes to pluralism is uncertain.

A few dozen working life and organization researchers are not a meaningful category in this context. The majority within the category advocate those perspectives which agree with traditional management ideas or union

---

[8]) On the other hand there is incentives for employers and corporate leaders to give activities a stamp which makes them correspond to the ideas of "the good organization" which in time is spread and institutionalized in the social environment (Meyer and Rowan, 1977). This should be done to give companies, commerce and industry legitimacy. Here it is less a matter of driving the value of work as an aim for business practice but rather of adapting formal structures so that legitimacy can be attained and measures and circumstances aimed at ensuring high efficiency can be taken and exist in peace respectively (Meyer and Rowan, 1977).

doctrines and do not make any independent, particularly relevant contributions to pluralism.[9]) Consequently, it is the trade unions, primarily LO (the Swedish Confederation of Trade Unions) and to a certain extent, TCO (the Swedish Central Organization of Salaried Employees), who make up the "exponent teams" behind the new perspective. The dequalification and proletarization of the work situation, which in recent decades has affected large groups of lower white-collar workers, has led to their bringing up of perspectives concerning, for instance, the value and meaning of work. Regarding the trade unions in relation to the from-within perspective, one can say consequently, that the categories (workers and proletarized collar workers), who address a similar problem (the dominance of the from-without perspective and its effects on working condition) with similar demands and values (the value of work, etc.), are similar.

The conclusion is that Sjöstrand's analysis of supplementary perspectives fits better in a more or less Marxist view of conflict (i.e. with focus on class conflicts) than in the pluralist frame of reference, as Sjöstrand assumes. The fact that he still chooses this, instead of a conflict theory, can be interpreted as ideological features coming into the picture. At least a presentation of contradictory perspectives in organizational practice, that neutralizes the conflict element in them by talking of discrepant pluralist perspectives, can serve an ideological function.

In conclusion, however, I would like to point out once again that the "ideological burden" of Sjöstrands analysis is relatively insignificant. The analysis does not lack critical thinking, and from an ideological viewpoint, it would be unfair to place it in the same category as, for example, Simon and Drucker. My reason for bringing up Sjöstrand's article is that I wanted to supplement the critical ideology analysis of organization theory, which includes ideology in a somewhat rougher form, with an examination of a more shaded text, where certain subtle features of ideology still occur.

7.7   Discussion

In prevailing, technological-capitalist social order and the management culture that denotes the leading administrative stratum guiding this order, is characterized by the following:

– economic growth is thought to be the main goals of society and business

---

[9]) This statement concerns the practice, i.e. the approaches and ideas that receive penetration power in reality. On this practice-level, the contributions of social and business researchers to "pluralism" – to the extent one can speak of such – are, to all appearances, insignificant. On a conceptual level, i.e. regarding theory, debate, etc. in society, the researchers' influence is greater. This does not warrant, however, the fact that Sjöstrand allows this category to, so to speak, improve on pluralism. Sjöstrands discussion is valid primarily for the practical reality of business, nor for the public debate.

– technical development is considered extremely positive and is seen as a decisive measurement of progress
– economic values compromise the predominant rationality criteria, and
– hierarchial social relationships are manifested in the form of a distinction between the leaders and the led, and an unequal distribution of priviledges are thought to be natural rather than socially constructed and well motivated from the striving for efficiency and success.

(See, for example Alvesson, 1984 a; Carter and Jackson, 1986; Littler and Salaman, 1982; Sandkull, 1981; Thompson, 1980; Zey-Ferrell and Aiken, 1981.)

These values, comprising the base of management ideology, are unreflectively echoed in large parts of management and organization theory.

One call well imagine a negation of this value which assumes another type of rationality: economic growth can be seen as an unnecessary goal in "the affluent society", the technical development can be understood to be destructive in many ways, economic values can be seen as only one of many ways of attempting to gain social values, and social hierarchies, as well as unfairly distributed privileges can be interpreted as arbitrary. From the standpoint of the conservative powers and interest groups, it is essential that this negative thinking does not arise, or, alternatively, can be fought in a flexible way.

Managers have an important task, partly because they should not act unnecessary in a practical way so that negative thinking is stimulated, and partly because it is essential that they manoeuvre ideologically in such a way that legitimizes the predominant goals, the currently pursued practice, and their own position. The latter is accomplished by, for instance, appropriate rhetoric, adequate ways of defining reality, influence on the socialization process, etc. Managers need, consequently, apart from technical knowledge, even ideological qualifications to do their jobs. They must be able to act ideologically correct towards others and, of course, their subordinates, They themselves must completely accept certain values. It won't do to have, for example, automobile presidents who are against private motoring, sceptical about advanced technology, think that a meaningful job is a more important value than high productivity, and who are in favour of the same pay for everyone. The dedicating of an ideology implies an individual's submission to a certain social context as well as his qualifying for it.

Organization theory's ideological features can be seen in light of this. One expresses an ideology under the legitimating cloak of science, which reproduces an order build upon the above-named and other values pursued by managers.

The demonstrated ideological features in the analyzed texts can be related to these values, Simon and Schein present the development of work as unproblematic in different ways. Simon claims that the consequences of the technical development, in the form of increased programming and routinization of work tasks, do not cause any problems for the staff – rather the opposite. Schein gives the impression that it is the technical development and the interest of long-range economic efficiency that drive forth a humanization of working conditions. The economic growth ideal is seen more as a guarantee for a humanized development. Managerial and individual goals are viewed as congruent and harmonious. Thus, Schein's book legitimizes the goals and the technological/economic rationality that is the basis of the prevailing social order. Simon's book includes the same ambition, even if its success is more doubtful here because the thesis is too crudely argued. While both books are supportive of the technological rationality's ideology, Schein is also expressing the ideologies of total harmony of management and individual demands and of future optimism. The latter two ideologies seem to be popular in an almost naively crude form in parts of recent popularized management texts (like in Arvedson and Rydén, 1983 and Deal and Kennedy, 1982) where Utopia is indicated to be on its way (Alvesson, 1985 b). There is a risk that texts of these types cover over problems with the quality of working life and thereby obstruct the humanization of work.

The clearest ideological theme in Drucker's and McClelland and Burnhams' texts is the value of pronounced hierarchical relationships and an elitist conceptualization of management. Drucker emphasizes the enormous meaning and heroic efforts of organizational managements. McClelland and Burnham regard a social responsible power orientation and the absence of strong needs of being well liked by everyone as decisive peculiarities of efficiency. A good boss wants to have power. Implicit here is the assumption that arrangements reducing managers possibilities to use power put spokes in the good boss' wheel – only bad bosses are thought to find themselves in such an order. However, it is claimed that a risk for undue exercise of power does not exist – organizational management is an objective function (Drucker, compare the technocratic ideology in management), good power-orientied managers are unselfish, driven by the desire to serve others (McClelland and Burnham). This is a clearly selective way of formulating the matter.[10])

---

[10]) Willmott (1984) expresses a similar view of management literature:
   "Overall, the *image* of managerial work that emerges from popular management books is that of the 'professional' who impartially carries out the universally and technically defined functions of management. Organizations are assumed to fulfil societal and communal needs and, by applying their professional expertise to organizations, the work of individual managers is seen to be socially responsible as well as personally rewarding." (p. 355)

The pluralist view in business and organization theory does not legitimize the predominant rationality and the hierarchical relationships in the same way. In Sjöstrand's text, ideology is regarded more as a restriction influencing the limits of what is taken up, than as something permeating the text. More generally, the great interest in pluralist organization theories in the recent decades can possibly be seen as an expression of organization theory's task as a cognitive instrument helping managers to develop and mediate advanced and ideologically efficient ideas.

". . . managers have now been carefully taught by sociologists to recite that it is more realistic to see an organization as 'a pluralistic system or a coalition of interests'." (Anthony, 1977: 242)

Anthony points out that managements' ideological actions are more efficient nowadays because they have become more advanced, subtle and realistic. Organization theory has contributed here, which is also said to be its task as a practical science. Management-oriented organization theory shall give a basis for efficient management within the framework of a capitalist economy. Efficient management requires, for instance, that managers have internalized management ideology and have the ability to efficiently produce ideological ideas among the company's staff and other interested parties. The same holds for getting legitimacy on the societal level. The stronger the impact of managerial ideologies in the public debate and on the thinking of decision making in politics and government the better for business leaders. These ideological aspects of management demand a basis, of course, and as mentioned, organization theory comes in here.

It appears from my discussion that at least parts of organization theory include ideological features submitting and qualifying the individuals they appeal to for an activity in business, working life and a society characterized by elitism and technological rationality. Of course, one can ask oneself how striking these features are. From my discussion, I would like to claim that they are rather important, at least in certain texts. It does seem as if the ideology permeates considerable parts of organization theory, especially when it concerns the defence of elitist condition and values (compare Laurent, 1978).

On these grounds it would be tempting to describe many organization researchers as the intellectual marketeers of management ideology. But even if this formulation does apply to an essential feature in numerous management-orientated approaches in research and texts, it would not be right to reduce the majority of reports, books and articles in management-orientated organization theory to being solely or even mainly concerned with ideology, even though there are many such cases. Numerous texts reveal an independent attitude to ideology. As has already been remarked, many management researchers are highly critical with regard to crude ideological distortions of the dominant perspective (e.g. Forsblad, 1978; Laurent, 1978 and to a considerable extent also Pfeffer, 1981 b and Sjöstrand, 1978). Thus there are considerable differences between "serious scientific" management literature and literature produced by company consultants.

Attention should also be drawn to differences between various nations. Organization theory is still dominated by Americans and organization theory therefore reflects, as Hofstede (1981) remarks, the cultural context of one specific society. But a change seems to be coming rapidly. This does not mean, of course, that the emphasis on ideology will cease in favour of more all-round and intellectually independent approaches to research. This sort of approach would mean that organization and management are not only viewed from a narrow management perspective but also from social-theoretical and social-philosophical points of view and on the basis of the interests and perspectives which characterize the subordinated/the managed, unions, etc. and other specific groups such as women and minorities. Even if, for example, Swedish management oriented organization research is often enough committed to management ideologies, these are not usually expressed so crudely but rather in a more subtle fashion, doubtless reflecting the Swedish social culture influenced by Social Democratic governments during a lengthy period, strong trade unions and relatively regarded far-reaching ideas of equality. Swedish management oriented organization theory is not therefore characterized by the hegemony of management ideology but also contains research from the perspective of the trade unions, e. g.. (For some comparative views on Swedish and North American organization theory from the aspect of ideology, see Alvesson, 1985 a).

Returning to the discussion of organization theory on a general level, it seems as if some of the rougher features of ideology in organization theory are becoming less prominent (compare Anthony's comments above). The growth of wage earner-oriented working life research and critical organization theory has contributed to this, at least in parts of Europe and it is considerably likely that it will do so to a greater extent in the future. At the same time, the management culture's predecessors might be forced all the more to refine the ideological aspects in the future. Even if periods of economic crisis can accidently reduce the need for flexible ideological actions from management's side, the long-range development points to the increase of managers' need of subtle ideologies, naturally influencing the ideology in organization theory. A list of reasons, which will be treated in the following chapter, points in this direction. It is conceivable that organization theory in the future will fill even more of an ideological function, which will probably then be mediated in a subtle and shaded way.

8. Organizations, Culture and Ideology

In this chapter I shall continue the discussion on the relationship between organization theory and ideology, but from a somewhat different point of view than that expressed in Chapter 7. There I tried to reveal the general tendency that an ideology permeates various management-oriented organization theories; in this chapter I shall tackle the perspective of development. The relationship theory – ideology shall be interpreted on the basis of the time context and the problems typical of the time which distinguish the social context in which the theory arises and spreads. Apart from a couple of brief examples from the history of organization theory during the last fifty years it is mainly organization theory which is typical of the 1980's, i.e. corporate culture and organization symbolism theory which will be treated.

It is reasonable to assume that the ideology which is reproduced, further developed and distributed in organization theory texts which in company practice and public debate (lectures, articles and propaganda material from interest party organizations and pressure groups) is not static but subject to continuous change. This can take place over long periods of time or as the result of relatively short-term drastic changes which have immediate ideological consequences. Thus the economic and political situation and development, the state of the labour market, changed values and the development of general knowledge leave their mark on both the direction of ideologies as well as on their degree of refinement. The further the "process of modernization" has advanced in a society, the more advanced the ideologies, we must assume, even if the spread and influence of mass-media can to some extent work in the opposite direction.

Different social changes call for different types of ideological responses from the elites who dominate society, business and organizations. This penetrates – even if only indirectly – the forming of ideologically-infiltrated theory. (It also influences theories in other ways – e.g. through the fact that certain problems come to the fore which guide approaches to research, but it would take much too long to go further into this aspect here.)

In this chapter I shall begin by taking up some characteristics of many late capitalistic societies which indicate an increased need, from the point of view of the business elite, of well functioning ideologies on companies, company management and jobs. In the next section I shall give some examples of organization theories, of which the origin, design and spread, can be related to those problems of social (and partly political) nature which were characteristic of the time of their spread. Organization theory, to the extent it is of practical relevance, is regarded here not only as "technical" answers to various demarcated company problems but also as ideological answers to more extensive social and political problems. Thereafter I shall discuss research on organization culture (-symbolism), which is typical of the 1980's, and relate this to the social context in which it exists. Some views on this direction, with regard to both its bases and content, are expressed from the standpoint of the critique of ideology.

8.1   Increased Need of Ideology?

There are signs indicating that managers' need of an ideology that contributes towards legitimizing their power, position and values, has increased of late. This applies, then, as much to those values and goals that management in the modern, technological-capitalist society is based upon, i.e. technological rationality (including economic rationality, technical progress and economic growth). I shall point out some lines of development (a total of 8) which suggest such an increased need of legitimacy.

Problems With Sanctions in Complicated Organizations

In modern, technologically-complex and hierarchical organizations, a hierarchical differentiation occurs, which results in people at different levels (or even at the same level) having different types of knowledge (Offe, 1970). A superior does not normally have mastery of all the knowledge that his subordinates possess and use in their work. This can be compared with the relationship of knowledge between a trained craftsman and his apprentice, where all trade-relevant knowledge that is held by the latter is even possessed by the former. The knowledge relationship of the workplace, combined with the complexity of the production, makes the possibilities of effectively punishing or even sharing responsibility more difficult because it is hard to know if anyone is "guilty" and, in which case, who it is. The sanction possibilities at the disposal of company management have been reduced in that society has become more »permissive« and that changed legislation (in any case in Sweden) has reduced the possibilities of sacking people. This leads to a need for a general legitimizing of the entire organization's activities.

Oppositional Actions can Have Great Financial Consequences

An aversion to accepting the goals and aims of the company can lead to an action counteracting this. Such an action can result in serious consequences, in particular for complex, capital-intensive production. Because industrial production has become all the more capital-intensive and complicated, the risks of this type of opposition are greater now than they were before.

One can question whether the development of advanced administrative and supervisory systems would not, if anything, limit the employee's scope of action. The employee has always a certain amount of space to object to the activities, however.

"While, as individual, he cannot modify, alter or overfulfil the regulations which make up his work role, he can at any time omit or even refuse to fulfil one or all of these norms. Thus, even by the strictest shaping by technology or the work procedures and the relationships of cooperation, the worker always has the opportunity to make mistakes, to produce rejects, to work carelessly, to create dysfunctional conflicts in the structure of cooperation and to 'fail' in every possible way." (Offe, 1970: 36)

This aspect implies the significance of the employees normatively joining in the activities of the company, considering the possibility that the individual could act, in some way, to sabotage the production. Ideological aspects have in this context, great influence, of course. The "wrong" ideology of the employee might create problems in terms of unreliable behaviour.

Development of the Work

The development of technical production entails a rather high frequency of fragmented and monotonous work. This leads to a motivation crisis for the workers who are to carry out the unqualified and administrative tasks. (Compare Chapters 2 and 5.) As many spokesmen for humanistic and democratic styles of leadership point out, the spread of longer education and higher expectations can lead to higher claims on the part of many younger workers, which can reinforce the problem of motivation.

An essentially different trend than the growing claims of the labour force in relation to frequently unskilled and tightly controlled job conditions in industry, but which nevertheless places the problem of motivation in the centre, is the spread of service trades. As Normann (1983) remarks, these are often dependent on their personnel displaying a "pleasant and attractive personality" and in the field it is difficult for managements to check the behaviour of personnel in more subtle respects. If their activities are to function satisfactorily, it is important that the personnel observe the correct values and standards and that is after all partly a matter of ideology. In this context it may be observed that the decline of the Protestant work ethic can also contribute to the problem of motivation. Habermas (1973a) points out that the loss of meaningful work and the work morale can contribute to the problems of the late-capitalist society. New and effective ideologies can be of interest to organization managers here, as well.

Growing Strength of the Trade Unions, and the Increased Extent of Government Interventions

is another development trend in working life and in the economy, which, at least in Sweden, can be thought to have changed, and possibly increased, the need for a well-functioning management ideology.

Government interventions are often of a positive nature for companies, but can also imply restrictions for the scope of action of company managements, not least in the form of legislation to advance the positions of the trade unions. In some parts of Europe the combination of trade union influence and Social Democratic governments is considered to be a problematical combination for commerce and industry.

Changed Attitudes to Authority

Throughout the entire Twentieth Century, but much more rapidly during the most recent decades, the traditional figures of authority have lost influence in relation to the position which they more or less automatically possessed. The entire process of socialization and social relations were formerly characterized by the clear relationship between paternal-/authority figure and child/subject (Ziehe and Stubenrauch, 1982). Fathers, teachers, clergymen, managers, and other persons in authority occupied more or less automatically their positions without necessarily being required to possess the qualities which motivated authority in relation to and the respect of people of lower status.

Today this is no longer the case to the same extent as 25 or 50 years ago and managers and other people in authority can no longer profit from the psychological dispositions for obedience which an authority-orientated socialization implies. This means that management requires new sources of legitimacy in order to be able to maintain it's hierarchical position and function without disturbance. New values and beliefs must develop or be created in order to assure the smooth functioning of leadership.

New and Other Values

The increasing weight that some people place on non-economic, non-technological values such as good environment, etc. is important. This trend can give rise to legitimation problems for management. If the environmental ideal is interpreted as antagonistic in relationship to such central management values as economic growth and technological rationality, it can become problematic for managers. Debates on nuclear energy, work environment, quality of life, consumer interests etc. suggest a displacement of the main point in the society where the productivity and growth ideals of many are given low priority to the benefit of other values. The "inner" life values have acquired importance in relation to material things (Zetterberg and Winander, 1983). Certain elements in organization theory can serve the purpose of providing ideological arguments (besides inspiring changes in practice) against some features in the critique of traditional priorities of economic and technological values.

Centralization of Power in Organizations

As pointed out by several authors, e.g. C. W. Mills (1959) the demand for explicit ideological legitimation has sharply increased because new institutions with great power have risen, while older power centres have become less influential. Mills points out that the power of the modern, large-scale enterprise cannot be automatically excused by referring to the old liberal doctrines of the Nineteenth Century, which constitute the main source in the legitimation of authority in capitalist societies.

This trend might be formulated as the centralization of power functions:

"Centralized power grows, both in large corporations and in government, but the loyalty and discipline this power can command from its subjects is uncertain. While control is ever more centralized, it is more and more difficult for the masters to make that control seem legitimate. This problem has appeared most strikingly in work, especially since the 1960's. Laborers now show their dislike for the institutions in which they work in ways that are affecting productivity, discipline in plants and offices, and orderly planning." (Sennett, 1979: 42)

Uncertainty about Wage and Consumption Increases

Steadily increasing wages and growing consumption have formed an important basis for the legitimacy of the prevailing social and economic conditions (see Gouldner, 1976). If reassuring the workers about increased opportunities for consumption becomes problematic even in the future, as seems to be the case now, then this basis for legitimacy can be torn down or reduced.

These eight trends, which to some extent overlap each other and may even on some point be slightly contradictory, apply to a varying degree to various countries. They are characteristic of Sweden, at least, in the 1980's and – I have the impression – that on most points they apply to post-industrial/late-capitalist society in general.

These trends can contribute to the questioning of management's authority and legitimacy. Furthermore, there is a risk that the motivation to participate willingly in the work process decreases while, at the same time, the possibility of being passive or even forcefully sabotaging the managements' ambitions increases. Each of these trends can be instrumental in making the employees refuse to cooperate on management's terms. The position of "technostructure" in society as a whole can end up under fire. A consequence of this would be an increased need for managers to create and spread new and effective management and working life ideologies. This influences the search for new theories and conceptions within, for instance, organization theory.

There are even trends which point in another direction, i.e. towards a decreased need of ideological legitimation. A possible example is the rising unemployment which probably often results in those who have jobs feeling fairly well off. The economic recession can also be instrumental in management's perspective being put forward more strongly. Another trend strengthening manager's position is the tendency towards weakened class conflicts. I mean, however, that there are more development lines resulting in an increased need of qualified ideological support than there are implying the opposite.

Naturally the trends described do not lead only to changes on the ideological level but also penetrate in various ways into the changed practice in companies and other organizations. Of special interest in this context, in which ideology is the principal subject of study, is the organization practice which is affected more by ideological and legitimizing factors than by strictly economic or technological considerations. Such practice is normally of little importance except that of influencing people's ideas and presenting circumstances in a more favourable light. This theme has been taken up by, amongst others, Meyer and Rowan (1977) who in an often quoted article say that the changed values of society force changes in organizations' formal structures, with the aim of affecting legitimacy and scarcely influencing the organizational practice in terms of technical effectiveness. Even Thompson (1980) emphasizes that ideological functions have a great significance for some organization principles which, lately, are thought to have come to characterize some companies:

". . . even business firms, which are not (supposedly) ideological agencies, nevertheless pay attention to criteria of symbolic-appropriateness in evaluating and selecting their structures and procedures. The engage in a certain amount of 'appearance-management' or 'window-dressing' . . . such considerations are really instrumental, aimed at disarming possible critics or opponents, or even attaining more legitimate ends such as efficiency and greater productivity. Certainly these are among the considerations that have prompted the adoption of schemes for worker participation in management, work councils and joint consultation schemes, job enrichment and enlargement. But a concern for the 'appearance' of structures and procedures can also stem in part from ideological concerns relating to symbolic-appropriateness or inappropriateness. (Thompson, 1980: 220–221)

A kind of confirmation that questions of ideology and legitimacy have been accorded greater importance in recent times may be seen in the fact that research on organization during the last ten years has devoted considerable and increasing interest to the subject, normally, however, without observing that this increase may be affected by a changed social situation which makes these aspects of special interest. (One exception is Meyer and Rowan, 1977.) I deal further with this point in Chapter 8.3.

8.2.   Theories as Ideological Responses to Problems in the Development of Society

When researchers in social science formulate or adopt a new theory they normally believe that the reason for this is that the new theory is in some way better than the previous one, e.g. pays regard to more aspects or more important aspects, is more precise or gives greater coverage, permits a better understanding or provides a better background of knowledge for the practical solution of problems than was permitted by the preceding theory. The background of new theories and areas of research should thus, according to the representatives of the theories, be inadequacies in the old theories or the neglect of vital areas of research and the intrinsic (intellectual) qualifications of the new theories. This point of view is expressed in principle by both the researchers concerned with developing the theory and modifying it within a certain tradition as well as researchers who change "paradigm" or even produce a new one.

When researchers in a particular field describe the theoretical development of the field, they often do so in terms suggesting that they are proceeding from rather simple models and forms of understanding to advanced equivalents. When e.g. Berg (1982b) describes current trends in organization theory, he says amongst other things that these proceed "from single and simple to multiple and complex images", "from a mechanistic logic to a social rationality" and "from a single level to multiple analysis". From the above, as from the majority of other surveys and works on the historical development of theory, the reader receives the impression that the theoretical development goes "forwards and upwards".

A somewhat different impression is given by authors who take note of the development of society and the sociological dimension of knowledge in order to understand the development of knowledge. Here it is now accepted that the theoretical autonomy of science is limited and that it is not only an academically determined work on the development of theory that lies behind whatever knowledge is produced, developed and spread. A series of social and political conditions play their part, from the economic foundations of society, political and cultural situations of current interest and other macro-aspects of whatever research policy is applied. (A kind of intermediate form between academic and social determination are the politics within the academic field, including the in and out definition processes of researchers and research with different interests in knowledge and methodologies which form a considerable part of academic life and where the fall-out is of great importance to whatever research is being produced.) According to this point of view, the knowledge which is developed and spread during a particular epoch is largely determined by the social conditions typical of the time. This idea or methodological principle is one of Marx' most important contributions to social science:

".. . all 'higher' expressions of culture and social organization are affected by the economic praxis of society. That this is an ingenious and fruitful concept on the part of Marx cannot be denied. As a methodological idea it is something to hold on to in all branches of humanistic and social science research, quite independently of the views of the researcher himself on the prevailing social system." (von Wright, 1978: 143)

The direction of many of the approaches to research treated in this study can be understood on the basis of this principle of interpretation. That research on working life for a long time "forgot" the central importance of job content for job satisfaction and mental health and that it was not until nearly the 1960's that this factor was rediscovered may be seen in an example (see p. 69–72). Thus theory can be developed and acquire respectability because it fits in with the prevailing way of thinking or with the interests of dominating social groupings, which are in turn closely associated with the way the economy functions. Insofar as the economic, political and cultural situation of a given epoch does not offer an intellectually superior basis for advanced theory than an earlier epoch, there is therefore no reason to assume that the development of theory is necessarily proceeding towards better and better forms of the production of knowledge.[1] Naturally this applies especially to fields of research which are closely related to the practical solution of problems and ideological interests, e.g. the management oriented organization theory.

The social determinations behind the powers of penetration of a particular theory or focusing of research are often difficult to detect but must instead be derived from a complicated network of different social, political, eco-

---

[1] According to Kuhn (1970) a new theory is different rather than more true than an older one. Kuhn points out, for example, that new theories at their birth are inferior instruments of clarification than their predecessors. Their are phenomena which the older theory explains better than the new and problems which the new theory does not in the main take up:
"There are losses as well as gains in scientific revolutions, and scientists tend to be peculiarly blind to the former". (Kuhn, 1970: 167)

nomic and scientific circumstances and interactions between these. It is more seldom that direct causality between social phenomena and the development of theory can be identified, whereas it is more often that social problems and circumstances can be seen as a background with which a certain theory is in agreement as far as its content is concerned. Thus, for example, the rise of academic social psychology about the turn of the century in some early industrialized countries is regarded as associated with the separation between individual and the neighbourhood community brought about by industrialization and urbanization (Asplund, Dreier and Mörch, 1975) and Freud's ideas on the central importance of psycho-sexual development to human psychological functioning may be regarded as influenced by the social conditions (patriarchy, strict sexual morals, etc.) characteristic of Vienna at the turn of the century.

A survey of the brief history of business economics-orientated organization theory reveals that it is often possible to point to rather clear connections between on the one hand social conditions and problems and on the other the development and spreading of a certain theory/school.

Organization theory as the technocratic and ideological response mainly to the problematical social conditions of business leaders, for example, is what clearly applies to the early human relations school in Mayo's version. The background to Mayo's works and the enormous popularity they achieved was the degree of industrialization which American industry had attained by the end of the 1920's, the depression chiefly during the early 1930's, and the social conflicts which this reinforced and made manifest, which amongst other things found expression in the form of militancy of labour.

"The depression had unveiled social antagonisms, stimulated unionism, promoted government intervention in industry and generally rendered workforce less tolerant and respectful of managerial authority." (Rose, 1975: 169)

Mayo's proposed solution for these emerging social problems and conflicts was to suggest that the work-group of large organizations should be made the focus of social living, responsibility for this integration being entrusted to an elite of socially skilled managers. Mayo took up central social problems and their expression at industrial places of employment in a manner which was attractive to heads of businesses and proposed a virtually simple handling of these: conflicts, quarrels and maladjustment were dressed up in a partly psychiatric jargon and »therapeutic« leadership was looked upon as a solution to the problems (see, for example, Mayo, 1949: 222–224). It was

»Mayo's ability to recognize the emerging social problems and to popularize attractive explanations and solutions, turned him into a kind of human relations superstar." (Rose, 1975: 114)

The powers of penetration of Mayo and the early human relations school swiftly became incredibly widespread and the Hawthorne experiments and their interpretation became one of the most renowned social science studies. If we look at the scientific value of the contribution of Mayo and the early human relations school, it seems to be generally agreed that it was not so great, most of the organization and implementation of the experiments into presented conclusions and theoretical speculation having been cut down by researchers from various schools and of differing political backgrounds (see e.g. Blumberg, 1968; Perrow, 1979; Rose, 1975 and Yorks and Whitsett, 1985). Obviously it was factors other than the purely scientific which lay behind the rapid spread and great powers of penetration of the tradition. Rose (1975) draws attention to an important factor of ideological nature:

"Mayoism emerged rapidly as the twentieth century's most seductive managerial ideology. What, after all, could be more appealing than to be told that one's subordinates are non-logical; that the uncooperativeness is a frustrated urge to collaborate; that the demands for cash mask a need for your approval; and that you have a historic destiny as a broker of social harmony.« (p. 124)

The arrival and spreading of the human relations ideas in Sweden can also be related to the social and political situation which left its mark on the country immediately after the Second World War. The marked radicalization of Swedish politics at the end of the war – comprising, amongst other things, the most extensive strike in Swedish history in 1945, a large proportion of votes in favour of the Communist Party and demands for nationalization and socialist policies – provided fertile ground for the considerable and rapid popularity of human relations ideas at that time (Björkman and Lundqvist, 1981: 30).

Another example of the way ideas and theories are developed and spread on the basis of a political situation rather than on the basis of the scientific development of the theories is the reception and spreading of socio-technics in Sweden during the late 1960's:

"The tremendous amount of attention which the Norwegian sociotechnical experiments aroused in that country in 1967 and 1968 also spread to Sweden. In 1969–70 the enthusiasm was comparable to that of the late 1940's for human relations. The social background scenes had certain common features. The general political situation was uneasy. Industrial peace was threatened by strikes, this time wild. Some companies had recruiting difficulties, others had a high turnover of personnel. Sociotechnics was thought to be a promising solution to all these problems." (Ibid page 42)

In this context it may be noted that both the practical as well as the theoretical interest seemed to have subsided since the late 1970's.

Yet another example of the way social conditions which are problematical for dominating elites affect the popularity of a certain theory is the spread of the participation idea. According to Ramsay (1977), this idea, at least in the United Kingdom, has been tied up with the state of the market. Participation as a field of research and practice has undergone different cycles with respect to the particular interest and force it comprises, depending on the political climate.

The examples quoted here illustrate how the prevalence and spreading of organization theories can be related directly to problematical social conditions. The latter appear to be just as powerful a factor behind the prevalence of the theories as the internal driving academic forces. We may very well assume that above all the social factors decide to what extent various theories are spread and to a lesser extent the content of the theories. Possibly there is a good deal of truth in this, but the influence of the social level is not limited only to guiding the extent of the propagation of various theories. The content which has dominated organization research during various periods can, at least in the examples above, be looked upon as in part directly determined by problematical social conditions to which organization theories may be regarded as answers characteristic of the times.

Another important aspect of the way social conditions influence the forming of theories is that social development reveals new phenomena and indicates new aspects of the researcher's object of study. Social development creates new objects of study by changes in social conditions – in the post-industrial welfare society severe cases of poverty are normally of little interest as objects for research, while the service-producing company makes its appearance as a common object of study. On a more subtle level social development means that a similar object of study in time acquires partly changed characteristics at the same time as the social context in which the research is included is also changed, while new perspectives and frames of interpretation are developed. One consequence of this is that the object is interpreted in a different way than previously. (An example might be motivation: Here the social man becomes the self-actualizing man in the course of a couple of decades.) This generates a certain flexibility between social development and the development of theory. This does not necessarily mean that the former penetrates into the ideological content of the theories. If now, as I stated in Chapter 7, a certain theory is dominated by an ideological bias in favour of dominating social interests and contributes to legitimizing these, we can assume from this that changes in the structure of these social interests and needs of legitimacy have affected the development of the theory. This, so to speak, over and above the general influence in favour of changes in the development of theory generated by social development via changes in the character of the object of study and in the forms of general understanding which influence how research is pursued at a given time. (These forms of understanding can, in their turn, be ideologically influenced, of the type strict positivism as an intellectual attitude which favours the status quo during a particular historical epoch. A form of understanding, e.g. a scientific theory or method can, however, be relatively independent in terms of ideology – in the sense I accord to the concept.)

The influence of the social conditions on organization theory is normally less direct and unequivocal than in the above examples. The social level, and in the first place the way the economy functions and the interests which are most closely related to this (i.e. those of the capital owners, business leaders and the political elite) usually have a long-term indirect influence on the choice of research method, the focus of research and the manner in which research poses and answers questions. The ideological bias which was revealed in the last chapter, with regard to both the perspective of the dominating management-oriented organization theory as well as the discourses which are expressed, indicates the "sensitivity" of the theory to the social conditions. At the same time there is, of course, a relative autonomy, possibly weaker in this research discipline than in the majority of other social sciences, but which nevertheless means that research cannot be reduced to being regarded as consisting only of reflections of contemporary social problems or as uncritically treated technocratic answers to the latter.

To sum up it may be said that it seems reasonable to suppose that the content of the organization theory is decided by non-scientific determinants, of the type social conditions characteristic of the time and the researchers' identification with dominating ideologies in society (especially those held by business leaders) as well as by the "purely" scientific discourses which, despite the influence of the former, hopefully make understanding in some sense increasingly advanced in the course of time. This should mean that in the long term there is a tendency for theory to move towards better forms of understanding without one direction succeeding another being necessarily intellectually superior to its predecessor. Intellectually weak theories can, if they appear at the right time and/or correspond to the interests of the dominating elite of society or of other important social groups, suppress stronger theories. (Naturally it is often difficult, if not impossible, to decide what is a strong and what is a weak theory.) The relative importance of the non-scientific and internal determinants varies, depending on the epoch, the social situation, the research-institutional and political conditions as well as the type of research in question. In general it is likely that the stronger the emphasis on the practical solution of problems and management interests, the stronger the non-scientific determinants.

The non-scientific determinants of a theory often (but not necessarily) have the consequence that the ideological element in the discourse becomes significant. This is illustrated rather clearly by the theories which have been discussed here in the light of history. These examples deal partly with the concrete solution of problems and not exclusively with ideology. However, they do indicate an overall relationship between the power of scientific theories and political problems which are of an ideological character. Social and political controversies are re-defined as technical problems, (e.g. supervision skills, job design, participative management), i.e. the problems are technocratized and presented as solvable with the assistance of demarcatable expert actions. The influence of the theories extends far beyond mere coverage of changes in concrete practice. They also function on an ideological level, by describing and explaining how work places function or will (be able to) function after the new organization principles have come into force. One example would be Mayo's ideas on how social conflicts are the result of inadequate social integration which has the effect of bringing out the neurotic characteristics of the workers. Another is the indications by proponents of sociotechnical systems on the possibility of harmonious integration of technical and social demands. Research and texts function as a basis of, and express also directly, arguments directed against criticism and protests against prevailing conditions. As I pointed out in Chapters 6 and 7, the discrepancy between the extensive spreading which humanistic organization theories have received in literature, education, company journals, etc., and the less marked effect they have had on concrete practice, may be regarded as an expression of such an ideological function.

8.3   Organizational Culture in the Societal Context

The variant or focusing which is most characteristic of organization theory in the 1980's is research into organizational culture/symbolism. (For reasons of space I generally refer only to culture and choose to concentrate on it when I then take up aspects where differences between the cultural and symbolic perspectives exist. However, what I have to say applies to a great extent also to research into symbolism, and thus much of what follows also includes that subject.) Culture/symbolism research has become very extensive within rather a short time. This indicates that behind the rise of this subject and its explosion-like spread there lie powerful non-scientific decision factors. It is hard to believe that only the purely theoretical advantages of this orientation would suffice for its rapid propagation (Alvesson, 1984b). Theories which are not backed up by being expressed at the "right time" are normally only slowly propagated.

The popularity of organizational culture research in academic circles as well as in the consultant and book markets can to some extent be accounted for by a number of economic problems in many western countries and western companies. The decline in productivity problems of motivation and severe competition on the part of successful Japanese companies are factors which pave the way for new points of view and theories. And particularly the cultural dimension seems to be relevant in this context. But the purely economic problems do not explain why just the culture/symbolism theme has aroused such great interest. This orientation also exists alongside all research on Japanese business management, quality circles etc. and the association with what is purely "Japanese" is so slight that for the greater part of the research that Japan's successes can scarcely fully explain the interest in organizational culture and symbolic management. Perhaps we could say that "the Japanese miracle" contributes to paving the way for theoretical novelties which promise revolutionary solutions without directly influencing these theories and solutions.

To some extent during the whole of the Twentieth Century, but to a rapidly accelerating degree during the past 10–20 years, the economic development, above all under late capitalism, has resulted in a previously uniform and cohesive culture beginning to break up. The transfer of more and more functions to formal organizations and to various professions, the introduction of an increasingly far-reaching functional division of labour in society and the sectional organization of need fulfilment for different areas of life has brought about a technocratization of social life and a destruction of the traditional cultural patterns (Ziehe and Stubenrauch, 1982). The tendency for a rapid destruction of (earlier) integrated cultural patterns includes a series of trends: reduced significance of religion and of morals determined by religion, the reduced significance of generation and sexual roles, changed attitudes towards authorities, parental figures, sexual morals and cultural attributes specific to classes, the decline of traditional labour ethics, the institutionalization of a hedonistic consumption way of life, etc. (See also e.g. Lasch, 1978; Jacoby, 1980; Kovel, 1980.)

In relation to the cultural patterns which existed merely a couple of decades ago, contemporary social culture is characterized by fragmentation and heterogeneity. This development has been brilliantly described by Ziehe and Stubenrauch (1982) who speak of "cultural isolation-liberation" ("Kulturelle Freisetzung"), i.e. people are set outside traditional culture in a kind of cultural vacuum, and analyse the psychological consequences of this. The latter implies, amongst other things, that young people today to an increased extent than was formerly the case are undergoing a process of socialization which means that an identity is formed which in some sense is weaker, more vulnerable, but possibly also more flexible and less inclined to permit itself to be disciplined under repressive social conditions (boring and harshly controlled work). In research on organization and leadership a similar theme has been studied by Maccoby (1981).

The general social fragmentation, the loss of integrated cultural patterns, the "anomic" character of social life, the loss of traditionally internalized work ideology, a "motivation crisis" towards traditional work conditions, the increasing scope of characters with forced confirmation of needs and the experience of purpose in different contexts, as well as the rapid changes in these conditions in recent years might be seen as a general cultural background of the greatest significance to research into culture/symbolism and similar topics.

The focusing of the culture aspect of organizations can be understood as an effort to counteract disintegration problems in society, (Alvesson, 1985f). The "strong" organizational culture thus becomes an attractive "solution" to problems involving fragmentary, anomic and vulnerable identities. From the point of view of the business leader the destruction of traditional culture, which provided the foundations of the morals of work, the acceptance of authority and social integration at work places raises the need of trying to counteract the consequences of cultural "isolation-liberation". It is no coincidence that the interest in the cultural aspects of organizations and the vision of the strong well-integrated organizational culture has acquired such a tremendous impact in the 1980's. It is the needs felt by, and the wishes of, managers and people in general that account for the vast sales of books like "Corporate Culture" (Deal and Kennedy, 1982) and "In Search of Excellence" (Peters and Waterman, 1982) in the 1980's. One way to understand organizational culture research and practice is to see it as a response to cultural fragmentation in society and, indirectly, at work places (Alvesson, 1985f). On this point, as also to some extent when it is a matter of the theoretical direction, there are obvious similarities between organizational culture research today and the human relations school of the 1930's.

8.4   Organizational Culture as Ideology: Preoccupation with Social Integration

For the observer who is involved in the critique of ideology much research on organizational culture offers him a great deal to tackle. One important aspect in an organizational culture (in the cultural perspective on organizations) is in fact ideology. Several authors who speak of organizational culture actually seem to mean by this the ideology of the organization rather than its culture, which is a very broad concept. (Ideology is then regarded in the "neutral" or "positive" sense according to the review of the concept in Chapter 7.) This mainly concerns the prescriptive, application-orientated literature (Westley and Jaeger, 1985). This, combined with the observation that organizational ideology, legitimacy in organizations, internal marketing, image management and several similar themes in recent times have become the objects of academic and application-orientated research and writing, indicate that ideology does not only set its stamp on the basic perspective of, and many discourses in, management research but has also become an important field of research in itself (although not necessarily recognized as such).

The social trends I mentioned earlier in this chapter and the fact that management and organization research takes up the theme of ideology explicitly and implicitly, shows that social integration has become problematical. An important aspect of this is that the earlier ideologies do not possess the correct or optimal impact and that there is room for improvements with regard to the content and refinement of the ideologies and/or the foundations on which they are based. As Geertz points out, ideology (and ideologies) will become of greatest importance when earlier cultural patterns and/or forms of concrete practice no longer pass on suitable ideas on the nature of the world and the political order.

"The function of ideology is to make an autonomous politics possible by providing the authoritative concepts that render it meaningful, the per suasive images by means of which it can be sensibly grasped.

It is, in fact, precisely at the point at which a political system begins to free itself from the immediate governance of received tradition, from the direct and detailed guidance of religious or philosophical canons on the one hand and from the unreflective precepts of conventional moralism on the other, that formal ideologies tend first to emerge and take hold." (Geertz, 1973: 218–219).

In this section and the following one research concerned with organizational culture and similar themes will be interpreted in the light of the need for social integration. As I mentioned in Chapter 7, the majority of the authors who take up the ideology concept, irrespective of whether the ideology is regarded in a primarily critical, descriptive or positive sense, relate ideology to social integration in a broad sense (including the generation of legitimacy, commitment, etc.). From the point of view of the critique of ideology, this research can be commented on in principle from two aspects. In the first place in terms of the obvious ideological elements which much of the organization theory texts express with regard to perspective, questions and discourses . . . (I then interpret the texts in the same way as in Chapter 7.4–7.6.) In the second place, knowledge of ideologies and how they function, aswell as of ways of refining and expressing them, which research may generate, are interpreted from the perspective of the critique of ideology. In this case it is rather the applications of the produced knowledge which lies in the extension of literature than the texts themselves which are of interest from the point of view of the critique of ideology. I shall begin by expressing some views on the overall perspective which distinguishes the main stream in cultural literature and in the following section I shall draw attention to some features of the organizational culture texts and interpret these with reference to the influence of management ideology.

A striking characteristic of the greater part of organizational culture research is its preoccupation with questions and aspects of the organizations which touch on social integration, i.e. the way a particular social order is reproduced and strengthened by reinforcing the consensus and solidarity of the members, by giving legitimacy to the order and by taking counter-measures against tendencies to disintegration and conflict. This direction already exists to some extent in the application of the cultural perspective to organizations. By regarding organizations as cultures (i.e. by using culture as a metaphor for organization) or by declaring that organizations possess a culture, researchers emphasize the common ideas, forms of thought, values, standards and ways of working in an organizations. The organizations' character of well-integrated units is quite commonly stressed. Organization researchers speak, for example, of "a system of shared and meaningful symbols" (Allaire and Firsirotu, 1984), symbols functioning as sources of "system maintenance" (Dandridge, Mitroff and Joyce, 1980) and "organizations as shared meanings" (Smircich, 1983b). Pondy deals with the way "the use of metaphors helps to couple the organization, to tie its parts together into some kind of meaningful whole; that is, metaphors help to organize the objective facts of the situation in the minds of the participants" (Pondy, 1983: 157).

The character of consensus in the great majority of cultures and in the researchers' conceptualization of organizations is marked. The overall dimension which Burrell and Morgan's term "the sociology of regulation" corresponds particularly closely with the main stream of organizational culture research, i.e. society (and the organizations within it) are regarded as being characterized by/can be understood on, the basis of concepts such as social order, consensus, social integration and cohesion, need satisfaction, etc. (See further Chapter 1.2.)

As Burrell and Morgan point out, the greater part of all organization research expresses a basic social science philosophy of this kind. Organizational culture research, however, compared with much other research, is extremely consensus and regulation oriented due to its focusing, its definitions and the concepts it uses. The majority of the other organization theories which, according to Burrell and Morgan, express a sociology of regulation orientation (e.g. contingency theory, structural-comparative organization theory of the Aston studies type, human relations etc.) do not speak so much or so explicitly about shared beliefs, values and meanings as typical of organizations (organizational cultures).

On the foundations of this basic perspective, culture and symbolism researchers have studied a series of various conditions and phenomena in organizations. Obviously it is possible to point to a symbolic meaning or cultural significance in practically everything which is characteristic of an organization, including receipts and the organizational chart (Daft, 1983). This is then regarded as corresponding to the social and emotional needs of the individual and to the organization's (the collective's) need of solidarity, commitment and control. The following are the most common categories, phenomena and aspects which culture researchers have studied on the basis of the above-mentioned idea of integration:

– rites and rituals
– ceremonies
– metaphors
– myths
– stories and jokes

This focus is typical of the organization theory of the 1980's, yet before the end of the 1970's it was scarcely the subject of organization research. (On the other hand a series of other aspects which lie close to culture, e.g. ideology, climate and attitudes to people in organizations have long been subjects of study. Culture research is partly associated with the human relations tradition.)

An illustrative example of the way culture research formulates and answers questions is a study by Martin and Powers (1983) on organizational stories. Their research problem is as follows:

"If organizational stories are a particularly effective means of generating commitment, they are a potentially powerful management tool. From a management point of view, it would be useful to know whether in fact an organizational story is a more effective way to generate commitment than other forms of communicating information. It would also be useful to know the conditions under which an organizational story would lose its impact." (p. 96)

The main result of this study is that stories constitute a more efficient means of influencing attitudes and creating commitment than many other ways, e.g. information based on statistical facts, but that the potency of the story can be lost if information which contradicts the story is available.

Research on organizational stories, like research on rites and other symbolic patterns of action, the use of metaphors in organizations, on cultures in their entirety or the symbolic dimension of organizational life in general, yields a systematic picture of those aspects and conditions of organizations which are normally accepted as spontaneous and "unconscious" with regard to the basis of their origin and function. This research provides a knowledgeable basis for control and checking of these (previously) spontaneous elements of organizational life. Certainly these elements, also previously consciously controlled or "functionalistically generated", have always been a part of the organizational control. As some organizational culture researchers point out, it is difficult to make up or guide a story or an introduction of new employees so that it functions as an organizational story or an inauguration ritual which assumes a "living" character, i.e. that it acquires meaning and has consequences throughout time and lives on in the organization (Westley and Jaeger, 1985). The consequences of this type of research for the action of business managements and for the possibility of gaining social control should not thus be exaggerated. Nevertheless this type of research does indicate an increase in business managements' systematic control of organizations and personnel to the point of also covering cultural and symbolical conditions. Culture research indicates that there is a large field which was not previously made the object of systematic control and also reveals way in principle of attaining such control and what potential advantages follow from this.

These advantages do not affect primarily productivity or efficiency in a narrow technical sense. Instead they deal mainly with social integration, with generating commitment and morale and with building up a positive image of the company in question, in other words with persuading the company personnel to accept the ideology the company management want their personnel to accept. (Cf. Alvesson, 1985f.) This latter can be specific to one organization but is probably more often a question of minor variations of general management ideology as mentioned in Chapter 7.

As I have already emphasized several times in this book, culture research includes a considerable number of different approaches and by no means all writers express a social-integrative interest in knowledge. Some researchers are exclusively engaged in working on questions of an academically oriented research nature and some even on critical research. (Academic research can in itself constitute the foundations for social integrative management research (i. e. applied research) and practice, but normally this does not display such a type of interest of knowledge. The primary aim is to contribute to a general development of knowledge. If, however, we envisage the field in its entirety, including all insights into the symbolic and cultural aspects of companies and other organizations which research has revealed, it does provide a basis for improved forms of conveying ideologies, above all from the perspective of top management.

8.5 Organizational Culture as Ideology: Some Examples

The above-expressed views on how organizational culture research can be understood as a production of knowledge as to how an advanced ideological influence can take place do not say very much about the extent to which research also expresses ideology (in the sense I apply to the concept in texts which claim to be of a scientific nature, see Chapter 7). The heavy emphasis on consensus and common values in the organization and on similarity with regard to ideas and "shared meanings" throughout entire organizations can appear to be ideologically as well as intellectually motivated: It is not necessary to represent a conflict or sociology of radical change perspective (see Ch. 1.2) in order to understand that organizations normally consist of a heterogenous collection of people with different backgrounds, job situations, professional and class membership, that differences in beliefs, values and meanings do exist, and that conflicts and disputes do in fact occur.

The reading, from the point of view of the critique of ideology, of a large number of texts on organizational culture and similar subjects, motivates the following comments. I shall only take up items which are to be found in several texts.

1.   It is to a Great Extent the Manager's Picture Which is Disseminated

Certain texts are based solely or mainly on business leaders' statements in descriptions of the cultures of a number of companies. This applies, for example, to Deal and Kennedy (1982), Pascale (1985) and Peters and Waterman (1982). (The latter are criticized on this point also by Carroll (1983).)

Two questions which arise here are, firstly, whether a business leader normally has sufficient knowledge and insight to make comments on the culture of his own organization which are valid from other than his own personal perspective, and, secondly, it must be a temptation for such leaders to express conditions as being just a little more positive than they really are. Culture research embodies the thought that individuals who are well adjusted to, and have pursued careers in, an organization with a "strong" culture possess values and a way of thinking which are specific to this (at least when it is a matter of their own culture). Consequently they are virtually by definition powerfully biased with respect to the questions concerned. These spokesmen certainly have important information to give, but this must be balanced against other information and worthy critical judgments to yield reliable results. This, however, is lacking in some research on organizational culture. An extreme example of this is to be found in an article dealing with organizational socialization and which states the following instances of risks involving heavy investment in this:

"What about the cost of conformity? As senior vice-president of IBM states: 'Conformity among IBM employees has often been described as stultifying in terms of dress, behavior and life-style. There is, in fact, strong pressure to adhere to certain norms of superficial behavior, and much more intensely to three tenets of the company philosophy – 1) respect for the dignity of the individual, 2) providing first-rate customer service, and 3) excellence. These are the bench marks. Between them there is wide latitude for divergence in opinions and behavior.'" (Pascale, 1985: 36)

Pascale allows this statement to stand as evidence for the factual conformity characteristic of IBM. There is no reason to suppose that the senior vice-president in this case would be able or willing to give a correct assessment of IBM in this respect. In this context it may be mentioned that the three virtues in the quotation feature in much of the "light" organizational culture literature and also that a number of serious commentators appear to consider that IBM is characterized by strict conformity with regard to dress, behaviour and life-style (Martin and Powers, 1983; Ott, 1979).

2. Top Management Culture is Placed on the Same Footing as Organizational Culture

As I have previously pointed out, organizations, whether they are seen as having a culture or as being a cultural unit, are often placed on the same footing as culture itself. Organizations are not differentiated on the basis of internal cultural differences between various strata in the organization. It should be added that it is probably rather the exception than the rule that organizations are stamped with a specific culture which distinguished one organization from another and which is characteristic of most or of all the personnel of the organization. Nevertheless many authors speak as though organizations constituted cultural units. In fact it appears that quite often they confuse organizational culture with business management culture, i.e. beliefs, values, meanings, etc., which are primarily held by the top leaders of a company are regarded as the culture of the (entire) organization. Two brief examples:

Smircich (1983b) studied, primarily by observing meetings, "shared meanings" in an organization. It was almost exclusively the top management, 10 people in all, who were studied. In her article Smircich keeps rather close to this empirical material, but in the title ("Organizations as Shared Meanings") and in parts of the text this group's shared meanings are regarded as characteristics of the organization in its entirety.

Berg (1985) writes in an article about organization change that an organizations can be regarded as "a symbolic field". About this it is said, amongst other things, that it is "essentially the holographic pattern created by the cluster of symbolic representations which constitute the reality in the organizations" and that "the symbolic field is a collective phenomenon". This collective phenomenon stands for the entire organization. At least it is never mentioned that the collective should be limited to only certain strata in the organization. The point of the article is, amongst other things to regard strategic planning as "rites of renewal". Strategic planning is thus looked upon as a symbolic operation of collective character. This implies a "a change in the shared images", the corporate "mission" and "vision". Since strategic planning is not normally an activity in which the majority of the employees of a company participates, it is more reasonable to demarcate it as a matter characteristic of the small group of top management who takes part in strategic planning. It is, of course, possible that a greater part of the organization is in some way affected by the symbolic aspects of a strategic change, but the difference between the top leadership and the others is probably very considerable. Many of the employees in numerous companies are probably in any case hardly affected by the company's strategic changes and could not care less about them. Berg's article thus speaks of the organization as a collective when what he is really talking about is the company management.

3. Socialization and Definition of Reality von oben[2])

Much of the literature on organizational culture emphasizes more or less explicitly the part played by company management with regard to the socialization of the personnel not only with respect to vocational qualification but also with respect to values, ways of thinking, forms of awareness, jargon, linguistic usage, etc. As previously pointed out, it lies in the extension of culture research, i.e. the practice towards which research is pointing and which it quite often represents, that business managements are moving forward their positions in order to influence the overall views of their personnel, not only in the form of issuing factual information or of distributing rewards and punishments or by argumentation but also by

---

[2]) The concept "socialization von oben" as the title for this section is inspired by W. F. Haug (ref. by Liedman, Mithander and Olausson, 1984) which makes a distinction between ideology and culture. Ideology means (alienated) socialization from above, whence dominant social strata leave their stamp on socialization. Culture stands for socialization which grows from below, on the basis of an equal interaction between people. In other words, ideology can be regarded as vertical socialization while culture can be regarded as horizontal socialization. The distinction is probably difficult to apply in analyses of empirical phenomena, but nevertheless appears to be fruitful in relation to the field of organizational culture. However, I have not the opportunity to apply it in this book.

indirect forms of influencing, e.g. by a metaphorical linguistic usage or by trying to spread organizational stories from top management.

Of examples of this manner of relationship in literature there are a number of different variants, from Deal and Kennedy's (1982) argument that business management is the most important group in society for influencing values to Smircich and Morgan's (1982) formulation of leadership as "the management of meaning". I am somewhat sceptical about arguing against the latter idea, which I find attractive to some extent, but regard it as in part an expression of inadequate clarity, significance and meaning in the work itself at present time. The latter is probably a phenomenon typical of its time. The management of meaning is a central aspect of leadership when the "task identity" and "task significance" of a job become unclear. To stress the part played by a chief in the formulation of the meaning of a task (or to reinforce this side of leadership) marks in a way an advance of the von oben determination of the definition of reality. This applies perhaps above all if Smircich and Morgan are interpreted as normative, i.e. recommend that leadership shall be conducted as "management of meaning". But even if their thesis should be interpreted as an attempt to draw attention to one aspect of leadership in order to describe it better (which probably is their ambition), this tends to support and legitimize a leadership which strongly influences the subordinates' definition of reality. (It would probably have been less problematical if they had introduced a historical perspective and placed "the management of meaning" in a diacronical context. As the management category is a very important group in society when it is a matter of making decisions for important sections of society and of organized life (which tends to be a larger and larger part of life in the organization society), the expansion of ideas about increased management of meanings, values, images, definitions of reality, etc., points to a hegemony of management ideology.

4. Cultural Phenomena are Judged on the Basis of Functional Value rather than of Truth Value

Ideologies in organizations (and among these I reckon also the main element in what many authors term cultures) are not described on the basis of how correct they are – although the ideologies concerned normally contain myths which can be judged or at least discussed in terms of truth or falsehood. Instead it is the functional value which is in focus.[3]) The concept

---

[3]) Elzinga and Jamison (1984) believe that the cherishing of a relativistic scientific attitude paves the way for far-reaching pragmatism in the view of knowledge. They declare that the exploitation of knowledge by dominant social elites constitutes an interest behind "objective knowledge" and "truth" is accorded less emphasis as a target for research. They point

of ideology is thus understood in a positive, consistent a-critical sense. (I.e. the position A in the figure on p. 152)

Research on organization culture does often concentrate itself on phenomena which are difficult to turn into subjects of "objectivistic" study, e.g. myth (in the non-critical sense culture researchers apply to the concept) and image. And here it is undeniably fruitful to see reality as a social construction. There is, however, a tendency to wish to make a virtue out of necessity, to see the difficulty in determining "the truth" as valuable rather than problematical, circumstances and the phenomenon of an ambiguous character is regarded as a possibility from the perspective of the business manager. Normann (1983) points out that, for example, business leaders can exploit image management for employees and neighbours to create an image of the company which is not truly based on reality, the object being to achieve a desired development. He also issued a warning that this can be a hazardous strategy which often fails. Pondy (1983) takes up metaphors and myths and recognises the following functions in these, amongst others.

". . . they place explanation beyond doubt and argumentation . . ." (p. 163)

". . . in myth, the ordinary rules of logic are suspended, anomaly and contradiction can be resolved within the mythical explanation." (p. 163)

"Because of its inherent ambivalence of meaning, metaphor can fulfill the dual function of enabling change and preserving continuity." (p. 164)

Pondy ends his article by concluding that "attention to symbolic aspects is necessary for the effective management of organizations." A somewhat malevolent interpretation of his text could be that metaphors and myths as far as possible should be managed so that the suitable combination of change and continuity is attained without being disturbed by "doubt and argumentation, the ordinary rules of logic, anomaly and contradiction."

A slightly different example of the way the functional value of different conditions and ideas is produced may be found in Peters and Waterman (1982). These refer with enthusiasm to a study which revealed that the majority of American men had a violently exaggerated idea of their own ability in several respects. Thus 70% of the randomly chosen, asked if they belonged to the best quarter with regard to leadership, said that they did so; and 100% believed that they belonged to the top half of the population with regard to the possibilities of getting along well with other people.

---

to "similarities between relativism and the pragmatism fostered in R & D bureaucracies where they also have a socially exploiter perspective and tend to disregard the internal conditions of science. There is also a tendency to mix up usefulness with truth or to disregard the latter in favour of the former. Such an argument should lead to the conclusion that the relativism of the new orientations reflects the social interests of the corporativistic forces." (p. 178)

Peters and Waterman conclude that the person is in accordance with what these results show. Companies should confirm this side of people and try to make them believe they are "excellent". People's exaggerated and wrong ideas about themselves are consequently regarded as an asset capable of exploitation.

5. Organization Cultures are Described Solely in Positive Terms

This thesis appears above all in the "light" prescriptive literature on cultural organization. There culture stands for inclusion, meaning, vision, commitment and integration. The more the culture, the more of the latter, according to a number of authors (including Deal and Kennedy, 1982). Sometimes the company cultures which pave the way for good performance are regarded as both strong and "good" in their content. This applies, for example, to Baker (1980) who writes that

"Good cultures are characterized by norms and values supportive of excellence, teamwork, profitability, honesty, a customer service innovation, pride in one's work, and commitment to the organization." (p. 10)

The frequent use of superlatives is typical. The attributes of a culture are described in positive terms. The choice of words in much of the literature is of such a calibre that one could believe that the authors belonged to the public relations departments of the firms concerned. The question is whether it is not seldom just that image of the companies that the managements wish to spread and which is therefore published. (See, e.g., Deal and Kennedy, 1982; Peters and Waterman, 1982.) The negative aspects are very seldom expressed. An exaggerated harmony seems to embody the relationship between the demands of individuals and of management with regard to activities.

Even if all the people involved in the companies in question appear to be relatively contented, it is hard to believe that all would be well. Consider, for example, the virtues which the IBM management and some culture authors claim to be characteristic of that corporation: respect for the individual, first-rate customer service and excellence. What will become of respect for the individual if he for any reason should find it difficult to live up to the second and third ideals? Is it not likely that strong emphasis on "excellence" can imply severe stress and even risk for unemployment for some of the personnel? But of the occurrence of the latter no mention is made in this kind of literature. Only the "positive" aspects are expressed the whole time.

In the (very comprehensive) culture literature which is not concentrated on highly efficient companies and the cultural dimensions to be found in these, organizational culture is not described only in positive terms. Instead the picture is given more shades of meaning.

6. Organizational Cultures are Described as Consistent rather than as Full of Inconsistencies and Contradictions

Organizational cultures and ideologies are often described as unequivocal and congruent. Such a point of view is expressed, amongst other things, when somewhat peripheral organization phenomena, type jokes, stories, parties and various rites and ceremonies are regarded as expressions of the organization in its entirety. Against this it may be said that organizations often contain dissimilar and even contradictory values, ideologies and other cultural forms. (See further Alvesson, 1985c.)

The contradictory character of organization ideologies has been pointed out by Abravanel (1983). He believes that ideologies operate in two dimensions: fundamental, morally pure questions on the one hand, practical, immediate operative considerations on the other. In reality ideologies are divided up into fundamental ideology and operative ideology. These are described in the following way:

"Ideology applied in actions inevitably bifurcates into fundamental and operative concerns. The fundamental dimension includes principles that determine the final goals, the ends towards which the organization is working, the vision of what should be done. The operative dimension includes principles that underlie actual policies and support the means used to pursue immediate ends. . . .

In the operative dimension, norms of efficiency or expediency give technical prescriptions priority over moral prescriptions." (p. 280–281)

Abravanel believes that contradictions and inconsistencies between the fundamental and operative principles are inevitable.

"The 'ideal' supportive matching of principles in organizations is both a rare and unstable condition. Principles collide and diverge within and between dimensions." (p. 281)

This view touches on some of the above-mentioned critical points of view. That the contradictions are seldom mentioned in culture literature can be due to the fact that it is largely the management image which is spread, and that in reality it is business management culture rather than organizational culture which is the subject of the discourse. Furthermore, there is a tendency to select and point out the "positive" features in the organizations' cultural dimensions. A propos the last point, it may be said that part of the theoretically light-weight, prescriptive culture literature is concerned with is virtually to describe an idealized variant of the fundamental ideology of the company under the pretence of shedding light on corporate cultures (in their entirety and inconsistency). The tendency to regard organization cultures as consistent rather than harbouring different and even contradictory values, basic beliefs, ideologies and other cultural expressions is, however, not restricted only to "consultant literature" in the field, but is also characteristic of the greater part of the total literature on organization cultures.

7. The Most Basic Cultural and Ideological Aspects of Companies and Organizational Life are Ignored

The absolute majority of cultural and symbolic dimensions of companies and other organizations assume a perspective centered on the organization which implies the neglect of the social dimension. Organizations are characterized to a great extent by the values, ideas and ideologies which distinguish society as a whole or important strata in society, e.g. a certain more or less general management or business culture. The large majority of companies constitute only minor variations of these social cultural conditions. Thus most organizations are imbued with the general highly-industrialized culture characterized by the following elements (amongst others) in the system of values and ideologies: efficiency, productivity, glorification of advanced technology, control, hierarchy, dominance of typical male values, etc. (Alvesson, 1985d).

The dominance of technological rationality, the core of the cultures of the majority of companies, is completely ignored. This dominance is not taken into account by the researchers on culture. These concentrate primarily on minor cultural variations between firms without regarding the way the general social patterns find expression in organizations. Much organizational culture research is concerned with rather narrowly demarcated aspects of the cultural patterns which distinguish organizations, in that the ideas, values, ideologies and symbolism are pervaded by the dominance of technological rationality and which constitutes the foundation for organizations in the late capitalist/postindustrial society is taken for granted. Very large sections of research on organizational culture give, in other words, a systematically selective image of companies as cultures.

Digression: On the Problem of Generalization and the Consideration of Various Aspects

One dilemma in my discussions of the relationship between organization theoretical texts and ideology is to avoid being able to make statements and interpretations which extend further than to applying only to the individual case without making myself guilty of unfounded generalizations. At the conclusion of this chapter, I relate the above sections to the themes of previous chapters and to the overall questions in this book, but first I shall express some views of the possibilities to generalize in my discussions in this (and to some extent in the preceding) chapter.

First of all, I wish once more to make clear that my comments and interpretations from the perspective of the critique of ideology are not intended to apply to all studies and texts in the organization culture field of research. In organizational culture research there is, for example, much research of an essentially basic research nature which is only to a limited extent characterized by what my expressed criticism concerns (one example is many of the articles in *Administrative Science Quarterly,* 1983, Vol. 26, No. 3).

The above-mentioned critical view-points come to light in a more or less evident manner in a number of texts in this field and the interpretations say something about the field of organizational culture research as a whole – even if they do not thus tell us anything about every or even the majority of research work on the subject. It is difficult to decide quantitatively to how many cases the expressed points of criticism apply. Often the criticism is valid to a minor or major extent. In any case it is hardly worthwhile trying to determine the number of cases covered by the point of criticism. This aims at illuminating one aspect of literature in the field under discussion – not at giving a complete analysis of this.

My interpretation of the almost explosive development of research on organizational culture during the 1980's as a theoretical answer to a general cultural fragmentation in society and working life introduces – in my view – a central and valuable aspect of this research. This does not mean, however, that there are not other important aspects for the understanding of the development of the direction of research. One is the theoretical value of the direction: this contributes to a broader and more informed understanding of organizations. For my part I regard organizational culture and symbolism research as exciting and fruitful, which does not thus prevent me from recognizing a large number of problematical features in much of the literature on this field. To introduce the theoretical value of research as a basis for the understanding of its spread is, however, rather pointless. This is taken as given by everyone and needs no special emphasis. One possibly less trivial point concerns the organizational researchers' own interest in what they want to engage themselves. In this way the expansion of research can possibly be understood as a sign that the collapse of the positivistic hegemony in the field of organization theory can enable researchers to work on interpretative approaches and follow unconventional lines in their studies, which they appear to appreciate and which possibly favour, amongst other things, the type of research to which reference is made here.

Now in this book it is not my task to produce comprehensive reports of all the possible reasons and causes which underlie the origin and propagation of various organization theories. My ambition is to contribute to the understanding of organizations – and in particular – thinking and constructing theories about these by introducing critical theory as a possible frame of reference and on this basis to reflect about one aspect of organizations and organization theory: the ideological. From this it follows that my presentation must be concentrated on this aspect. But naturally this does mean that I claim that other aspects are unimportant.

8.6 Discussion

Many of the views expressed above are linked to a couple of themes I treated in Chapter 6. This primarily applies to my statement that many texts speak of entire organizations without differentiating between different parts or hierarchical levels in companies and other organizations. The texts convey a thought of equality, suggesting that we can regard organizations as homogeneous units in which people have an identical situation and are treated according to identical principles. In Chapter 6.7 and 6.8 I declared that this way of presenting the conditions conceals the fact that different forms of work organization and principles of organization tend to leave their mark on different organizational levels. In the previous chapter research on organizational culture has been criticized because, amongst other things, it starts from, and describes conditions as though considerable differences with regard to group and class specific values, beliefs, cultural competence and symbolic operations did not exist. The company hierarchy and differences in people's job content closely related to this are ignored, although it is reasonable to suppose that these conditions must be of decisive importance to the concrete significance of the cultural conditions.

The comments I expressed in Chapter 6 on differences in modern human relations, at least in McGregor's version, between rhetoric and concretizations have also to some extent a counterpart in that which is characteristic of many organizational culture texts. Rhetoric and assiduous use of seductive concepts and descriptions but little in the way of "substantial" concretizations are characteristic of these. As in the case of old human relations, organization conditions are promised which can create satisfaction, but those aspects of the job situation which, according to the psychology of working life are of the greatest importance to the more profound satisfaction of needs and mental health at work, i.e. control of the job and the level of skill of the job, are hardly touched upon at all.

The present chapter, however, is primarily linked to Chapter 7. Several of the views expressed above on research on organizational culture agree closely with the criticism of the dominant perspective in organization research which has been expressed by Zey-Ferrell (1982) and to which reference was made in Chapter 7.4. It should be observed that Zey-Ferrell was concerned with an organization theory other than culture research. Still, the agreement holds good of the way this research poses and answers questions of interest to business leaders and administrators, that it is the images held by these groups that research scholars rely on, that there is a consensus on the objectives of the company among the members of the organization who are united in a well-integrated system and that it is assumed that the company management and the workers have the same values and interests, that these are neither contradictory nor antagonistic and that in consequence conflicts do not exist or are of little significance.

The classification of various kinds of management ideologies (or rather parts of these) which I made in Chapter 7.3 and illustrated in Chapter 7 correspond rather closely to the points described above. Failure to take note of the cultural dimension in the dominant rationality which underlies the most central ideas, systems of values and ideologies can be regarded as if this was taken for granted more or less like a natural law. This, i.e. Point 7 above, corresponds in part to the basic management ideology concerning the fundamentals of activity or basic rationality. Management ideologies concerning hierarchy and elitism in companies find expression to some extent in Points 1, 2 and 3, i.e. that it is the business manager's image which is spread, that top management culture is presented as company culture and that the operators of the management function are assigned the task of defining reality for other groups. Management ideology as the satisfaction of needs in organizations is expressed mainly by describing efficient organizational cultures in positive terms and by formulating the needs of individuals at work in terms of purpose, solidarity and confirmation (Point 5 above).

As stated in the above account, the ideological elements in research on organizational culture are sometimes most apparent in the lighter, application-orientated, type of literature.[4]) This applies mainly to Points 1, 3 and 5. Even in the heavier more theoretical types of literature the propagation of

---

[4]) The distinction between "heavier", theoretical and "lighter" and application-oriented literature respectively is important to draw because culture literature is extremely heterogeneous with respect to aims, style and "scientific" standard. Some "lighter" studies are characterized by the rapid, somewhat superficial and unconcentrated perspective of consultants and are written mainly for a target group of practicians. Others, the "heavier" studies, are more exact with regard to concept and focus and proceed more warily. The latter are of the greater interest from the academic point of view, but also the former are of great interest as they generate many ideas and suggestions and also have the greatest striking power (if we except the narrow circle of university graduates who have specialized in organization theory) Not seldom it is quite simple to refer different texts to either category, but my distinction between "heavier" and "lighter" organizational cultural literature is aimed primarily at pointing to opposite poles and serving a reminder that we cannot make general statements about the literature in its entirety without noticing differences within it.

ideology is not seldom evident. The stress on social-integrative aspects of culture, ideologies, images and similar phenomena in relation to "false" or misleading ideas, etc., is also characteristic of the theoretical type of literature on culture. To some extent this is more "ideological" than application literature as the latter is openly "manipulative" by stressing the need that the business leader must deal with cultural, symbolic and/or image management, i.e. emphasizing that cultural integration must be *created*. The heavier, theoretical literature often rather postulates an extreme social integration as a kind of natural state, in which business leaders constitute a small central group with regard to influence, their role being more concerned with paying careful regard to "shared meanings" and similar aspects and the way that metaphors, myths, rituals, stories, etc. more or less automatically contribute to harmonious social integration. In this way theoretical research is often in a certain sense more intimately ideologically linked to consensus thinking.

The presentation in this chapter attempts to give further and more profound support to the central thesis of this book that considerable areas of primarily the humanistic school of management and organization theory have been ideologically penetrated, i.e. inadequacies in intellectual stringency due to the bias in favour of management interests and ideology in texts and discourses. In the brief and not always glamorous history of organization theory concerned with social-psychological aspects there are a number of cases in which it is possible to regard research almost as a response to current social problems. These answers, e.g. classical human relations and socio-technics in Sweden in 1969–70 should, of course, be looked upon both as social engineering and as ideology. Both elements aim at contributing to social integration of a social order which is threatened by disintegration and conflict (in addition to there being a knowledge-developing element which cannot be reduced solely to being concerned with ideology or social engineering.)

The "soft", social-psychological, organization theory which is characteristic of the 1980's and which partly constitutes an extension of the theme of the human relations tradition can also be understood in this manner. The relationship between acute social problems and research-based technocratic and ideological answers to these is, however, not at all so direct and dramatic as in the two examples referred to. Nevertheless research on organizational culture can be regarded as one of many theoretical responses to the social and cultural fragmentation tendencies characteristic, above all, of the late capitalist society of the 1970's and 1980's. (As examples of other such responses mention may be made of the dramatic increase within a very brief period of youth research and of psychological and culture-theoretical research on "narcissism".)

Partly linked to this background, research on organizational cultures and similar themes can be understood as an organization theoretical offensive on the ideological front, comprising both the development of methods for conveying ideologies, i.e. research on the ways stories, myths, etc. affect the ideas and behaviour of people, as a continued refinement of the management ideologies which are conveyed by means of organization theoretical texts. In connection with culture research it is interesting to note that a book such as "In Search of Excellence" (Peters and Waterman) has a circulation far beyond narrow vocational groups. The book has been sold in editions of millions and has provided the basis for video and TV programmes which reach a very large public with the seductive message of the book: truly successful companies are genuinely oriented towards people's – employees' and consumers' – needs, listen to consumers and regard their personnel as the corporations' most important resources, are dynamic, anti-bureaucratic and integrate, fully and completely, the demands of efficiency and excellence with the individuals' job satisfaction and involvement in the companies.

9. Working Life and Technological Rationality

In this chapter I shall try to tie up some of the very different subjects which have been treated in this book. First, however, I shall give a brief summary of what has been dealt with so far. The study made of research in the disciplines work sociology and working life psychology stated principally in Chapters 2 and 3 indicates that modern working life in Sweden (and in comparable countries) is characterized to a great extent by working conditions which cause employees to suffer from mental and psychosomatic problems, dissatisfaction, etc., and also bring about a continuous socialization which results in reduced competence in action and restricted opportunities in life.

Whereas my discussion in Chapters 2–4 was mainly from the employee's point of view, in Chapters 5–6 I treated the quality of job conditions from the point of view of management. In this context I made a critical examination of the relations between certain organization theoretical and psychological aspects of working conditions. I reached the conclusion that the management aspect scarcely contains incentives for action which *radically* changes and humanizes working life. What we do find is some regard paid to the importance of job satisfaction and motivation, even some interest in counteracting excessive frustration, but not the will to reconstruct the work organization from the ground in accordance with human needs.

Nevertheless, spokesmen of the modern human relations school favour the idea of presenting the demands for efficiency as though a far-reaching integration of the interests of management and of the individual were possible. I have stated that this type of argument is partly of an ideological character. It gives the false impression that the free forces of the market, competition and compulsory long-term economic rationality gradually combine to bring about a humanization of working conditions. Increased employee influence or extensive social changes are, according to this opinion, therefore unnecessary to attain this goal. In previous chapters I have shown how ideology can assume different forms in organization theory. There are, however, signs that organization theory is on the offensive when it is a matter of formulating and spreading ideology. This brings me to the subject-matter of this chapter, which is intended to fulfil an integrating function. With my point of departure the previously described psychological and sociological aspects of working life today, I shall now discuss both working life research as criticism of technological rationality and also some parts of organization theory which defend it. I do so on the basis of terms of reference which are highly influenced by Marcuse's views on technological rationality. In one or two sections I outline possibilities of overturning the dominance of this rationality over economy and working life.

9.1   A Working Life which Causes Sickness?

On the basis of the extensive references and discussions of research results and theories in Chapters 2 and 3 I consider that we can formulate the following conclusion on the overall influence of working conditions on the conditions of human lives: contemporary working life creates widespread mental and social problems and exercises a negative influence on satisfaction with life for a large number of people, thereby harming the whole of society. As I have already indicated, this conclusion is based on extensive empirical material and it seems that most people engaged in research on working life accept such a conclusion. For example Lawler (1977) writes that "the whole society is injured when employees work in environments harming their mental health and sense of well-being« (p. 125).

The injuries of unqualified, repetitive work appear as farreaching if mental health is defined in a way that takes into account not only the absence of psychic symptoms and a sense of well-being, but also a personality development which includes increased rather than restricted capacities and aspirations of the individual. Mental health is thus defined as anti-thetical to an adjustment which limits the action potential of the person (see Ch. 4).

Despite considerable research in the field of work and mental health, it is unusual for working conditions to be related explicitly to mental disturbances and social problems. For some reason not much seems to have been done in this field, so the following presentation must be regarded as tentative.

It appears to be generally agreed that mental and social problems are widespread in our society. These problems form a contrast to our material welfare. Nervous troubles, alcoholism, crimes of violence, social isolation and suicide are hardly rare phenomena in the industrial community, and there are signs that mental and social disturbances have been increasingly apace with economical and industrial development.[1] In fact it is somewhat

---

[1] For a report on the data and a discussion of this question, see e.g. Lohmann (1972), Cullberg (1979) and Adler-Karlsson (1979).

difficult to prove this. However, there is no reason to believe that mental and social problems have diminished despite the growth of the welfare apparatus, the increase in consumption resources and the expansion of education – changes which at least to some extent might be supposed to bring about a reduction of these problems. The fact that the problems in spite of this, and in spite of numerous other positive changes from the point of view of "mental hygiene", have not been reduced totally indicates that there are tendencies in social development which point in the other direction. It would take us far beyond the already broad framework of this book to discuss these, so here I shall only touch on the importance of working life to various mental and social problems in social development.

The research surveyed in Chapter 3 showed that in particular low-skilled and strictly controlled job conditions, especially in combination with demanding job requirements, resulted in a series of problematical mental consequences. Of the studies mentioned, two – above all – point to far-reaching and extensive mental problems in consequence of these types of job conditions. Karasek (1981) shows for example that symptoms of depression occur about twice as often in people having little personal control and demanding job requirements than is in the case with employees on the average. (The study covered an American and a Swedish population, both consisting of men aged 20–65 in employment.) As compared with people who had in this respect optimal conditions, easy job requirements and a high degree of personal control of their work, the category with the worst conditions had slightly more than six (the American material) and four (the Swedish) respectively times as high frequency of serious problems. (Extensive support for these results may be found in the referred studies and analyses by Frese, 1978.)

Kornhauser (1965) found in his study that workers with low-skilled jobs enjoyed poorer mental health than workers with more qualified jobs. He also found that job conditions correlated with a disharmonious family life. A further important result from this extremely extensive, thorough and rich study was that a connection was established between job conditions and aggressiveness. On the basis of questions of the type "Do you ever feel like smashing things for no good reason?" Kornhauser was able to produce a "hostility-index". It turned out that factory workers had higher numbers in this respect than the comparison groups. Within the factory worker group those who had jobs at a lower level of skill (i.e. with a less qualified and monotonous job content) were rather more "hostile" than those who had more skilled tasks.[2])

---

[2]) It should be pointed out that it can be difficult to draw exact conclusions as to what it is in the job situation which generates the mentioned problematical consequences. That unskil-

Of course not everyone who has frustrating job conditions becomes disturbed in his development. Nor will anyone claim that job conditions are the only or even a principal cause of various social problems. When it is a matter of mental disturbances such as neuroses or psychoses it is probably less likely that any strong link exists between the disorders and job conditions. However, Kornhauser's study does point to certain relations between working conditions and neurotic problems.

In general we can regard mental disturbances and social problems as the result of disorders both of an early nature and of events, circumstances and living environments in later (adult) life which give rise to or reinforce the problem. Naturally the relative importance of early experiences and later environmental factors respectively differs from disorder to disorder. Thus it would appear that psychoses, for example, are mainly the result of numerous early disorders (and to some extent also of biological factors), whereas current job conditions, for example, have a relatively clearer influence with respect to depressive reactions and symptoms.

It may seem as though mental problems which can be explained mainly on the grounds of upbringing and experiences during early development have nothing to do with the way working life functions. After all, small children do not work. But their parents do. And the influence of working life on the parents may reasonably be supposed to affect the parents' way of relating to their children. At least the material referred to in Chapter 3 and above provides evidence for this conclusion: if the individual's mental health and social life situation are affected by his/her job situation, it is likely that his/her way of bringing up children is also affected.

Studies on what parents' working conditions mean for children and their upbringing are remarkably enough rather rare. This applies not least to job content (cf. a survey by Näsman et al., 1983).

It would be interesting to have answers to questions of the following type: do the qualities of the job conditions contribute to generating inadequate upbringing of children and in consequence to mental problems for children, adolescent crime and problems of drug abuse, etc., and if so, to what extent? About this we know little, but we do have a sufficient basis to formulate a number of hypotheses.

---

led and semiskilled workers have disharmonious family conditions to a greater extent than others can be due to facts other than job content, such as low wages or inconvenient working hours. There is, however, reason to believe that it is job content which is the decisive element in these low qualified jobs, the central determining factor behind all the different problems referred to. (Cf. Kohn, 1980.)

Kornhauser's (1965) study provides some support for the assumption that parents' job conditions exert influence on the rising generation. The people whom Kornhauser questioned were of the age groups 20–30 and 40–50 years of age. A certain but rather weak connection between mental health and parent's (father's) occupation was found in the case of the latter group, while the connection was very strong in the case of the former. Of those fathers who were skilled workers, according to Kornhauser's study, 63% enjoyed good mental health, whereas of those whose fathers were unskilled workers only 23% were equally fortunate. (The assessments of mental health were made by clinical psychologists.) The results can be interpreted in this way: the father's job situation is of great importance to the family environment, which exerts a strong influence on the individual's mental development mainly up to early adult life.

Westlander (1976a) reports some results indicating that a person's job situation influences his or her capability as a parent. In a study of a group of male factory workers she found, amongst other things, that the level of self-decision and competence (considered together as a single unit) had a positive connection with emotional involvement in the children's situation and experienced own value as parent (belief in meaning something as a parent). It is, however, difficult to establish the last two factors.

Even though some of the thoughts described above are tentative, there is absolutely no doubt that working life today offers job conditions which exercise negative effects on the mental health and well-being of very large groups, mainly of the working class. What are the implications of such a conclusion? Naturally this is in part a political question with its roots in pure evaluations. Working life psychologists who deal with research on mental health cannot avoid being involved with this problem. It is hardly enough to say that prevailing job conditions constitute a danger to large groups of wage-earners without diving any views on what this insight should lead to.

We can, like Westlander and Baneryd (1970), pose the question whether we are

"... prepared, over and above sacred values such as efficiency and productivity, to introduce, for example, job satisfaction per se, a value which might even disturb the other two." (p. 63)

Gardell (1979) expresses a similar criticism:

"If development is to be allowed to continue to be governed by the prevailing 'attitudes' among business leaders and technologists, this is going to mean continued impoverishment of work, increased mental stress and increased elimination from employment, all of this, of course, in the supposed name of efficiency.« (p. 254)

Many working life psychologists regard the now prevailing values as dubious. The allocation of priorities to productivity, efficiency and economic rationality to such an extent as has been and is at present the case is thus in conflict with the results of research on working life. Therefore the majority of research scholars on working life do not consider that contemporary working life is particularly "rational" in relation to objectives such as mental health and job satisfaction.

9.2   The Problem of Rationality

I have now come into the question of "rationality" in contemporary working life.[3]) This question can be divided into at least three problems, which I have previously dealt with. These are:
1. Is contemporary working life rational from the business economic point of view? That is to say, are the jobs designed to make high productivity and efficiency possible?
2. Is working life rational from the social economic point of view?
3. How rational is the allocation of priority to economic efficiency as "means" regarded in comparison with alternative priorities in relation to the "good" life and the "good" society as overall objectives? To what extent is it reasonable to stress economic rationality and economic growth before the meaning of work and quality in relation to satisfaction in life, for example?

Many worters on organizational psychology (e.g. McGregor, Marrow, Schein) are prepared to answer the first question, i.e. whether working conditions in modern working life are rational (here used in the sense of economically efficient) as seen from the business economic point of view, in the negative. They declare that efficiency in working life could be improved by more humane working and organization conditions orientated so as to permit participation. In this work I have argued that the parallel humanization and attainment of greater efficiency which could be brought about in this way would be limited. The main driving force behind contemporary working life is business economic efficiency, and I assume that contemporary working life may be regarded as for the most part rational in the business economic sense.

---

[3]) As Hyman and Brough (1975) point out, the concept of rationality is a difficult concept in sociology. There is a marked difference between speaking of rationality in something which functions as a means in relation to a certain target and the rationality of the target as such. The latter is a matter of a more or less pure statement of evaluation. (As Habermas remarks, however, evaluations can be more or less rationally based, depending on whether or not they have been preceded by undistorted or systematically distorted communication. Cf. Chapter 1.1.) Hyman and Brough write that it is customary for both senses to be mixed up. In this section rationality is treated in both senses but hopefully without confusion.

A rather larger gap is to be found between the design of working life and what is social economically rational. Unsatisfactory job conditions have economic consequences which only in part affect the companies. Absence due to sickness, for example, admitted causes trouble for companies with regard to the placing of personnel, problems of operation, etc., but the costs of sickness benefit and medical care are borne by society or by the individuals themselves. The same applies to early retirement. If we also agree that working life contributes to the creation or reinforcement of social problems, mental disturbances, etc., and that the inadequacies of job conditions can even affect the rising generation, then the gap between social economic rationality and contemporary working life is further widened. However, I am dubious about pressing this argument too far. Some mental and social problems do not lead to any major economic costs for society. Mental suffering and social problems can hardly be translated into economic terms. By just pointing at the economic consequences of these problems, the nature of these is misunderstood and their importance severely underestimated.

A more interesting problem than the economic is perhaps the relationship between economic efficiency (i.e. conditions for high consumption) and a work which is in harmony with people's needs. To management-oriented organization psychologists this conflict of objectives is of no interest. They look on the prevailing social order as given and the efficiency target as a guiding rule, its legitimacy being beyond question. As we have seen, they try to evade the problem by presenting humane working conditions and efficiency as compatible and mutually supporting objectives in working life.

To working life psychologists who are not management-oriented the long-term efficiency demands do not imply any guarantee for the humanization of job conditions. Therefore they ask themselves whether satisfying work conditions should not be increased at the cost of efficiency, or declare that the prevailing attitudes must be changed if the negative effects of the job conditions are to be stopped (Westlander and Baneryd and Gardell respectively, above). In affluent or post-scarcity society, the quality of work seems to be more important for mental well-being and a "good life", than increased consumption of material commodities.

A questioning of the efficiency ideals seems to be more or less automatically followed by knowledge of the quality of working life in combination with its psychosocial consequences. In itself it is scarcely possible on the basis of research results to determine any suitably detailed way of weighing up on the one hand regard for the meaning of work and satisfaction and on the other efficiency demands and consumption possibilities. But there is no doubt whatever that research results can form the basis for questioning prevailing conditions and practice, as well as for laying down some guidelines. This is the task of critical research, or to put it in other words, the critical task of research.

In order to realize this critical 'potential' which is to be found in empirical working life research, it must be related to a reference system which can throw light on the relation between the quality of work and the efficiency ideal. In my opinion the critical theory – and within this principally Marcuse's analysis of technological rationality – can fulfil such a function.

9.3   Marcuse, Habermas and Technological Rationality

To Herbert Marcuse, technological rationality and technological domi-nance are concepts of fundamental importance to anyone who wishes to understand the late-capitalist and highly industrialised society. Technologi-cal rationality stands (as mentioned in chapter 1.1) for a basic attitude to social life and to Nature – an attitude in which instrumental control, supported by scientific and technological knowledge, is a crucial compo-nent. On such a basis, it is argued, maximum resources can be generated; the idea is that social and economic shortages, and other problems concern-ing the Man-Nature relationship as well as relationships between people, can in fact be successfully dealt with. The technological – or, to apply a similiar concept, the instrumental – rationality constitutes a model of social practice where any problems are defined in technical terms and assumed to be soluble with the aid of scientific knowledge and advanced technology. In a number of publications (cf. for instance Marcuse 1964, 1965 and 1969), Marcuse has attacked the totalising influence of this rationality, particularly in the late-capitalist, highly industrialised society. In "One-Dimensional Man" (1964), Marcuse develops the proposition that advanced technology and administration, developed on a scientific basis, constitute the prevailing elements in our time. He writes,

"Society reproduced itself in a growing technical ensemble of things and relations which included the technical utilization of man – in other words, the struggle for existence and the exploitation of man and nature became ever more scientific and rational. The double meaning of 'rationalization' is relevant in this context. Scien-tific management and scientific division of labor vastly increased the productivity of the economic, political, and cultural enterprise. Result: the higher standard of living. At the same time and on the same ground, this rational enterprise produced a pattern of mind and behavior which justified and absolved even the most destructive and oppressive features of the enterprise. Scientific-technical rationality are welded together in new forms of social control." (Marcuse, 1964: 146)

According to Marcuse, technological "rationality" tends to become totalita-rian. It tends to create one-dimensional thinking, a one-dimensional soci-ety, and a one-dimensional human being – that is, a kind of thinking (society, man) without negations, and without dialectics.[4]) The ideology of the technological rationality penetrates people's minds, exercising a constantly growing influence there. During the period of liberal capitalism, the organized society and its institutions largely kept out of the private spheres of individual people. The mass production and mass distribution of the advanced industrial society, aided and abetted by industrial psychology, communication technology, and sales psychology, call for a kind of social control which incorporates the whole person – including his/her mental depth structure.

Advanced capitalism, Marcuse says, has created a second human nature in which man is tied to the form of the products, "libidinously and aggressively". This second nature serves as a basis not only for the technological ideology itself, but for the legitimacy of that ideology, too. Its importance to the preservation of the existing social order, and to the blocking of the negation, can hardly be overestimated. In a publication issued a few years after "One-Dimensional Man", Marcuse writes:

"The second nature of man is thus opposed to every change that might interrupt, perhaps even abolish, this dependence of man on a market which is being filled with an increasing number of commercial products, abolish his existence as a consumer who consumes himself by means of buying and selling. The needs created by this system are thus to a large extent stabilizing, conservative needs: the counterrevolution attached to the instinctive structure." (Marcuse, 1969: 19)

Hence, Marcuse does not discuss technological rationality merely in terms of its influence on the manufacturing sphere. The point is that not only production and labour, but social and "private" life at different levels, are affected by technological rationality and by the methodological-scientific apparatus in which rationality is transformed into action and practice:

"This apparatus has been built with the aim of calculable efficiency; its rationality organizes and controls things and men, factory and bureaucracy, work and leisure." (Marcuse, 1965: 205)

Marcuse accords rather less space to political economy and class conflicts than orthodox Marxists are in the habit of doing. Instead, he emphasises the repression generated by technological rationality and its ideology. Especially in "One-Dimensional Man", Marcuse expresses a view which is actually pretty far removed from Marx. Marcuse argues that the ruling class is, more than anything else, made up of bureaucrats and technocrats. However, even these people seem to be caught up in that repression which penetrates into the instinctive fundament of our species. In his more recent works, he is apt to dwell on a particular aspect of technology, namely its

---

[4]) As Giddens (1982) states in a criticism of Marcuse, this thought cannot be pursued too far. I believe that Marcuse should be interpreted as though he is describing a central tendency rather than an absolute state, when he speaks of one-dimensionality.

character of an instrument whose repressive influence serves the interests of a certain class. The technology itself, and the machinery, are not the source of the oppression, according to Marcuse; that source is found in

"the presence of the masters in these things, which determines their number, their life-span, their power, their positions in our lives, and our need of them." (Marcuse, 1969: 20)

Marcuse is thus somewhat ambivalent when it comes to deciding whether his analysis applies to the highly industrialised capitalist society alone, or whether it is valid for all technologically advanced societies. In addition, he is ambivalent where the chances of liberation are concerned, at least in "One-Dimensional Man". Still, the student revolt of 1968 induced a more favourable point of view on that score.

Marcuse's critics – even those whose basic attitude to him is one of approval (see for instance Israel, 1971 and Schroyer, 1973) – have concentrated on these problems. Obviously, the question whether the repressive effects of the advanced technological society are integral components in the highly industrialised society as such, or whether they constitute a function of the use of technology in the relevant society, is of fundamental importance. Schroyer argues that Marcuse is suggesting that the development of "one-dimensionality" is ineluctable. Consequently, Schroyer feels that there is no need to study those social interests that started, and maintained, the processes which have in their turn led to the technological rationality reifying socio-cultural and cognitive conditions (Schroyer, 1973: 205). I cannot agree with this criticism. Marcuse regards technological rationality as being related to the interests of capitalists and of the technological structure itself (as the above quotation shows). Marcuse may well be a pessimist in "One-Dimensional Man", but he does not express any determinist viewpoint with regard to the influence of technology. Other works testify to the truth of this last statement even if in some works he expresses views which are rather hostile to technology (see e.g. Marcuse, 1941). Marcuse's standpoint could be briefly summed up as follows: on the one hand modern science and technology are instruments which express the interests of the élite, partly in opposition to the interests of the majority of the population, while on the other hand science and technology lead lives of their own, containing in themselves a source of repressiveness and obstacles to the freedom of action of decision-makers and ordinary people. Thus Marcuse balances between a "sociologistic" standpoint, where technology is regarded in itself as neutral while the social decisions behind it are decisive, and a "technologistic" standpoint, where technological rationality in itself, without being dependent on social interests, is regarded as the universally prevailing element.

To Marcuse, liberation means that the supremacy of technological rationality is made to yield to a kind of rationality in which technology becomes the servant of mankind, assisting in the liberation of man, not the master it is now. Consequently, production and consumption must be subservient to the needs of human beings. Today, one might almost say that the reverse is true. Marcuse feels that a large proportion of what is produced and consumed today can and should be dispensed with. This is a prerequisite, as well as a consequence, of the rupture of the "vicious circle" adhering to the technological rationality – that is, the process where production and consumption are geared to satisfying those needs which the manufacturing and distributing apparatus has created in order to establish a market for the products.

The analysis presented by Habermas (1971) resembles Marcuse's approach in several ways, but the former's focus is partly different. As Habermas has to a limited extent influenced the discussion on the following pages, a brief recapitulation of his attitude towards technological rationality in late-capitalist society seems indicated. Here I deal only with a small part of Habermas' extensive and versatile production, mainly on the basis of his book »Towards a Rational Society« (Habermas, 1971).

Habermas makes a fundamental distinction between "purposive rational (instrumental) action systems", or "work(ing)", and symbolic interaction systems, or "interaction". The former denote human activity governed by technical rules based on empirical knowledge. Symbolic interaction systems refer to actions and conditions involving social norms and frames of reference for human activity – that is, to the world of socio-cultural life. Instrumental actions are directed by a wish to satisfy man's material and other needs, whereas the symbolic interaction creates institutional frameworks for political, social, and cultural issues. According to Habermas, the individuals of a late-capitalist society characterised by advanced technology are apt to lose their awareness of the difference between instrumental and interactive action systems:

"As long as the productive forces were visibly linked to the rational decisions and instrumental action of men engaged in social production, they could be understood as the potential for a growing power of technical control and not be confused with the institutional framework in which they are embedded. However, with the institutionalization of scientific-technical progress, the potential of the productive forces has assumed a form owing to which men lose consciousness of the dualism of work and interaction." (Habermas, 1971: 105)

Habermas indicates a line of development in the course of which, he argues, society's institutional frame of reference tends to become absorbed by the sub-systems of instrumental actions. The dominance of these sub-systems acts as an ideology for new forms of politics which are adapted to technological problems, blocking questions associated with practical reason. In other words, technical-scientific solutions to a society's problems are apt to supplant political discussions about those problems, legitimizing themselves as the highest form of rationality. As a result of the development, instrumental logic has come to function as a model for the sphere of symbolic interaction, reducing the scope of that sphere in the process.

"Practical questions, or questions about societal goals, are reduced in public discussion to technical questions: problems which can only be solved according to the objective standards of science and technology." (Schroyer, 1973: 218)

"In the face of research, technology, the economy, and administration – integrated as a system that has become autonomous – the question prompted by the neo-humanistic ideal of culture, namely, how can society possibly exercise sovereignity over the technical conditions of life and integrate them into the practice of the life-world, seems hopelessly obsolete. In the technical state such ideas are suited at best for 'the manipulation of motives to help bring about what must happen anyway from the point of view of objective necessity." (Habermas, 1971: 59)

Habermas' approach is akin to Marcuse's and constitutes an attempt to take the latter's ideas about technological rationality a step further. Habermas' division into an instrumental and a symbolic sphere does not correspond directly to any one component in Marcuse's approach, though. Nor does Habermas proceed from the view that the state of tension between the ascendancy of instrumental rationality and its negation constitutes a basic aspect of the societal totality. While Marcuse's criticism is levelled at that ascendancy *per se,* Habermas is concerned with this rationality's pushing the distinction between instrumental and symbolic spheres aside, commanding the latter sphere as well.

Marcuse's and Habermas' approaches focus on complementary aspects. The following discussion will refer to both, but first and foremost to Marcuse. One important reason why Habermas remains in the background is that his work concentrates on a more abstract level (in relation to concrete living conditions); another is found in the fact that his fundamental concepts do not lend themselves very easily to an analysis of problems in working life. In fact, the focus of Habermas' interest can almost be said to exclude the sphere of working. (This aspect of Habermas has come in for some criticism; see for example Eyerman and Shipway, 1981.)

9.4   Working Life Research as Critique of Technological Rationality

It is now appropriate to relate working life research and critical theory (especially in Marcuse's version) to each other. Working life research and some critically oriented organization theory (which is treated in Chapter 10) should be able to supplement, specify and to some extent concretize the criticism of the dominance of technological rationality which Marcuse, amongst others, expressed.

Working life research should be able to produce a supplementary basis for criticism of technological rationality in above all three ways:

1. By proving that the efficiency ideal leads to mental and social problems for many workers and their families, thereby causing extensive problems in society, e.g. passivism and alienation. Much psychological and sociological working life research is concentrated on this field. But few of these studies embody an overall perspective in which an attempt is made to take up the importance of individual environmental factors and place them in a broader context. Often no attempt, or very little, is made to relate the mental and social effects of the job conditions to the social totality. In studies on stress the effort is seldom made to show in what way the observed stress can be connected to overall summary concepts of technological rationality type. The greater part of organization theoretical research appears in the main to be still more directly and uncritically allied to the representatives of technological rationality in companies and working life.

2. By questioning the results for employees which can be attained by allocating priority to instrumental rationality, e.g. higher wages, shorter hours of work, longer vacations, higher standards of living, etc. the overspread effects make it problematical to claim that economic possibilities of rich leisure time should be able to compensate for an impoverished job. The frustration and passivity normally resulting from such a job tend to affect an individual's leisure time as well as his total life situation. Working life research can here provide a basis for critique of the consumption-orientated style of life as an ideal which legitimates the prevailing dominance situation.

3. By proving that the dominance of technological rationality generates many of the problems which legitimate it. Medical care, public assistance, psychiatry, etc., are central functions requiring massive resources in the welfare state. The productivity of industry and commerce must create the economic basis of these activities. But the high productivity of working does not only make possible, but also to some extent creates, the undeniable need of an extensive public sector on the basis of contemporary social conditions. The need of medical care, psychiatry, correctional care, early retirement, etc., is to a great extent called for on social grounds. The significance of job conditions to mental disorders and psychosomatic symptoms has been clearly proved. In the course of an argument in favour of the humanizing of working life André Gorz

wonders whether the allocation of priority to a technology which enables workers to communicate with each other, vary their rate of work and increase their knowledge would really need to cost enormous sums:

"Who nowadays really bothers to estimate the costs of fatal accidents, reduced span of life due to mental and physical exhaustion, vocational diseases, the splitting up of families working on shifts, children to whom their stressed parents do not have the time to show tenderness, etc.?" (Gorz, 1980: 180)

I shall not proceed further into the world of social economics, because this is not my field and also it is *not* desirable from the standpoint of critical theory to attempt to determine any kind of optimal economic state of affairs. However, we can ask ourselves whether or not the prevailing social and economic order is partly based on a self-generating vicious circle. People must work under physically, mentally and socially expensive production demands in order to support a social apparatus capable of taking care of the damage caused to working life by the demands of the production apparatus.[5])

As in the case of point 2 above, this type of argument implies criticism of the central legitimation of the dominance of technological rationality.

On the basis of research on working life we may conclude that the continual allocation of high priority to instrumental rationality in social practice is difficult if not to say incompatible with human needs (manifested in the form of mental well-being, satisfaction with life, etc). Cf. Erich Fromm who express the conflict between paying regard to economic factors and to factors concerned with human needs as follows:

"... do we need to produce defects in the system man in order to have an efficient system of management and economic production? Or, do we need to produce sick men in order to have a healthy economy? I have no doubt that it is possible to build an industrial society centred on the full development of man, and not on maximal production and consumption. But this would mean a radical change in our social structure, in our overall goals, in the priorities of production and in our methods of managing." (Fromm, 1968: 96)

Fromm's ideas sum up the views which large sectors of modern working life research more or less strongly represent. These views imply a heavy attack on the logic, the interests and the interested parties which dominate the economy and working life.

---

[5]) A task for the critical theory can be to daw up a balance sheet of contemporary working life which against its technical rationality contrasts its humanistic sense. Attempts in this direction mentioned in the present study point to a conclusion similar to that of Schneider: "Not until the mental balance account of the so-called welfare state is exposed to the sight of everyone together with the balance account of profit and impoverishment (and salaries, my comment) will the welfare and consumption ideology be definitely discredited." (Schneider, 1973: 247–8)

9.5   Organization Theory as a Defence of Technological Rationality

Attacks, amongst others in the form of the above-mentioned type of working life research, naturally meet response in defence strategies devised by the dominant interests. Some organization theory can be regarded as a strategy of this kind. In Chapter 7 I indicated the ideological foundations of organization theory and its importance to maintaining the legitimacy of working life and thereby also the legitimacy of the prevailing social order and of technological rationality. "Humanistic" organization theory gives the impression that technological rationality does not lead to oppression, but is highly compatible with humanistic practice in working life.

Far from all organization theory encourages such a line of thought. Some organization theory gives a more all-round picture of the conditions and points to various problems. This applies above all to organization theory which is not too closely bound up with a management perspective. Another side of organization theory expresses a harsh attitude in which the management perspective is regarded as the only aspect of interest and for which the attainment of goals in accordance with this interest is in the main the only legitimate course, even if this should generate unsatisfactory job conditions for employees. In a textbook Robbins (1983), for example, speaks of the advantages of bureaucracies and many highly formalized jobs in many cases. Here the dominance of technological rationality – and of the actors who support it – is perceived as so self-evident that it is quite unnecessary to legitimate it by declaring its compatibility with the needs of the employees, etc.

In recent times, however, some management-oriented organization theories which emphasize the possibilities for, and even the need of business leaders to integrate production demands and efficient behaviour (which includes creativeness) with the satisfaction of the employees' needs have begun to gain ground. Peters and Waterman (1982) and other corporate culture writers express themselves, at least in parts, in attractive terms from the point of view of needs – even if a closer examination reveals a somewhat different picture. These authors express the following view:

"... the excellent companies are among the most fiscally sound of all. But their value set *integrates* the notions of economic health, serving customers, and making meanings down the line. As one executive said to us, 'Profit is like health. You need it, and the more the better. But it's not why you exist.'" (p. 103)

In this book, of which a million copies were sold, and in the literature which followed in its wake, ideas are expressed which contradict the criticism of impoverished and meaningless jobs, alienation and stupidity in working life, etc. Much of the popularity acquired by this kind of thinking is to be found in the attractive and almost seductive picture of the way companies can and actually do function. To some extent the background to this may be a certain reversal of the employees' values from instrumental and economic values to an increased emphasis on what Zetterberg and Winander (1983) call "inner world values", e.g. self-realization, the creative spirit, awareness of health and environmental questions (cf. Chapter 8.1).

Even if such changes in human values can affect working life in the long term, ideas of the kind expressed by Peters and Waterman must be regarded as more ideological than realistic.

The "humanistically" oriented organization theory and the practice in its spirit scarcely challenge technological rationality: on the contrary, they reinforce it. Although Argyris, McGregor, Peters and Waterman and others stress the importance of the satisfaction of needs and of self-realization, it is nevertheless the raising of organizational and business economic efficiency which constitutes the indisputable guiding rule.[6]) The companies studied by Peters and Waterman were graded as "excellent" exclusively on the basis of economic criteria such as growth and yield from capital.

In this book I have endeavoured to show that organization theory based on the design of work in relation to needs, participation, etc. as a strategy to achieve long-term business economic efficiency can only lead to limited improvements in job content and other central dimensions for job satisfaction and the meaning of work (see above all Ch. 5.5 and 6.7). According to this argument the conditions do not exist in working life to unite instrumental rationality and "practical reason", and thereby to bridge the basic conflict which has increasingly come to characterize the late industrial social structure.

Admittedly the humanistic organization theoreticians are right when they say that there are certain points of contact between more humane job conditions and increased or at least maintained efficiency. However, what they do is thoroughly to overemphasize these very points of contact, ignoring the conflicts between the allocation of priority to the content of the work and the result of the work. They concentrate on questions where the practical and technical rationalities coincide, leaving other problems out of account. In this way they give the impression that no such conflict exists. The principles which should, and in time will, be the guidelines for the

---

[6]) Edlund and Kjellin (1974) illustrate this in a study based on Likert's model, in which amongst other things "confidence" and "trust" are regarded as examples of "intermediate variables" while "high productivity", "high profit" and similar are classed as "result variables". It would hardly be possible to illustrate more clearly what is to be regarded as means and what is to be regarded as end, respectively.

design of working life are declared to be those which will satisfy instrumental as well as humanistic demands.

Against this we can oppose the critical view which is primarily concentrated
on abolishing the conditions which cause alienation and the repression of
human needs. I shall give a couple of examples of the way representatives of
a "bourgeois" perspective and of a critical school respectively adopt
attitudes towards and present the conditions for the humanization of
working life.

The first example illustrates the bourgeois and the critical attitudes to
participation. Here instrumental rationality and practical reason confront
each other in a rather narrow field. The representatives of both standpoints
believe participation to be good. But does this hold good without any
reservations and how far can the principle of participation be driven? (The
problem with this concept, as is also the case with many of the concepts of
humanistic organization theory, is that they are broad and non-committal.
Cf. McGregor's Theory Y.) Dunnette and Blumberg both express the view
that participation is a good thing in principle. Yet the dissimilarities in the
basic view are considerable, as is evident from the following two quotations:

"The effective manager ... is first of all a diagnostician and a flexible and rational
human being ... an effective manager will behave in a variety of styles depending
upon whether he is task or relationship oriented, his level of control and influence
... his tenure in his current superior-subordinate hierarchy, the time he has
available, the completeness of his information, how important subordinate acceptance is for implementation to occur, and whether development or 'growth' of
subordinates is desired as a consequence of the particular task or problem which is
being addressed." (Dunnette, 1975)

"It is true that participation has lately become quite fashionable in management and
business school thinking in the United States, having replaced the human relations
approach which was considered too manipulative and thus self-defeating; and the
new fad has given rise to concepts and approaches such as bottom up (!) authority
styles, theory 'Y', T-Groups and an assorted alphabet soup of participative and
pseudo-participative techniques.

Our approach, of course, differs from all of these in that we do not see participation
as a device to lower costs, to improve quality, to increase productivity, to undercut
trade union or workers' demands, or to give workers the illusion of power without
its actuality, the more easily to guarantee jealously guarded managerial prerogatives
within the framework of private enterprise. We are interested in the question of
participation as it bears on the larger sociological and philosophical issue of the
alienation of labour, and we are prepared to follow wherever this research leads."
(Blumberg, 1968: 123, 129)

I shall give one more illustration of the way organization theoreticians/
working life researchers deal with the conflict between the instrumental/
technological and the practical/humanistic knowledge interests:

"I have found that organizations can improve business results in a humane way and improve the quality of the human experience in a business-like manner by identifying the work cultures that promote both improvements simultaneously."

"A commitment to dual outcomes is congruent with the values increasingly held by knowledgeable people, but also it has proved to be the most practical approach to making significant advances toward either end. ... a commitment to dual objectives sets in motion a search for the limited set of changes that will promote both human and economic ends." (Walton, 1979)

Humanizing changes, according to Walton, should thus only be implemented when they are motivated on economic grounds. We can, for example, oppose this with the following view:

"I think it is necessary to anchor research not in economic but in social and humanistic values, where health, well-being and use of creative resources are fundamental goals in their own right ... I deliberately play economic and administrative goals against human and social goals in an effort to make clear the basic differences of approach to the practical use of psychological knowledge which are inherent in these two models." (Gardell, 1977b)

Gardell's emphasis on the conflict between economic and humanistic targets and his attitude to the latter naturally agree with the argument presented in this book.

The solution to the problems of working life is thus according to Dunnette, Walton and other management orientated organization theoreticians and working life researchers to humanize working life by measures for which the humanizing elements are economically profitable. Representatives of this school stress to a varying extent the scope for combined solutions, in which the practical interest can be subordinated to the overall instrumental rationality. Often the interests are depicted as converging (this line is followed by Maslow, Schein, Marrow and McGregor, for example). The relationship between the two rationalities is thus declared to be at root of a consensus nature. (Dunnette and Walton above are more cautious, however.)

Burrell and Morgan characterize this point of view as follows:

"All the so-called neo-human relations theorists who advocate a humanist approach to the design of organizations, technology, etc., do so from a perspective firmly grounded in the functionalistic problematic. Their humanism represents a plea for reform rather than a well-founded and consistent theoretical perspective committed to an alternative view of society. For the most part, their perspective is grounded in a philosophy of social engineering and piecemeal reform within the problematic which defines the status quo." (Burrell and Morgan, 1979: 325)

On purely empirical grounds we can point to the limited success of this standpoint in practice. Braverman-inspired working life sociology reveals a falsification of the idea that the fusion of efficiency and humanism has at least until now been able to pave the way for the decisive humanization of job conditions. In this study I have attempted, partly on theoretical and partly on empirical grounds, to prove that this point of view is no guarantee for any large-scale humanization.

Management-oriented organization theoreticians believe in a one-dimensional spirit that the practical and technological interests are compatible in important respects, and that we cannot therefore speak of a basic conflict between them. My discussion concludes that it is much more reasonable to speak of such a conflict.

On the basis of the perspective presented in this book stand the researchers who claim that the possibilities of integration are only illusory representatives of the humanistic point of view. The dominance of technological rationality is not questioned; it is rather a question of choosing, within the framework of the various methods and principles permitted by this rationality, the "most" humanistic possibilities – and furthermore these must in turn generate still more productive and efficient behaviour. Thus it is only if this supremacy of rationality is regarded as given, which the authors I discuss do in fact, that we can speak of humanism. Naturally we can, however, assert that they are speaking for and possibly going as far as to present a (limited) change in a humane direction.

On the basis of a critical perspective in relation to the dominance of technological rationality and of offering support to the "practical"/humanistic interest, this organization theory assumes the appearance of pseudo-humanism. Rather maliciously we could refer to it as "piecemeal social engineering humanism". When humanistic organization theory speaks of questions concerned with human needs and possibilities of development in work can be solved with the aid of suitable company management methods and techniques, we are confronted by "technocratic consciousness", i.e. a kind of notion implying that social, ethical and political problems can be formulated as technological problems.

"Technocratic consciousness makes this practical interest disappear behind the interest in the expansion of our power of technical control." (Habermas, 1971: 113)

To put it more simply: the meaning and value of work and undistorted communications about these things are reduced to questions of motivation and job design to be dealt with by company managements and organization experts.

Technocratic consciousness or, to use Marcuse's concept, one-dimensional thinking, contributes to keeping basic conflicts latent.

"As long as the incompatibility of claims and intentions is not recognized by the participants, the conflict remains latent. Such forcefully integrated action systems are, of course, in need of ideological justification to conceal the asymmetrical distribution of chances for the legitimate satisfaction of needs (that is, repression of needs.) Communication between participants is then systematically distorted or blocked." (Habermas, 1973b: 27)

The organization theory with which I am dealing here can be understood in the light of this. By glossing over the conflict between the practical and the technological, prevailing conditions and ultimately the prevailing social and economic order are made legitimate.[7])

9.6   Can a Society be Better than its Working Life?

By asking this question I am not claiming that working life should mean everything to the individual or to society. This would be to glorify the importance of work in accordance with the crudest kind of Protestant labour ideology – an ideology into which it is all too easy for working life researchers to fall into. Yet my question is worth asking and thinking about. For many people and for society as a whole working life is a central institution. Its quality affects to a varying extent more or less directly most aspects of society, from family harmony to the need of medical and social care as well as political activity and quality.

A judgment on working life cannot therefore be separated from a judgment on society as a whole.

---

[7]) This is certainly a consequence which some of the organization and working life researchers who favour "humanistic methods" do not wish and which they may not even want to be aware of. Nor can their influence be reduced to dealing only with ideology and legitimation. Their ideas, theories and concrete proposals for change also have a positive influence in many cases. Probably it is necessary to argue that a reforming of job conditions pays for itself economically if it is to be possible to bring about practical changes. This positive side of the humanistic organization theory is important and deserves mention so that the criticism expressed in this book should not be altogether biased. The problem is that an entire field of knowledge allows itself to be subordinated to what permits itself to be implemented in practice in "reality" and fails to review this reality on the basis of a wider and independent perspective.

It is too much to expect researchers with ambitions – directly and not only via the stimulation of reflections – to influence practice that these should support the critical theory – anything of this kind is by definition impossible. What is reasonable is to conceive that these authors argue for the changes they regard as desirable and possible *at the same time* – they avoid flattering descriptions of actual conditions, changes in progress or possible changes

– state problems and borders for what can be attained under prevailing conditions

– in their presentation express the possibility of a negation of the dominance of technological rationality, i.e. they should not present existing conditions and their framework as irrevocable (as equally unchangeable as the laws of nature).

Much of the core of my criticism is that this is not happening.

This book has argued fiercely in favour of reducing to problems the basic rationality which permeates working life and which lies behind the fact that many people have fragmented, impoverished as well as mentally and socially costly jobs in the affluent society. To break away from the dominating rationality would naturally require basic economic and social changes because

". . . no matter how rapidly productivity may grow, no matter how miraculous the contributions of science to this development, no satisfactory level can ever be attained. Thus, a century after the beginning of the Industrial Revolution, the problem for capitalism which towers over all others, and which takes the form of a crises threatening survival itself, remains: *more productivity*." (Braverman, 1974: 207)

Braverman's point is thought-provoking. Still, despite a rise in material standards which in the global and historical perspectives is unprecedented, technological rationality continues to be the supreme aim of our practice. Is it not remarkable that the central social problem in the most affluent countries in the world should be the productivity and efficiency of commerce and industry?

10. A Critical Framework for Organizational Analysis[1])

This final chapter differs in various respects from the content of this book in general. The aim of this chapter also deviates somewhat from that stated in the introduction. Hitherto I have primarily been concerned with existing organization theory. I have tried to re-interpret and reveal partly concealed implications in these theories (mainly of the ideological type) and I have attempted to create an increased critical understanding as a contribution towards better theories. This corresponds to my two aims formulated in the introduction: the integration of knowledge and the critique of ideology.

In this chapter I shall endeavour to formulate some theoretical points of departure for critical organization theory and working life research. Thus I no longer remain within the framework for a critical examination which so to speak functions in relation to existing research and theory. The alternative organization theory which I present in outline, however, accepts as one of its points of departure criticism of the prevailing theories.

This chapter is structured as follows. First I review and express brief comments on some important criticism which has been directed against the dominant organization theories in recent times. Then I take up some alternative approaches which are based on this criticism. The studies dealt with are related to my own and thus form a contribution to the formulation of a critical organization theory.

In the following section I make, partly on the basis of the critical analysis in the previous chapter, my own contribution to such an organization theory. I formulate some main characteristics in a critical, Frankfurt-inspired organization theory and I discuss this in relation to other alternative organization theories and to different interests in knowledge.

---

[1]) This chapter is a slightly modified version of an article published in *Organization Studies*, 1985, Vol. 6, No. 2.

10.1 Some Examples of Critical Approaches in Organization Theory

In recent years, a fair amount of fundamental criticism has been levelled at the predominant conceptions in the field of organization theory. This criticism has been based on different critical viewpoints, Marxist aspects among them; see for instance Benson (1977a; 1977b), Burrell and Morgan (1979), Clegg and Dunkerley (1980), Salaman (1981), Zey-Ferrell (1982) and some of the papers in anthologies by Morgan (1983), Salaman and Thompson (1980) and Zey-Ferrell and Aiken (1981). The critics have objected to those perspectives which emanate from the assumption that consensus is characteristic of social relationships and norm systems. Research in which such a perspective is employed – that is, contingency research, structuralist and modern human-relations approaches, as well as certain variants of pluralistic organization theory – is summarized by Burrell and Morgan (1979) under the collective heading 'sociology of regulation'. By far the largest part of all organization theory can be said to belong to this category. According to its critics, this kind of research expresses an asociological view of organizations. They hold that there is no social analysis, or only a very primitive variety. Management interests are promoted in the tacit assumption that they also constitute general public interests; the conceptions and interests of the predominant élite are transmitted and reinforced and an ideologically conservative picture of organizations is expressed, confirming the status quo with regard to influence, privileges, and target priorities in organizations. Furthermore, the critics argue that the majority of organization-theoretical studies are primarily geared to issues which are mainly of interest to business management circles, whose chief objective is to augment the efficiency of organizations. For a summary of this criticism, see Zey-Ferrell (1982).

A large part of critical organization research – which has, as earlier mentioned, not been in evidence for very long, and the proportions of which are as yet fairly modest – has aimed at supplying critical scrutinies of the mainstream in organization theory, as well as articulating the problems with which it is associated. Up to now, the formulation of an "independent" critical organization theory has not progressed very far. The following pages offer a few examples of approaches indicating some theoretical guidelines for analyses, where the implications inherent in the above-mentioned criticisms are taken into account.

Benson (1977a) presents the basic components of a dialectic organization theory. He chooses four principles of a dialectic analysis as starting-points – social construction, totality, contradiction, and praxis – and attempts to apply them to organization theory.

Social construction refers to the constant creation of the social world performed by individual people – by means of interaction with one another, and by means of building, and rebuilding, institutional structures. As a result, the social reality is constantly being modified. However, there are potent forces at work, trying to ensure that the prevailing social structure is reproduced.

An organization forms part of the social reality and is, as such, in a state of flux. Its central characteristics – aims, structural conditions, technology, informal relationships, etc. – are the outcome of the social construction. Dialectic analysis attempts to elucidate the emergence (the production) of specific organization forms; the mechanisms employed in efforts to retain (reproduce) those forms; and the constant change that organizations undergo (reconstruction). Conceptions, actions, interests, and power conditions thus turn out to be particularly absorbing objects of study.

The interest in *totality* on the part of the dialectic approach means that social structures are illuminated in their capacity of forming parts of a larger whole, rather than being discussed as an isolated, abstract phenomenon.

"Dialectical analysis is not to be restricted to the narrow, limited, conventional reality promulgated by administrators. Its focus is the total organization from which this limited segment has been wrenched. It analyzes the intricate ways in which the organization as a rationally articulated structure is linked to its unrationalized context; it explores and uncovers the social and political processes through which a segmental view becomes dominant and is enforced; and, it anticipates the emergence of new arrangements based on shifting power relations." (Benson, 1977a: 271)

The principle of totality involves the relating of organizational conditions to society as a whole – not merely to macro-structural conditions of an economic and political description, but also to the everyday lives of individual people (that is, after working hours, too).

According to the dialectical way of thinking *contradictions* are built into the social order and into the construction of social conditions. The social construction does not form a rationally governed, centrally supervised process. Despite the efforts of leaders and administrators anxious to remain in charge of the process, some of its components end up beyond rational control. Certain contradictions are generated within the organization, for instance as a result of the division of labour, and the various structures dispensing rewards or exercising control. Individuals and groups in different positions, working under different conditions, can develop views and patterns of action which go against the predominant rationality.

The fourth principle is what Benson (1977a) calls *praxis*. The concept, as he uses it, stands for the free and creative reconstruction of social conditions on the basis of rational analysis of the limitations and opportunities inherent in social forms today (Benson, 1977a: 267). The interest in praxis is of descriptive as well as normative significance. In this context, the descriptive significance entails an ambition to build on people's capacity to reconstruct the social situation on the basis of their own rational analysis based on their role as active actors, and their view of certain circumstances. Where the normative aspect is concerned, dialectic organization theory aspires to contributing insights which stimulate such reconstruction. In other words, the interest of knowledge is emancipatory.

The dialectical approach entails criticism of limited perspectives blocking the praxis, as well as the construction of alternatives to the current organization forms.

Another alternative approach in organization theory is outlined by Burrell (1980). Burrell criticizes Benson (1977a) for regarding organizations as wholes, rather than as parts of wholes. This objection supplies a clue to the main feature of Burrell's (1980) own approach. He feels that it is the modern capitalist society as a totality, rather than the organizations, that should provide the focus for what he calls radical organization theory. Within the framework of this totality, however, there is a need for understanding organizations, as this is where capital and labour meet, where the working process takes place, and productive and unproductive work interact.

"It is organisations which represent the point of production, the meeting place of deep-seated contradictions, the initial locus of class-based conflict. Thus, it would seem of some importance to recognise that under 'late capitalism' some of the crucial processes of the totality take place within an organisational form. Radical organisation theory takes this as its fundamental starting point and as its raison d'être." (Burrell, 1980: 90)

Among other things, Burrell (1980) writes that organizations act as mechanisms integrating economic, political-administrative, and ideological social structures within the framework of one totality. Burrell argues that the essential task when developing a radical organization theory – at present, anyway – does not consist in pursuing field studies. Rather, the main job is to solve the philosophical and theoretical problems that are associated with the development of an alternative organization theory.

The articles by Benson (1977a) and Burrell (1980) are examples of attempts to suggest an outline for a critical organization theory, rather than attempts to express a complete, finished theory. Both approaches are firmly connected with a frame of reference derived from the theory of science. They are also influenced by Marxist theory; both authors, however, interpret it along the lines drawn up by the Frankfurt tradition rather than in accordance with "orthodox" Marxism. Vital research problems and problem areas have been defined within the framework supplied by several approaches towards a critical organization theory. For instance, Burrell and Morgan (1979:323–324) hold that it is urgently necessary to subject the following matters to critical scrutiny:

– The concept of instrumental rationality as the predominant and most highly appreciated line of thought in organizational contexts.
– The ideological mechanisms through which the worker becomes accustomed to accepting the roles, rules, and linguistic usage belonging to the workplace.

While Burrell and Morgan emphasize the critical aspect, Benson (1977a) also dwells on the construction of alternative organization forms as an important task for critical organization theory. According to Benson, the following issues are essential: the humanization of working processes; the development of participative systems (autonomy); the creation of alternatives to bureaucracy; the removal of conditions of dominance; the development of ways of exploiting expert knowledge without creating technological élites, etc. Benson is well aware of the fact that these fields of research entail great difficulties, but he is content to mention them in passing; like the other authors mentioned above, he does not advance beyond the "approach stage".

This section has supplied a brief review of conceivable research problems which a critical organization theory should be prepared to tackle. At the same time, the survey has provided some pointers to the directions in which efforts to concretize a critical organization theory should proceed.

10.2   Six Theses for a Critical Organization Theory

The critical organization theory outlined in the ensuing pages is set forth under six main headings, or "theses". They are not in any way strictly separate; on the contrary, the theses are closely interrelated.

Thesis 1: In organizations, there is a state of tension between technological rationality and the negation of that rationality.

The latter element can be regarded as "practical reason", but I prefer to use the concept "negation" in order to stress the presence of a form of rationality that is merely suggested, not definite and complete. Besides, this concept emphasizes the state of tension vis-à-vis the predominant technological rationality. The negation or practical reason denotes a rationality which serves as a basis for efforts to mould the "good", or "free", individual and social life by abolishing repressive conditions. In comparison with technological rationality, practical reason assumes an entirely different starting-point for rational thought and action, proceeding from an endeavour to maximize freedom and minimize repression. By contrast, the purpose of technological rationality is to maximize resources and minimize shortages.

The relationship between the rationalities is thus dialectic rather than dualistic. The contradiction between these principal rationalities can be more or less "objectively" far-reaching and more or less "subjectively" accentuated. The latter depends to a large extent on ideological matters (which will be dealt with later on). The scope of the contradiction is determined by such factors as technological issues, the state of the market, and class conditions. Where the establishing of working conditions is concerned, different technologies can be seen to produce different degrees of freedom. The fewer are those degrees of freedom, the more striking is the contradiction between the manifestation of the prevailing rationality and its negation. The market situation for a business company or, to select another level of analysis, a country, may be more or less strained: a short-term compulsion to maximize profits may strengthen the contradiction.

The working class may be more or less socially and ideologically integrated in the prevailing conditions of dominance, and more or less apt and able to express its demands in accordance with technological rationality. The resistance, if any, against the predominance of technological rationality can produce different results; depending on the selection of strategies made by the leading strata – that is, by the managers and actors of technological rationality – such resistance can either reinforce or reduce the state of tension. Together with the development of the economy, the market, and the technology, the actions of the interested parties create contradictions which make it difficult to carry out previously designed strategies belonging with the range of the prevailing rationality. Such contradictions may, in fact, necessitate changes in that rationality. Three types of modifications involving the realization of technological rationality will be discussed in the following paragraphs.

A. The contradiction between technological rationality and its negation can be *reduced.* Reactions in the form of active opposition (sabotage, strikes set off by poor working conditions, etc.) or passive protest (absenteeism, working-to-rule etc.) on the part of the employees, directed against the expressions of the prevailing rationality, can enforce changes in those conditions that caused the reactions – which are regarded as manifestations of the negation. In other words, the actors of technological rationality (mainly business leaders and others belonging to the technical-administrative élite) may, to some extent, try to take steps to remedy the causes of the reactions. Hence, a realization of technological rationality does *not* necessarily entail an inhuman technocracy; some consideration must be given to social conditions and people's needs, or it would be impossible to achieve an optimum control over the maximum output. As Bosquet (1977) puts it:

"... Some of the more enlightened big bosses have begun to discover that the organizational passion of technocrats trained and hired to rationalize production down to its last detail can backfire in a way which the technocrats are unable to foresee ..." (p. 375)

To the actors of the predominating élite, however, the causes of discontent, protest, alienation, and other expressions of the negation, are not interesting in themselves; their sole interest lies in the fact that they place obstacles in the way of further technological and organizational development. Such reactions as mental ill-health and social misery due to various forms of elimination – reactions which can be viewed, in some degree, as effects caused by the predominance of technological rationality – do not impede, though, the realization of the rationality. At least, they do not do so unless the cause-and-effect relationship is highlighted and the prevailing conditions subjected to critical scrutiny, some sort of active opposition emerging on the strength of it. It is not in the dominating actors' direct interest to try to abolish the causes of the kind of reaction; all they have to deal with are the consequences which disturb the realization of technological rationality. Such organizational principles as job enrichment, socio-technical measures, and democratic leadership supply examples of attempts to remedy the causes of the problems, reducing the contradiction between technological rationality and its negation in favour of a more undisturbed realization of the former. As I have tried to show in previous chapters it is hardly possible to speak of a synthesis of the two rationalities except in very rare cases; rather, it is a matter of a minor adjustment on the part of expressions of the negation within the scope of the predominating instrumental rationality. (As has already been pointed out, this concept is used as a synonym for technological rationality.)

B.   On the basis of this rationality, however, the disturbing *manifestations* of the negation can be handled in a way that does *not* reduce the contradiction; on the contrary, the contradiction remains and may even be exacerbated. One way of doing this is to push labour management (the supervision of work) and the de-qualification of work further beyond the state of affairs that prevailed when the contradiction produced those expressions that disturbed the rationality. This can be, and seems to have been, a strategy which facilitates the retention of the prevailing rationality, as it ensures that the expressions of the negation are easy to deal with. True, labour management and de-qualification may lead to discontent, absenteeism, lack of motivation, etc.; but the effect of these reactions is in some cases minor and can even be brought into the estimates made before an anticipated rationalization. In this way, the employees' chances of being able to influence the prevailing technological rationality in an effective manner are reduced. The development of working life during the twentieth century has partly been controlled by this logic. The contradiction between the prevailing rationality and practical reason has become more and more obvious, but the opposition brought forth by the negation has been dealt with in a manner that did not weaken the contradiction. The attempts that have been made in order to reduce the state of tension by rectifying the causes of opposition against the predominant rationality have not been influential.

C.   Another way in which the expressions of the negation can be averted so as not to disturb the order of things is by resorting to the fruits of instrumental rationality, that is, to increase consumption. This can be worded in such a manner as to suggest that the profits engendered by technological rationality can be *distributed*. The culture of consumption is intimately associated with the dominance of technological rationality, and contributes to its legitimization. The fabrication of standardized "needs" which are easily satisfied by way of mass consumption forms a central part of this rationality.

This has important consequences for man's values in respect to work and – consequently – to actions within organizations:

"... society encourages its citizens to orient their search for satisfaction of their needs more and more exclusively toward consumption activities, in part by neglecting all other possibilities for individual self-fulfilment (such as participation in creative and satisfying work environments)". (Leiss, 1978: 38)

The increase in wages and mass consumption has made it possible to persuade the working class to "toe the line" after rationalizations, division of labour, and de-qualification. Channelling protests against dehumanization in such a way as to make them collide with a desire for the favourable effects of advanced technology has been, and still is, the most apparent method of neutralizing negative thinking and acting.

Thesis 2:   The dominance of technological rationality over the operational process corresponds to the interests of the predominating social strata.

By "predominating social strata" I mean, primarily, business leaders and other members of the technical-administrative élite as well as owners of large capitals. These people can be described as being the actors of technological rationality. Leading politicians and members of the trade-union élite can also be counted among them. The negation of the predominant rationality corresponds more to the interests of the workers and salaried employees at lower levels than to anybody else's, although these categories and their spokesmen certainly do not always act with reference to this negation. In fact, the reverse is more common. According to empirical working-life research, these are the groups that suffer most as a result of the logic governing present-day working life. The reverse side of that logic affects their situation at work more than that of any other group. Their working conditions are not seldom characterized by monotony, unqualified tasks, and strict supervision and control. These conditions generate mental disorders and psycho-somatic symptoms while also contributing to making the individual's leisure hours and entire situation in life more passive. Of course, the prevailing order may also adversely affect many people higher up in the organizations – for instance in the form of an over-sized workload and 'manager's stress' – but in relation to the lower occupational categories at least, it is more in their interest to uphold the dominance of the prevailing rationality. Generally speaking, the job satisfaction of different groups follows the organizational hierarchy; the more exalted the post, the greater the satisfaction (Berger and Cummings, 1979).

On the basis of purely empirical results recorded by specialists in occupational research, it is possible to maintain that current conditions in working life do not correspond to the interests of the majority of the population. The same thesis can also be proposed with reference to Marxist class analysis or Marxist alienation theory.

Organization-theoretical analysis may well engender a similar view; at the very least, it makes it easy to argue that the contradiction between technological rationality and its negation is usually more pronounced among the lower strata in organizations. Those organizational principles which aim to surmount the contradiction are much more likely to achieve results at higher levels in the organizational hierarchy than at lower levels, where conditions are far less conducive to favourable change (see Alvesson, 1982 and Chapter 6 in this book).

Thesis 3:   A society and an organizational practice built around the dominance of technological rationality calls for a highly developed ideology which is capable of covering the contradictions and the criticism caused by technological rationality.

What this means is that "disturbing" thoughts and actions whose purpose is to reduce the dominance of this rationality are obstructed and counteracted. In his description of the supremacy of such an ideology, Marcuse (1964) spoke of the one-dimensional society, one-dimensional thinking and the one-dimensional individual.

The totalizing character of the predominant ideology should not be exaggerated, though. There is no lack of expression of resistance to it, ranging from passive reactions (such as absenteeism) to oppositional political commitments and radical trade-union activities. For instance, negative employee reactions (such as strikes) due to the arrangement of the operational processes can provide an essential impetus for new ways of organizing those processes (cf. Edwards, 1979). Still, ideology is essential to the maintenance of order in the society of today. In that society, and in its organizations, the one-dimensionality and hegemony tendencies express the normal functions of power (Clegg and Dunkerley, 1980: 492 ff). In addition to force, consent is a vital organizational principle when it comes to generating appropriate behaviour on the part of subordinates in the operational process (Burawoy, 1979).

The advocates of instrumental rationality require, and make various efforts to stimulate the production of, consensus around the dominance of this rationality. To be successful, they need an ideology production comprising general social conditions as well as matters specifically connected with business policies. Against this background, the prevailing organization theory – in particular the organization theory which belongs to the field of business administration – can be more readily understood. Here, research and the formation of a theory contribute to the emergence of a consensus.

One way of achieving a consensus is to emphasize, at the theoretical level, problems relevant to a realization of instrumental rationality. Problems connected with the alternative rationality are, however, reduced or taken for granted. In the technological-capitalist society, there is a general tendency to re-define problems concerning purposes, aims, and values so as either to make them appear to be technical issues, or to make them seem irrelevant. Questions involving such matters as alienation, and the content and value of work, are defined as problems which socio-technical and other organizational principles should solve within the framework of prevailing conditions. When, in due course, social engineering views tend to absorb free discourses on values and aims, a "technocratic consciousness" (Habermas, 1971) may be said to assert itself. In the technocratic consciousness, the distinction between communication concerning political frameworks and social norms on the one hand and technical problem-solving on the other has been erased, at the expense of the former. This consciousness may be regarded as an aspect of one-dimensional thinking, and it contributes to the blocking of a dialectic where the negation of prevailing conditions is envisaged as a possibility. In this way, a world picture which supports the predominant rationality is transmitted.

This is the general tendency in the way in which problems are conceived and articulated. The prevailing social order is thus held to be given, and impossible to modify except by the application of socio-technical measures. In addition, the predominant ideology is expressed in a variety of specific ways. One of them is the myth according to which technological development is a good thing in itself. The predominance of instrumental rationality raises obstacles in the way of critical and many-faceted evaluations of different technologies, as well as preventing the restrictive application of those technologies. In organizations, for example.

"There is, instead, often a common acceptance that any technological development is inherently good and to be welcomed and that trade unions are somehow acting illegitimately and archaically if they oppose technological 'progress'. That such opposition is rationally in their interests is rarely discussed, nor that the introduction of the technology is clearly in the owners' and controllers' interests. ... Since the link between technology and progress is so closely established, to oppose technology is to oppose progress – it is as outrageous as to suggest that the earth is flat. Technology, therefore, has become institutionalized: its development is seen as inevitable, natural and neutral." (Clegg and Dunkerley, 1980: 341)

Another important theme in the ideologies which support the dominance of technological rationality is the development of concepts and conceptions which lend to it a humanistic dimension. Such a development suggests that efforts are compatible with humanism and that the latter is almost a prerequisite for the former. Modern human relations theory (Maslow, 1954; McGregor, 1960; Schein, 1980, etc.) and authors inspired by this (like Peters and Waterman, 1982) have contributed to the development and extension of these lines of thought. This organization theory has had a greater impact on the level of conceptions and ideas than in the field of concrete practice. In the formation of a consensus, it can be used in two ways. To start with, the organization theory bestows legitimacy on the predominant rationality, at a societal-ideological level and in respect to conditions in working life. In the second place, it constitutes a link in the process of qualification in the course of which individuals are fitted for practice within technological rationality (business leaders, for instance, as well as administrators and technicians, at the intermediary management level and higher up). With the aid of this organization theory, they are prepared for their practice in more ways than one. For one thing, the humanistic character of those theories helps them dismiss their own doubts and critical reflections concerning prevailing conditions; in addition, they learn to master a humanistic language and certain techniques (democratic leadership, for example) which make it easier to counteract other people's critical views on their conditions. (It might also make life more satisfying for these people.) All this increases their ability to execute their obligations as business managers, etc. Hence, these organizational theories contribute to socializing and qualifying the individual for a kind of activity in which the ideology facilitates adjustment and success (Chapter 7). This favourable aspect of the acquisition of an ideology is obvious to business managers and other leaders acquainted with management ideologies.

Thesis 4: An organizational practice which corresponds to the mental make-up of human beings as well as to the interests of the popular majority must break with the supremacy of technological rationality.

Apart from some exceptional cases, this supremacy does not agree with the needs of the people in late-industrial working life. This rationality must be overcome, or such values as the "free" development of man will never be realized.[2])

In this context, a problem-solving philosophy in the field of organization theory and working-life research which proceeds from the 'constructive' accommodation of humanism within the framework of the predominant rationality is of little use. In most cases, such a philosophy can merely reduce the unfavourable aspects of the liberty and development potential of mankind; actually supporting the favourable ones is beyond it.

The dominance of technological rationality was not prescribed by a law of nature; it originates in social factors. Hence, it is possible to surmount it. The predominating interests, however, try to make this dominance look inevitable, presenting it as a fundamental restriction in respect to, for instance, the humanization of working life:

"Systematic efforts to suppress transcendental consciousness characterize bureaucracies throughout the industrialized world." (Brown, 1978: 372)

The knowledge interest of critical organization theory combats this suppression and supports transcendental thinking. Its aim is to contribute to organizational *praxis,* which refers not only to the technical transformation of the environment (i.e. the realization of instrumental objectives), but also to conscious self-transformation of collective actors, including the increase of communicative competence in the organization (Heydebrand, 1983). The critical attitude is a step in the right direction. At the very least, it tries to create the intellectual prerequisites for overcoming restrictions affecting organizational practice as well as for structuring productive activities on the basis of a practical reason.

One important feature in such an activity would consist in the free communication of members within the organization and the free selection of

---

[2]) The implications involved in the use of the expression "the free development of man" (or words to that effect), where normative considerations can cause quite formidable difficulties, are indicated in the following quotation:

"Contemporary industrial civilization demonstrates that it has reached the stage at which 'the free society' can no longer be adequately defined in the traditional terms of economic, political, and intellectual liberties, not because these liberties have become insignificant, but because they are too significant to be confined within the traditional forms. New modes of realization are needed, corresponding to the new capabilities of society.

Such new modes can be indicated only in negative terms because they would amount to the negation of the prevailing modes. Thus economic freedom would mean freedom *from* the economy – from being controlled by economic forces and relationships; freedom from the daily struggle for existence, from earning a living. Political freedom would mean liberation of the individuals *from* politics over which they have no effective control." (Marcuse, 1964: 3–4).

various aims and values. This would govern the practical schemes of the organization. The maximizing of efficiency, productivity, and profit would not be a decisive criterion and would definitely not be held to be prescribed by some law of Nature. To state absolute guidelines for an alternative organizational practice is not altogether compatible with the dialectical idea which characterizes the critical organization theory. In this theory, the focal point is the possibility of – and encouragement towards – finding a negation of the prevailing practice, and of the institutionalizing of the rationality behind it. An organizational practice where the following ideals are given more attention, and perhaps also priority, than is the case in most organizations today is compatible, though, with practical reason:

– Participation and democracy are central values
– The value inherent in the work itself is at least as important as the work in its capacity of an instrumental action. In other words, learning, development, meaningfulness, and satisfaction are certainly no less vital ideals than high productivity ratings and consumer-oriented leisure characterized by a large supply of goods.
– The labour process is designed in a way that allows for personal decisions and a variated, well-qualified job content for all employees.

In most cases, these values and priorities will entail certain consequences with regard to the technology, size, and management/decision-making structures that are deemed to be suitable (cf. Alvesson, 1983). Collective production schemes where social, democratic, and economic aims are all held to be of equal importance form examples of organizations where the negation of the predominant rationality has been expressed in a decisive manner. Some examples of this in practice are described in Sandkull (1984).

Thesis 5:   Business companies and quasi-industrial organizations can be regarded as instruments for reproducing technological rationality. At the same time, they can be viewed as being determined by, and dependent on, the dominance of that rationality in society.

In other words, organizations (the leading strata of organizations) create, maintain, and propagate this rationality and its concrete forms of expression in economic, social, and cultural contexts. We can, as Forester (1983) writes, see that organizations, besides producing goods and services, also produce and reproduce their member's knowledge and beliefs, their trust in limited spheres of social cooperation, and their attention to a systematically selective range of organizational problems and tasks. At the same time, though, organizations are subservient to those restrictions with regard to their operations that are due to the dominance of technological rationality. In a capitalist society, those restrictions are relatively severe, as

"the capitalist mode of production can be comprehended as a mechanism that guarantees the *permanent* expansion of subsystems of purposive-rational action and thereby overturns the traditionalist 'superiority' of the institutional framework to the forces of production". (Habermas, 1971: 96)

That means that aspects such as scientific-technological development, economic rationality, productivity maximizing etc. have their own forceful dynamics; this reduces the chances of achieving a rational, free political communication. The necessity of further developing the productive forces in capitalism is thus apt to generate to technocratic consciousness.

In respect to its relationship with the technological rationality, the company – or, to be more precise, various strata within the company – forms a subject as well as an object: while reproducing this rationality and contributing to its dominance, the company is governed by that same rationality. Thus business companies also form expressions of the dominance of technological rationality. This subject/object dimension can serve as a starting-point for a differentiation of the actors in the company. The leading stratum of the company – chiefly actors whose actions are intentional and influence the environment – is a subject rather than an object. Conversely, employees working at the lower levels of contemporary business companies are often reduced to objects, that is, to passive, controlled operators obliged to adjust to the demands of the market and of the manufacturing process, demands passed on to them by way of the company's leading stratum. Of course, this differentiation according to a subject/object dimension is partly a question of power; but it involves the demands of highly advanced, large-scale technology, too. Limited scope is left for the subjectivity, intentional resources, and acting capabilities of the individuals, and what scope there is is to a large degree reserved for managers (cf. Thesis 3, above).

It should be noted, however, that the objectifying of the workers must not be pushed too far, if there is to be an optimal reproduction of the prevailing social and economic conditions. As Burawoy (1979) points out, certain chances of being able to make a choice – whilst limited – are called for; so is a degree of uncertainty in the supervision of the workers. If these factors are not present, the workers will be unable to express a certain minimal subjectivity, and the consensus on which reasonably undisturbed operation depends cannot be engendered:

". . . securing worker cooperation rests on a minimal uncertainty, the possibility that workers will assert some control over the labor process, if only of a limited kind". (Burawoy, 1979: 87)

However, this uncertainty – and the slight chances of making choices that are its corollary – is surrounded by relatively narrow boundaries, limiting the scope for action with a view to maximizing worker supervision and generating productive behaviour. The point of Burawoy's reasoning is that the workers' status as objects governed by, and subordinated to, the predominant rationality only works – or works best – if there is scope for a limited subjectivity. Hence, to advanced attempts to exercise control would counteract the purpose of those very attempts.

The subject dimension – the scope for intentional action, as opposed to passive response and adaptation – differs not only *within* the hierarchy of the single company but also *between* various stratas of different companies. This applies to business managements as well as to workers' groups. After all, the latter are no mere passive objects affected by external forces, and by management attempts to exercise control; they can also mobilize forces to help them exert influence on their situation. The workers' chances of being able to act independently, as subjects, vary; they depend on the strength of the workers' groups and on the current economic and political situation. Usually, though, managements have far greater chances of taking subjective action. Still, the scope for action differs from one management to the next. It goes without saying that the management of a multi-national company in a strong internal position and with an assured position on the market commands a wider scope for action than a management which has to contend with a well-mobilized group of organized workers and/or fierce market conditions and the necessity of a short-term maximization of profits. In the economy of today, where science and technology are essential factors in the production process and play a vital part in the competition, the leaders of big companies often find themselves in a strong position (cf. Karpik's argumentation concerning technological capitalism, Karpik, 1977; see also Galbraith, 1967).

These aspects concerning the subject dimension are not only valid for the realization of technological rationality, that is, the process where technological rationality is put into actual practice; it applies to the ideology production surrounding this rationality as well. Theories and ideas about the rationality, and about that reality which is a consequence of its dominance, are influenced, to a large extent, by the leading actors of technological rationality. Cf. the following remarks:

"In hierarchical organizations (or in a bureaucratized society) it is not only the means of economic production that become concentrated, but also the means of theoretical reflection. As large organizations emerge, elites exercise their powers more broadly, controlling complex interconnections over an ever widening field ... There comes to be not only a concentration of control over the contents of reality (the means of production), but also over the definition of reality ..." (Brown, 1978: 376)

There is no such thing as a sharp line of demarcation between the controlling of the "content" of reality on the one hand, and the controlling of the definition of reality on the other. To the actors of technological rationality, an important part of the controlling of reality lies precisely in the controlling of ideas, theories and conceptions concerning this reality, and its nature, in terms of inevitable necessity (as opposed to superfluous repression).

Thesis 6:   The functioning of organizations must be comprehended within the compass of that rationality which dominates the given historical and social context.

Normally, it does not make sense to talk about organizational laws of universal validity. An understanding of the manner in which organizations work, and of the individual's situation in an organization, cannot be reduced to the point where it only comprises the organizational level – perhaps complemented by an 'environmental' concept where the actions of the organization are regarded as responses, and adaptations, to the "demands of the environment" and changes in "the environment". As Perrow (1979) and others have pointed out, the "environment" of an organization chiefly consists of other organizations. Hence, an imprecise environment concept, used as a determinant ruling the functioning of organizations, can be misleading. Another common problem which crops up whenever you voice assumptions about a surrounding environment is that they are apt to turn out to be too vague to be of any use.

"To the extent that the outside world does impinge on the structure and functioning of organisations, it is conceptualised not as a source of interests, values, class loyalties, ideologies, market developments, etc., but as the organisation's 'environment'." (Salaman, 1978: 26)

Traditional organization theory justifies concentration on the organization itself as the central component in the analysis, on the basis of the assumption that organizations are separate, target-oriented, delimited systems. In some cases, like large parts of the organization culture literature, this assumption becomes almost absurd, as when organizations are seen as cultures, or are assumed to have cultures of their own (cf. chapter 8). This view can be confronted with the starting-point of anti-organization theory:

"(The anti-organisation theory) stresses the importance of the *mode of organisation* reflecting a particular totality, rather than the importance of organisations as discrete middle-range units of analysis worthy of attention in their own right." (Burrell and Morgan, 1979: 311)

The idea that the significance of the organizational level can be reduced to the point where it merely reflects a social totality is a very dubious one, though. The fact that such relatively different types of "totalities", such as those developed by the Western and Eastern societies, can generate similar working organizations suggests that manufacturing conditions and organizational matters possess a logic of their own in relation to technology, the aims of production, etc. (See further Alvesson, 1983) After all, the organization also consists of individual people, whose characters are determined not only by social conditions, but also by such matters as man's biological constitution, psycho-sexual development, intellectual restrictions, etc. Organizations are affected by the cognitive and emotional traits of human beings, by group phenomena originating in psychological factors, etc. – and these things cannot simply be dismissed as being reflections of the social totality. To a critical organization theory, however, this type of restriction is not of pressing interest. Instead, it is vital that organizational conditions be related to generate social characteristics.

The internal relationships that exist in companies – the labour/capital relationship first of all – and the construction of the working organization are all affected by conditions on the labour market, division of labour according to the sex of the employees, political and cultural conditions, and matters to do with wages and salaries, at the national as well as at the regional level. An analysis which keeps within the framework of a closed organization concept or an organization theory which only takes diffuse surroundings into account – an environment that has an external relationship with the organization – is no help when it comes to trying to understand these aspects. The concept 'technological rationality' can make it easier, to some extent, to steer clear of a dualism involving two levels, the social and organizational level, in that this concept makes it possible to move freely from one level to the other. The concept can serve as a bridge supporting an analysis of relations between societal and organizational levels. It also provides a convenient instrument for relating life within the organizations to life outside them. The predominant rationality does not only condition working life, it also exerts a powerful influence on the form and content of leisure and consumption. This facilitates the conducting of an analysis which avoids suggesting too severe a demilitation between different existential and social sectors. That way, artificial pictures of the relations between these sectors are prevented, too.

10.3   Brief Summary: Organizational Outputs of the Prevailing Rationality

Starting from the state of tension between technological rationality and its negation, the 'total' output of organizations belonging to the sphere of business economy can be described in the following, most summary, fashion:

From the 'positive' point of view of production, instrumental rationality is concerned with

- Transforming Nature with the aid of technology and science;
- Supplying social utilities to consumers;

- Training individuals along technical and scientific lines, adapting them to that kind of knowledge and thinking (far from the world of magical thinking);
- Satisfying needs and desires rooted in biological and/or cultural and historical factors.

This description is quite reasonable. It yields a certain picture seen from *one* special point of view – a point of view which is predominant and rarely questioned. However, it is possible to present a 'negative' point of view of production, too, supplying the following description:

- Maximizing man's control of Nature in order to transform it into utilities for human use demands a far-reaching social control, in which man's liberty, personal development, and thought are subjugated under instrumental rationality.
- This calls for the production (generation) of certain individual and social patterns and sacrifices. For many people belonging to the lower social classes, this process involves a personality development which corresponds to operational processes where the 'social component' is objectified as a part of the technological development. The personality of individuals is permanently affected in the process (Chapter 4).
- The formation of social life and the socialization of the individual in a manner which brings social and mental structures into agreement with superior technological interest does not affect man as a producing creature only. The physical functioning of the production and the legitimization of the predominant rationality both demand that there be a need, or at least a powerful desire, for the output of the transformation process. Such needs and desires are in some degree conditioned by biological factors, but in the 'affluent society' they are primarily inculcated by cultural circumstances. The cultural determination must be such that requirements harmonize with the instrumental rationality, and with that which can be achieved within its compass.

Another way of expressing the final item is as follows: the predominating interests in the organizations create and adjust needs and desires according to technological rationality. Its dominance in the production apparatus is matched by a corresponding dominance in the spheres of leisure activities and consumption. The formation of these spheres is not just a consequence of the techniques by which consumption is manipulated. Instrumental rationality also affects the consumer sector by way of its sovereignty over people's working situation. It is reasonable to assume that the diffusion effects from the working situation to the existential situation – meaning the development in the course of which the jobs handled by working people become less qualified and they themselves more passive – influence consumption, too. This is Horkheimer and Adorno's description of the relationship between mechanized labour and leisure activities:

"Amusement under late capitalism is the prolongation of work. It is sought after as an escape from the mechanized work process, and to recruit strength in order to be able to cope with it again. But at the same time mechanization has such power over a man's leisure and happiness, and so profoundly determines the manufacture of amusement goods, that his experiences are inevitably after-images of the work process itself. The ostensible content is merely a faded foreground; what sinks in is the automatic succession of standardized operations. What happens at work, in the factory, or in the office can only be escaped from by approximation to it in one's leisure time." (Horkheimer and Adorno, 1947: 137)

The dominance of technological rationality over the content of leisure and consumption is thus, these authors argue, transmitted via advertising, sales promotion, and other efforts in the way of manipulating consumption. The structure which characterizes the internal operation of organizations, and which has left its mark on the existence of working people during their working hours, is actually reproduced at the level of consumption. Modern working-life research supports this idea (see, for instance, Karasek, 1981).

The "external interested parties" of the manufacturing organizations – that is, the consumers – are usually active in manufacturing or 'quasi-industrial' organizations, hence it is doubtful whether they can accurately be referred to as 'external'. The productive system, that is, the aggregate of companies and quasi-industrial organizations, affects cultural conditions – including people's reaction patterns and behaviour – in a manner conducive to satisfying needs within the range of instrumental rationality.

Attempts to present comprehensive analyses, using organization-theoretical approaches, of all the aspects upon which I have touched tend to run into difficulties – too unwieldy and far-reaching studies may well be the outcome. In certain cases, of course, it is possible to accept a kind of critical study which concentrates on internal organizational conditions, relating organization phenomena to the social totality or to the "extra-organizational" life of human beings – not that it is ever completely "extra" – in a sketchy, general, and recapitulatory fashion, rather than in a thorough, analysing manner. Still, a critical organization theory must always aspire to avoid focusing on the organization itself as an analytical entity. If anything, social theory must be given at least the same significance as organization theory.

10.4 Concluding Comments

It is important to emphasize that my approach is *not* an alternative to traditional organization theory in the sense that it would in any way be more capable of answering the questions posed by the latter. In this respect, the present approach does not differ from those of other authors whom I have reviewed above. An essential point is that the critical organization theory is founded on an emancipatory knowledge interest. The vital problem for research to solve is not how to remedy technical difficulties as efficiently as possible, deferring to the prevailing restrictions, instead, it is one which Marcuse summed up in the following terms:

"How can the people who have been the object of effective and productive domination by themselves create the conditions of freedom?" (Marcuse, 1964: 6)

This research issue leads up to analyses dealing with problems and aspects that are fundamental, far-reaching, and, pragmatically speaking, of little use – compared to, say, OD ideas and socio-technical approaches which normally concentrate on clearly delimited, technically malleable problems, proceeding from a desire to make a "constructive" effort (in the narrower sense of that word). While traditional organization theory is subordinated to the technological rationality, regarding it as a given, ineluctable restriction and an absolute criterion, critical organization theory views the dominance of this rationality as a problem to be dealt with.

The relationship between traditional and critical organization theory can also be described in terms of Habermas' (1971) basic concepts. The former regards the functioning of organizations as a problem constellation belonging within the purposive-rational action system. Optimal technical-instrumental functioning is the prime object of interest. To critical organization theory, the organizations constitute a field of study which should be elucidated from the point of view of the symbolic interaction system, that is, actions, conditions, and discourses concerning social norms and frames of reference for human activity. The question of value systems, and unrestrained communication about such systems, is an essential issue. Critical organization theory attempts to increase the "communicative competence" (Habermas, 1970) where the functioning of organizations is concerned, thus contributing to the chances of conducting discussions undisturbed by repressive conditions. On the basis of these discussions, rational choices can be made concerning targets, values, and priorities in organizational practice. In other words, the aim is to contribute to maintaining the dialectic between instrumental rationality and its negation in organizations. Criticism of the predominant organization theory and its ideology, which represents a kind of "communicative disturbance", is an important component in this context.

By investigating and demonstrating prevailing conditions with regard to ideology and dominance in society, in working life, and in organizations, critical organization theory can contribute to increasing the "communicative competence" and – to express much the same idea in somewhat different terms – contribute to the development of a line-of-thought which forms a primary prerequisite when it comes to surmounting repressive organizational structures. Herein lies the constructive function of the critical organization theory.

References

Abrahamsson, B. (1978): Den organiska kicken, paper, Stockholm: Arbetslivscentrum.

Abravanel, H. (1983): Mediatory Myths in the Service of Organizational Ideology, *Organizational Symbolism*, Pondy, L. et al. (Eds.), Greenwich, CT: JAI Press.

– (1984): Corporate Culture and Leadership, paper, Université du Québec à Montréal.

Adler-Karlsson, G. (1979): Ofärdens etiologi, *Socialmedicinsk tidskrift*, 4–5.

Adorno, T. W. (1951): Cultural Criticism and Society, *Critical Sociology*, Connerton, P. (Ed.) Harmondsworth: Penguin 1978.

– (1967): Sociology and Psychology, *New Left Review*, 46.

Adorno, T. W., Frenkel-Brunswick, E., Levinson, D. and Sanford, N. (1950): *The Authoritarian Personality*, New York: Harper.

Agurén, S., Hansson, R. and Karlsson, K. (1976): *Volvo Kalmar-verken*, Stockholm: Rationaliseringsrådet SAF-LO.

Ahlmann, H. (1978): Den fulländade arbetsorganisationen, *Lundaforskare föreläser*, Lund: Gleerups.

Ahrne, G. (1976): *Den gyllene kedjan. Studier i arbete och konsumtion*, Stockholm: Prisma.

– (1978): Om klass, arbete och medvetande i Sverige mot slutet av 70-talet, *Sociologisk forskning*, 4.

Alderfer, C. (1969): An Empirical Test of a New Theory of Human Needs, *Organizational Behavior and Human Performance*, 4, 2.

Allaire, Y. and Firsirotu, M. (1984): Theories of Organizational Culture, *Organization Studies*, 5, pp. 193–227.

Alt, J. (1976): Beyond Class: The Decline of Industrial Labor and Leisure, *Telos*, 28, Summer.

Alvesson, M. (1982): The Limits and Shortcomings of Humanistic Organization Theory, *Acta Sociologica*, 25, 2.

– (1983): Om alternativ organisatorisk praktik. Några organisations- och samhällsaspekter på betingelser för arbetslivets humanisering, *Psykologi i tillämpning*, Lunds Universitet, 1, 4.

– (1984a): Questioning Rationality and Ideology. On Critical Organization Theory, *International Studies of Management and Organization*, 14, 1, pp. 61–79.

– (1984b): On the Idea of Organizational Culture. Remarks on Its Popularity, Its Limitations and an Idea for an Alternative Conceptualization, Paper presented to The First International Conference on Organizational Symbolism and Corporate Culture, Lund, June 1984, Revised March 1986.

– (1985a): Organization Theory in Practice and as Ideology, Working paper series

85-007, Montreal: Faculty of Commerce and Administration, Concordia University.

- (1985b): Optimism, heroism och det goda ledarskapet, Paper: Dept. of Business Administration, Åbo Academy. Finland.
- (1985c): On Focus in Cultural Studies of Organizations, *Scandinavian Journal of Management Studies*, 2, 2.
- (1985d): The Cultural Perspective on Organizations: Instrumental Values and Basic Features of Culture, working paper, Dept. of Management and Economics, Linköping University.
- (1985e): Organizational Culture and Societal Culture, working paper, Dept. of Management and Economics, Linköping University.
- (1985f): Image, Substance and Organizations, *Dragon*, 2, pp. 45–54.
- (1986): *Consensus, Control, Critique, On Paradigms in Research on Organization of Work*, Aldershot, U. K.: Gower.

Anthony, P. D. (1977): *The Ideology of Work*, London: Tavistock 1978.

Arbnor, I., Borglund, S.-E. and Liljedahl, T. (1980): *Osynligt ockuperad*, Stockholm: Liber.

Argyris, C. (1960): The Impact of the Formal Organization upon the Individual, *Organization Theory*, Pugh, D. S. (Ed.), Harmondsworth: Penguin 1978.

- (1964a): *Integrating the Individual and Organization*, New York: Wiley.
- (1964b): T-groups for Organizational Effectiveness, *Readings in Managerial Psychology*, Leavitt, H. and Pondy, L. (Eds.), Chicago: The University of Chicago Press 1973.
- (1973): Personality and Organization Theory Revisited, *Administrative Science Quarterly*, 18, 2.

Arvedson, L. and Rydén, B. (Eds.) (1983): *Våga leda!*, Stockholm: SNS.

Asplund, J. (1979): *Teorier om framtiden*, Stockholm: Liber.

Asplund, J., Dreier, O. and Mörch, S. (1975): Socialpsykologi og social integration – en inledning, *Udkast*.

Astley, G. (1984): Subjectivity, Sophestry and Symbolism in Management Science, *Journal of Management Studies*, 21, 3.

Aubert, V. (1970): Om metoder og teori i sosiologin, *Häften för kritiska studier*, 7/8.

Baker, E. L. (1980): Managing Organizational Culture, *Management Review*, June, pp. 8–13.

Baran, P. and Sweezy, P. (1966): *Monopoly Capital*, New York: Monthly Review Press.

Benson, J. K. (1977a): Organizations: A Dialectical View, *Complex Organizations: Critical Perspectives*, Zey-Ferrell, M. and Aiken, M. (Eds.), Glenwiew Ill.: Scott, Foresman and Co 1981.

- (1977b): Innovation and Crises in Organizational Analysis, *Sociological Quarterly*, 18, Winter.

Berg, P. O. (1979): *Emotional Structures in Organization*, Lund: Studentlitteratur.

- (1982): Seven Trends in Contemporary Organization Theory, *Traditions and Trends in Organization Theory*, Part 2, Berg, P. O. and Daudi, Ph. (Eds.), Lund: Studentlitteratur.
- (1985): Organization Change as a Symbolic Transformation Process, *Organization Culture*, Frost, P. et al. (Eds.), Berverly Hills: Sage.

Berger, C. and Cummings, L. (1979): Organizational Structure, Attitudes, and Behaviors, *Research in Organizational Behavior*, Vol. 1, Staw, B. (Ed.), Greenwich, CT: JAI Press.

Berggren, C. (1980): Changes in the Rationalization Pattern and Organization of Work within Mass Production in the Swedish Engineering Industry, *Acta Sociologica*, 23, 4.

– (1982): Braverman – och sedan? *Sociologisk forskning*, 1.

Berglind, H. (1976): Strukturförändringar, arbetsmiljö och utslagning, *Arbetsmiljöutredningen – rapport i psykosociala frågor*, Stockholm: SOU, p. 3.

Beyer, J. (1981): Ideologies, Values and Decisionmaking in Organizations, *Handbook in Organizational Design*, Nystrom, P. and Starbuck, W. (Eds.), Oxford: Oxford University Press.

Björkman, T. (1978): De lönsamma arbetsmiljöerna, *Sociologisk forskning*, 2.

Björkman, T. and Lundkvist, K. (1981): *Från MAX till Pia. Reformstrategier inom arbetsmiljöområdet*, Stockholm: Arkiv.

Blumberg, P. (1968): *Industrial Democracy: The Sociology of Participation*, London: Constable.

Bolinder, E. and Ohlström, B. (1971): *Stress på svenska arbetsplatser*, Stockholm: Prisma.

Bosquet, M. (1977): The Meaning of 'Job Enrichment', *Capital and Labour*, Nichols, T. (Ed.), Glasgow: Fontana 1980.

Bradley, G. (1977): *Datateknik, arbetsliv och kommunikation*, Stockholm: Delegationen för långsiktsmotiverad forskning.

Brante, T. (1980): *Vetenskapens struktur och förändring*, Lund: Doxa.

Braverman, H. (1974): *Labor and Monopoly Capital*, New York: Monthly Review Press.

Brecher, J. (1979): Roots of Power: Employers and Workers in the Electrical Products Industry, *Case Studies on the Labor Process*, Zimbalist, A. (Ed.), New York: Monthly Review Press.

Broady, D. and Helgeson, B. (1985): Farväl till arbetsdelningen? Den västtyska diskussionen om Horst Kerns och Michael Schumanns nya studie, paper, Stockholm: Skolöverstyrelsen.

Brosseau, K. and Prince, B. (1981): Job – Person Dynamics: An Extension of Longitudinal Research, *Journal of Applied Psychology*, 66, pp. 59–62.

Brown, R. H. (1978): Bureaucracy as Praxis: Toward a Political Phenomenology of Formal Organizations, *Administrative Science Quarterly*, 23, pp. 365–382.

Brunander, L. (1979): *Griptången. Hur organisationen påverkar människan*, Stockholm: Rabén and Sjögren.

Brunsson, N. (1982a): The Irrationality of Action and Action Rationality, *Journal of Management Studies*, 19, pp. 29–44.

– (Ed.) (1982b): *Företagsekonomi – sanning eller moral?* Lund; Studentlitteratur.

Bruzelius, L. and Skärvad, P. H. (1975): *Integrerad företagsadministration*, Lund: Studentlitteratur.

Burawoy, M. (1979): *Manufacturing Consent*, Chicago: Univ. of Chicago Press.

Burrell, G. (1980): Radical Organization Theory, *The International Yearbook of Organization Studies*, Dunkerley, D. and Salaman, G. (Eds.), London: Routledge and Kegan Paul.

Burrell, G. and Morgan, G. (1979): *Sociological Paradigms and Organizational Analysis*, London: Heinemann.

Carroll, D. T. (1983): A Disappointing Search for Excellence, *Harvard Business Review*, Nov.–Dec.

Carter, P. and Jackson, N. (1986): Management, Myth and Metatheory – From Scarcity to Post-scarcity, paper, Dept. of Management Systems and sciences, Univ. of Hull.

Clegg, S. and Dunkerley, D. (1980): *Organizations, Class and Control*, London: Routledge and Kegan Paul.

Colignon, R. and Cray, D. (1981): New Organizational Perspectives: Critiques and Critical Organizations, *Complex Organizations: Critical Perspectives*, Zey-Ferrell, M. and Aiken, M. (Eds.), Glenview, Ill.: Scott, Foresman and Co.

Connerton, P. (1976): Introduction, *Critical Sociology*, Connerton, P. (Ed.), Harmondsworth: Penguin 1978.

– (1980): *The Tragedy of Enlightenment*, Cambridge: Cambridge University Press.

Cooley, M. (1980): Computerization – Taylor's Latest Disquise, *Economic and Industrial Democracy*, 1, 4.

Cooper, M. R. m. fl. (1979): Changing Employee Values: Deepening Discontent?, *Harvard Business Review*, Jan.–Febr.

Crompton, R. and Reid, S. (1982): The De-skilling of Clerical Work, *The Degradation of Work?*, Wood, S. (Ed.), London: Hutchinson.

Crozier, M. and Friedberg, E. (1977): Organizations as Means and Constraints of Collective Action, *Traditions and Trends in Organization Theory, Part II*, Berg, P. O. and Daudi, Ph. (Eds.), Lund: Studentlitteratur.

Cullberg, J. (1979): Psykisk ohälsa i välfärdssamhället, *Socialmedicinsk tidskrift*, 4–5.

Daft, R. (1983): Symbols in Organizations: A Dual-Content Framework of Analysis, *Organizational Symbolism*, Pondy, L. R. et al. (Eds.), Greenwich, CT: JAI Press.

Dandridge, T. C. (1984): Ceremony as an Integration of Work and Play, Paper presented at "The First International Conference on Organizational Symbolism and Corporate Culture". Lund, June 1984.

Dandridge, T. C., Mitroff, I. I. and Joyce, W. F. (1980): Organizational Symbolism: A Topic to Expand Organizational Analysis, *Academy of Management Review*, 5, pp. 77–82.

Davis, L. (1979): Optimizing Organization – Plant Design, *Organizational Dynamics*, Autumn.

– (1980): Individuals and the Organization, *California Management Review*, 22, 2.

De Geer, H. and Giertz, E. (1980): Näringslivets rationalisering – Några perspektiv på ett triangelspl mellan stat, företag och fackliga organisation, *Datateknik*, ekonomisk tillväxt och sysselsättning, Stockholm: Liber.

Deal, T. and Kennedy, A. (1982): *Corporate Cultures*, Reading: Addison-Wesley.

Dickson, D. (1974): *Alternative Technologies and the Politics of Technical Change*, London: Collins 1977.

Drambo, L. (1981): *Ekonomi och samhällsförändring*, (diss.), Linköping University, Dept of Management and Economics.

Drucker, P. F. (1973): *Management. Tasks, Responsibilities, Practices*, London: Heineman.

Dunnette, M. (1975): The Hawthorne Effect: Its Societal Meaning, *Man and Work in Society*, Cass, E. and Zimmer, F. (Eds.), New York: Van Nostrand.

Edlund, C. and Kjellin, A. (1974): Organisationsutveckling vid AB Industriproduktion, *Organisationsutveckling*, Rohlin, L. (Ed.), Lund: Gleerups.

Edqvist, C. (1977): Teknik och arbetsdelning i arbetsprocessen, *Sociologisk forskning*, 2.

Edwards, R. (1979): *Contested Terrain. The Transformation of the Workplace in the Twentieth Century*, London: Heinemann.

Ehn, P. (1978): Arbete – teknik – samhälle, paper, Stockholm: Arbetslivscentrum.

Ehn, P. and Sandberg, A. (1982): Facket och den nya tekniken, *Arbetsorganisation och medbestämmande*, Sandberg, T. (Ed.), Stockholm: Tiden.

Ekvall, G. (1969): Om arbetstillfredsställelse, paper, Stockholm: PA-rådet.

Eliasson, S. (1980): Det samhälleliga sterbhuset, *Bokcaféts månadsbull.*, 52, Nov.

Elzinga, A. and Jamison, A. (1984): Forskningssociologi, *Forskning om forskning*, Bärmark, J. (Ed.), Stockholm: Natur och Kultur.

Emery, F. and Trist, E. (1960): Socio-Technical System, *Systems Thinking*, Emery, F. (Ed.), Harmondsworth: Penguin 1969.

Eyerman, R. (1981): False Consciousness and Ideology in Marxist Theory, *Acta Sociologica*, 24, 1–2.

Eyerman, R. and Shipway, D. (1981): Habermas on Work and Culture, *Theory and Society*, 10, pp. 547–566.

Faucheux, C., Amado, G. and Laurent, A. (1982): Organizational Development and Change, *Annual Review of Psychology*, 33.

Fjellström, R. (1975): Anteckningar om positivismen, *Försvarar vetenskapen det bestående?* Halldén, S. et al. (Eds.), Stockholm: Prisma.

Forester, J. (1983): Critical Theory and Organizational Analysis, *Beyond Method*, Morgan, G. (Ed.), Beverly Hills: Sage.

Forsblad, P. (1978): Synen på företagsledarens arbete – en nyansering, *Människan i organisationen*, Forsblad, P. m. fl. (Red.), Stockholm: Liber.

French, J. R. P. and Caplan R. (1972): Organizational Stress and Individual Strain, *The Failure of Success*, Marrow, A. (Ed.), New York: American Management Association.

French, W. and Bell, C. (1973): *Organizational Development – Behavioral Science Interventions for Organizational Improvement*, Englewood Cliffs: Prentice-Hall.

Frese, M. (1978): Partialisierte Handlung und Kontrolle. Zwei Themen der Industriellen Pathologie, *Industrielle Psychopathologie*, Frese, M. et al. (Eds.), Bern: Hans Huber.

Friedlander, F. and Brown, D. (1974): Organization Development, *Annual Review of Psychology*, 25.

Friedman, A. (1977): Responsible Autonomy Versus Direct Control over the Labour Process, *Capital and Class*, 1.

Fromm, E. (1941): *Escape from Freedom*, New York: Farrar and Rinehard.

– (1955): *The Sane Society*, London: Routledge and Kegan Paul.

– (1968): Humanistic planning, *The Crises of Psychoanalysis*, Harmondsworth: Penguin, 1978.

Furstenberg, F. (1974): Work Experience and Family Life, *Work and the Quality of Life*, O'Toole, J. (Ed.), Cambridge, Mass.: MIT.

Galbraith, J. K. (1967): *The New Industrial State*, Boston: Houghton-Mifflin.

– (1979): *The Affluent Society* (3rd. ed.), Harmondsworth: Penguin.

Gardell, B. (1976): Psykosociala problem sammanhängande med industriella produktionsprocesser, *Arbetsmiljöutredningen – rapport i psykosociala frågor*, 3, Stockholm: SOU.

– (1977a): *Arbetsinnehåll och livskvalitet*, Stockholm: Prisma.

– (1977b): Psychological and Social Problems of Industrial Work in Affluent Societes, *International Journal of Psychology*, 12, 2.

– (1979): Problem i arbetslivet, *Socialmedicinsk tidskrift*, 4–5.

Gardell, B. and Dahlström, E. (1966): Arbetsanpassning och teknologisk struktur, *Teknisk förändring och arbetsanpassning*, Dahlström, E. m. fl., Stockholm: Prisma 1970.

Gardell, B. and Gustavsen, B. (1980): Work Environment Research and Social Change – Current Developments in Scandinavia, *Journal of Occupational Behavior*, 1, 1.

Gardell, B. and Gustavsson, R. Å. (1979): *Sjukvård på löpande band*, Stockholm: Prisma.

Gardell, B. and Svensson, L. (1981): *Medbestämmande och självstyre*, Stockholm: Prisma.

Geertz, C. (1973): *The Interpretation of Culture*, New York: Basic Books.

Geuss, R. (1981): *The Idea of a Critical Theory*, Cambridge: Cambridge University Press.

Giddens, A. (1979): *Central Problems in Social Theory. Action, Structure and Condition in Social Analysis*, London: McMillan.

– (1982): *Critiques and Profiles in Social Theory*, London: McMillan.

Glenn, E. N. and Feldberg, R. (1979): Proletarianizing Clerical Work: Technology and Organizational Control in the Office, *Case Studies on the Labor Process*, Zimbalist, A. (Ed.), New York: Monthly Review Press.

Goldman, P. and Van Houten, D. (1977): Managerial Strategies and the Worker: a Marxist Analysis of Bureaucracy, *Sociological Quarterly*, 18, Winter.

– (1980): Uncertainty, Conflict, and Labor Relations in the Modern Firm I: Productivity and Capitalism's 'Human Face', *Economic and Industrial Democracy*, 1, 1.

Gorz, A. (1980): *Farewell to Working Class*, London: Pluto Press.

Gouldner, A. (1976): *The Dialectic of Technology and Ideology*, London/New York: McMillan.

Greenbaum, J. (1976): Division of Labor in the Computer Field, *Monthly Review*, 28, 3.

Gunnarsson, L. (1980): *Att förändra arbetsprocessen*, (diss.) Dept. of Sociology, Lund University.

Gustavsen, B. (1980): From Satisfaction to Collective Action: Trends in the Development of Research and Reform in Working Life, *Economic and Industrial Democracy*, 1, 2.

Habermas, J. (1966): Knowledge and Interest, *Inquiry*, 9, pp. 285–300.

– (1971) *Toward a Rational Society*, London: Heinemann.

- (1973a): Problems of Legitimation in Late Capitalism, *Critical Sociology*, Connerton, P. (Ed.), Harmondsworth: Penguin 1978.
- (1973b): *Legitimation Crises*, London: Heinemann 1979.
- (1979): *Communication and the Evolution of Society*, Boston: Beacon Press.
Hackman, J. R. (1975): On the Coming Demise of Job Enrichment, *Man and Work in Society*, Cass, E. and Zimmer, F. (Eds.), New York: Van Nostrand.
Hackman, J. R. and Lawler, E. (1971): Employee Reactions to Job Characteristics, *Readings in Organizational Behavior and Human Performance*, Scott, W. and Cummings, L. (Eds.), Homewood, Ill.: Irwin 1973.
Hackman, J. R., Oldham, G., Janson, R. and Purdy, K. (1975): A New Strategy for Job Enrichment, *Psychological Foundations of Organizational Behavior*, Staw, B. (Ed.), Santa Monica: Goodyear 1977.
Hartley, J. (1983): Ideology and Organizational Behavior, *International Studies of Management and Organization*, XIII, 3.
Hartmann, G., Nicholas, I., Sorge, A. and Warner, M. (1984): Consequences of CNC Technology: a Study of British and West German Manufactoring Firms, *Micro-processors, Manpower and Society*, Warner, M. (Editor), Aldershot: Gower.
Hang, F. et al. (1978): Teorier om automationsarbete, *Arbetets krav och mänsklig utveckling*. Aronsson, G. (Ed.), Stockholm: Prisma.
Held, D. (1980): *Introduction to Critical Theory*, London: Hutchinson.
Helgeson, B. (1978): Arbete, teknik och produktionsprocess, *Sociologisk forskning*, 4.
Heneman, H. and Schwab, D. (1972): Evaluation of Research on Expectancy Theory Predictions on Employee Performance, *Readings in Organizational Behavior and Human Performance*, Scott, W. and Cummings, L. (Eds.), Homewood, Ill.: Irwin 1973.
Herzberg, F. (1968): One More Time: How Do You Motivate Employees? *Harvard Business Review*, Jan.–Feb.
Herzberg, F., Mausner, F. and Snyderman, B. B. (1959): *The Motivation to Work*, New York: Wiley 1966.
Heydebrand, W. (1983): Organization and Praxis, *Beyond Method*, Morgan, G. (Ed.), Beverly Hills: Sage.
Hofstede, G. (1981): Culture and Organizations, *International Studies of Management and Organization*, XI, 1.
Horkheimer, M. (1937): Traditional and Critical Theory, *Critical Sociology*, Connerton, P. (Ed.), Harmondsworth: Penguin 1978.
Horkheimer, M. and Adorno, T. (1947): *The Dialectics of Enlightenment*, London: Verso 1978.
Hunt, J. and Hill, J. (1969): The New Look in Motivational Theory for Organizational Research, *Readings in Managerial Psychology*, Leavitt, H. and Pondy, L. (Eds.), Chicago: The University of Chicago Press 1973.
Hyman, R. and Brough, I. (1975): *Social Values and Industrial Relations, A Study of Fairness and Inequality*, Oxford: Basil Blackwell.
Håkansson, P.-A. (1976): Industriarbetets karaktär och arbetarklassens villkor, *Sociologisk forskning*, 1.
Ingelstam, L. (1980): *Arbetets värde och tidens bruk*, Stockholm: Liber.

Israel, J. (1971): *Alienation – från Marx till modern sociologi*, Stockholm: Rabén and Sjögren.

– (1972): *Om konsten att lyfta sig själv i håret och behålla barnet i badvattnet*, Stockholm, Rabén and Sjögren.

– (1979): *Om relationistisk socialpsykologi*, Göteborg: Korpen.

Jacoby, R. (1980): Narcissism and the Crises of Capitalism, *Telos*, 44, pp. 58–64.

Jain, H. and Murray, V. (1984): Why the Human Resources Function Fails, *California Management Review*, XXVI, 4.

Jay, M. (1972): The Frankfurt School's Critique of Humanist Marxism, *Social Research*, 39, 2.

Johns, G. (1983): *Organizational Behaviour*, Glenview, Ill.: Scott, Foresman and Co.

Jones, B. (1982): Destruction or Redistribution of Engineering Skills? *The Degradation of Work?* Wood, S. (Ed.), London: Hutchinson.

de Kadt, M. (1979): Insurance: A Clerical Work Factory, *Case Studies on the Labor Process*, Zimbalist, A. (Ed.), New York: Monthly Review Press.

Kahn, R. (1975): In Search of the Hawthorne Effect, *Man and Work in Society*, New York: Van Nostrand.

Karasek, R. (1978): Job Socialization: A Longitudinal Study of Work, Political and Leisure Activity, paper, Stockholm: Swedish Institute for Social Research.

– (1981): Job Socialization and Stress, *Working Life*, Gardell, B. and Johansson, G. (Eds.), Chichester: Wiley.

Karlsson, L.-E. (1982): On the Road to Soft Cushion Technology, Paper presented to the "Symposium on division of labour, specialization and technical development", Linköping, June 1982.

Karpik, L. (1977): Technological Capitalism, *Critical Issues in Organizations*, Clegg, S. and Dunkerley, D. (Eds.), London: Routledge and Kegan Paul.

Katz, D., Kahn, R. (1978): *The Social Psychology of Organizations*, N.Y.: Wiley.

Kern, H. and Schumann, M. (1970): *Industriearbeit und Arbeiterbewußtsein*, Frankfurt: EVA.

– (1984): *Das Ende der Arbeitsteilung? Rationalisierung in der Industriellen Produktion*, München: Beck.

King, T. and Fitzgibbons, D. (1985): Power, Conflict and Ideology: The Dialectic of Chaos and Order, Paper presented at conference on "Critical Perspectives on Organizations" September 5–7, New York.

Kling, M. and Stymne, B. (1982): Varför inte direktinflytande? *Arbetsorganisation och medbestämmande*, Sandberg, T. (Ed.), Stockholm: Tiden.

Kornhauser, A. (1965): *Mental Health of the Industrial Worker*, New York: Wiley.

Korpi, W. (1978): *The Working Class in Wellfare Calpitalism*, London: Routledge and Kegan Paul.

Kronlund, J. (1975): Duger Sociotekniken? *Sociologisk forskning*, 4.

Kronlund, J. and Wigblad, R. (1981): *Boxholmsprojektet del III. Att arbeta vid finvalsverket i Boxholm. Arbetsförhållandena förr och nu.*, Dept. of Management, Linköping University.

Lasch, C. (1978): *The Culture of Narcissism*, New York: Norton.

Laurent, A. (1978): Managerial Subordinancy: A Neglected Aspect of Organizational Hierachy, *Academy of Management Review*, 3, pp. 220–230.

Lawler, E. (1971): The Role of Pay in Organizations, *Readings in Organizational Behavior and Human Performance*, Scott, W. and Cummings, L. (Eds.), Homewood, Ill.: Irwin 1973.

– (1973): Satisfaction and Behavior, *Psychological Foundations of Organizational Behavior*, Staw, B. (Ed.), Santa Monica, Cal.: Goodyear 1977.

– (1975): Control Systems in Organizations, *Handbook of Industrial and Organizational Research*, Dunnette, M. (Ed.), Chicago: RAND/McNally.

– (1977): Measuring the Psychological Quality of Working Life: The Why and How of it, *The Psychological Foundations of Organizations Behavior*, Staw, B. (Ed.), Santa Monica, Cal.: Goodyear.

Lawler, E., Hackman, R. and Kaufman, S. (1973): Effects of Job Redesign: A Field Experiment, *Journal of Applied Social Psychology*, 3, 1.

Leiss, W. (1978): *The Limits to Satisfaction*, London: Marion Boyars.

Lichtman, C. and Hunt, J. (1971): Personality and Organization Theory: a Review of Some Conceptual Literature, *Psychological Bulletin*, 76, 4.

Liedman, S.-E., Mithander, C. and Olausson, L. (1984): Projekt Ideologi Teori, *Hälften för Kritiska Studier*, 1.

Likert, R. (1961): *New Patterns of Management*, New York: McGraw-Hill.

Likert, R., Likert, J. G. (1976): *New Ways of Managing Conflicts*, N.Y.: Wiley.

Littler, C. and Salaman, G. (1982): Bravermania and Beyond: Recent Theories of the Labour Process, *Sociology*, 16, pp. 251–269.

LO (1978): *Arbetsorganisation*, Stockholm: LO.

Lohmann, H. (1972): *Psykisk hälsa och mänsklig miljö*, Stockholm: Liber 1978.

Locke, E. (1975): The Nature and Causes of Job Satisfaction, *Handbook of Industrial and Organizational Research*, Dunnette, M. (Ed.), Chicago: RAND/McNally.

Lorsch, J. (1975): Managers, Behavioral Scientists, and the Tower of Babel, *Man and Work in Society*, Cass, E. and Zimmer, F. (Eds.), New York: Van Nostrand.

Maccoby, M. (1981): *The Leader: A New Face for American Management*, New York: Simon and Schuster.

March, J. and Olsen, J. (1976): *Ambiguity and Choice in Organizations*, Bergen: Universitetsforlaget.

Marcuse, H. (1933): On the Philosophical Foundations of the Concept of Labor in Economics, *Telos*, 16, Summer 1973.

– (1941): Some Social Implications of Modern Technology, *Studies in Philosophy and Social Science*, 9, 4.

– (1954): *Eros and Civilization*, Boston: Beacon Press.

– (1964): *One-Dimensional Man. Studies in Ideology of Advanced Industrial Society*, Boston: Beacon Press 1966.

– (1965): Industrialization and Capitalism in the Work of Max Weber, *Negations*, Harmondsworth: Penguin 1972.

– (1969): *An Essay on Liberation*, Boston: Beacon Press.

Marrow, A. (1975): Management by Participation, *Man and Work in Society*, Cass, E. and Zimmer, F. (Eds.), New York: Van Nostrand.

Martin, J. and Powers, E. (1983): Truth or Corporate Propaganda. The Value of a Good War Story, *Organizational Symbolism*, Pondy, L. et al. (Eds.), Greenwich, CT: JAI Press.

Maslow, A. (1943): A Theory of Human Motivation, *Readings in Managerial Psychology*, Leavitt, H. and Pondy, L. (Eds.), Chicago: The University of Chicago Press 1973.
– (1954): *Motivation and Personality*, New York: Harper and Row.
– (1955): Deficiency Motivation and Growth Motivation, *Toward a Psychology of Being*, New York: Van Nostrand 1968.
Mayo, E. (1949): Hawthorne and the Western Electric Company, *Organization Theory*, Pugh, D. S. (Ed.), Harmondsworth: Penguin 1977.
McCarthy, T. (1976): Translators Introduction, *Legitimation Crises*, Habermas, J., London: Heinemann 1979.
McClelland, D. and Burnham, D. (1976): Power is the Great Motivator, *Harvard Business Review*, March–April.
McGregor, D. (1960): *The Human side of Enterprise*, McGraw-Hill.
Mead, G. H. (1936): *On Social Psychology*, Chicago: The University of Chicago Press 1972.
Mendner, J. (1975): *Teknologisk utveckling i den kapitalistiska arbetsprocessen*, Göteborg: Röda bokförlaget 1977.
Menninger, W. (1975): The Power of Emotions: The Role of Feelings, *Man and Work in Society*, Cass, E. and Zimmer, F. (Editors), New York: Van Nostrand.
Meyer, J. and Rowan, B. (1977): Institutionalized Organizations: Formal Structure as Myth and Ceremony, *American Journal of Sociology*, 83, pp. 340–363.
Mills, C. W. (1959): *The Sociological Imagination*, Harmondsworth: Penguin 1978.
More, C. (1982): Skill and the Survival of Apprenticeship, *The Degradation of Work?* Wood, S. (Ed.), London: Hutchinson.
Morgan, G. (1980): Paradigms, Metaphors, and Puzzle Solving in Organization Theory, *Adminstrative Science Quarterly*, 25, 4.
Morgan, G., Frost, P. and Pondy, L. (1983): Organizational Symbolism, *Organizational Symbolism* Pondy, L. et al. (Eds.), Greenwich, CT: JAI Press.
Morse, J. and Lorsch, J. (1970): Beyond Theory Y., *Harvard Business Review*, May–June.
Myrdal, G. (1968): *Objektivitetsproblemet i samhällsvetenskapen*, Stockholm: Rabén and Sjögren.
Near, J., Rice, R. and Hunt, R. (1979): Work and Extra-Work Correlates of Life and Job Satisfaction, *Academy of Management Journal*, 21, 2.
Nichols, T. (Ed.) (1980): *Labour and Capital*, Glasgow: Fontana.
Noble, D. (1979): Social Choice in Machine Design: The Case of Automatically Controlled Machine Tools, *Case Studies on the Labor Process*, Zimbalist, A. (Ed.), New York: Monthly Review Press.
Normann, R. (1983): *Service Management*, Lund: Liber.
Nygren, P. (1979): *Den sociala grammatiken*, Stockholm: Esselte.
Näsman, E., Nordström, K. and Hammarström, R. (1983): *Föräldrars arbete och barns villkor*, Stockholm: Arbetslivscentrum.
Offe, C. (1970): *Industry and Inequality*, London: Arnold 1976.
Oldham, G. and Hackman, J. R. (1981): Relationships Between Organizational Structure and Employee Reactions: Comparing Alternative Frameworks, *Administrative Science Quarterly*, 26, 1.

Ott, K. (1979): Are Wild Ducks really Wild? Paper, Northeastern Anthropological Association.

Pascale, R. (1985): The Paradox of "Corporate Culture": Reconciling Ourselves to Socialization, *California Management Review*, 27, 2.

Pateman, C. (1970): *Participation and Democratic Theory*, Cambridge: Cambridge University Press 1978.

Perby, M.-L. (1978): SAF: s "nya fabriker" – några kommentarer, Arbetslivscentrum, Stockholm (stencil).

Perrow, C. (1973): The Short and Glorious Story of Organization Theory, *Organizational Dynamics*, Summer.

Perrow, C. (1979): *Complex Organizations: A Critical Essay*, Glenview, Ill.: Scott Foresman and Co.

Peters, T. and Waterman, R. (1982): *In Search of Excellence*, New York: Harper and Row.

Pettigrew, A. (1979): On Studying Organizational Cultures, *Administrative Science Quarterly*, 24, pp. 570–581.

Pfeffer, J. (1981a): Management as Symbolic Action: The Creation and Maintenance of Organizational Paradigms, *Research in Organizational Behavior* 3, Cummings, L. and Staw, B. (Eds.), Greenwich, CT: JAI Press.

– (1981b): *Power in Organizations*, Boston: Pitman.

Pondy, L. R. (1983): The Role of Metaphors and Myths in Organization and in the Facilitation of Change, *Organizational Symbolism*, Pondy, L. R. et al. (Eds.), Greenwich, CT: JAI Press.

Rhenman, E. (1974): *Organization Theory for Long-Range Planning*, New York: Wiley.

Ramsay, H. (1977): Cycles of Control: A Social History of Worker's Participation in Management, *Sociology*, 11, 3.

Rim, Y. (1977): Significance of Work and Personality, *J. of Occup. Psych.*, 50, 2.

Robbins, S. (1983): *Organization Theory: Structure and Design*, Prentice-Hall, Englewood Cliffs, N. J.: Prentice-Hall.

Rohlin, L. (1974): *Organisationsutveckling*, Lund, Gleerups.

Rose, M. (1975): *Industrial Behavior*, Harmondsworth: Penguin 1978.

Rosen, M. (1984): Myth and Reproduction: The Contextualization of Management Theory, Method and Practice, *Journal of Management Studies*, 21, pp. 303–322.

Rosenbrock, H. (1979): The Redirection of Technology, paper, Council for Science and Society.

Salaman, G. (1978): Towards a Sociology of Organizational Structure, *Complex Organizations: Critical Perspectives*, Zey-Ferrell, M. and Aiken, M. (Eds.), Glenview, Ill.: Scott, Foresman and Co.

– (1981): *Class and the Corporation*, Glasgow: Fontana.

Sandberg, T. (1978): Självstyrande grupper på försök, *Sociologisk forskning*, 4.

Sandberg, Å. (Ed.) (1979): *Computers Dividing Man and Work*. Stockholm: Centre for Working Life.

– (1981): Kunskapsuppbyggnad och aktivering, *Forskning för förändring*, Sandberg, Å. (Ed.), Stockholm: Arbetslivscentrum.

Sandkull, B. m. fl. (1981): *Koncerner, teknik, inflytande*, Dept. of Management and Economics, Linköping University: research report no 106.

Sandkull, B. (1982): Konsekvenser för de anställda vid förändringar i produktionsteknik, *Arbetsorganisation och medbestämmande*, Sandberg, T. (Red.), Stockholm: Tiden.

– (1984): Managing the Democratization Process in Work Cooperatives, *Economic and Industrial Democracy*, 5, pp. 359–389.

SCB. (1978): *Levnadsförhållanden. Rapport 12, Arbetsmiljö 1975*, Stockholm: Liber.

SCB. (1985): *Arbetsmiljön i siffror. Miljöstatistisk årsbok 1985*, Stockholm: Statistiska Centralbyrån.

Schein, E. (1975): The Hawthorne Group Studies Revisited: A Defence of Theory Y., *Man and Work in Society*, Cass, E. and Zimmer, F. (Eds.), New York: Van Nostrand.

Schein, E. (1980): *Organizational Psychology*, (3rd, ed.), Englewood Cliffs N. J.: Prentice-Hall.

Schmid, H. (1981): On the Origin of Ideology, *Acta Sociologica*, 24, 1–2.

Schneider, M. (1973): *Samhället som sjukdom. Till kritiken av den borgerliga psykologin*, Stockholm: Rabén and Sjögren 1975.

Schroyer, T. (1973): *The Critique of Domination*, Boston: Beacon Press 1975.

Schwab, D. and Cummings, L. (1970): Theories of Performance and Satisfaction: a Review, *Readings in Organizational Behavior and Human Performance*, Scott, W. and Cummings, L. (Eds.), Homewood, Ill.: Irwin 1973.

Sennett, R. (1979): The Boss' New Clothes, *New York Review of Books*, Feb. 22.

Shaw, J. (1972): The Personal Imperative: a Study of the Evidence for Self-actualization, *Six Approaches to the Person*, Ruddock, R. (Ed)., London: Routledge and Kegan Paul.

Shrivastava, P. (1986): Is Strategic Management Ideological?, *Journal of Management*, forthcoming.

Sievers, B. (1984): Motivation as a surrogate for Meaning, Arbeitspapiere des Fachbereichs Wirtschaftswissenschaft, Nr. 81, Bergische Universität, Wuppertal.

Simon, H. (1965): *The Shape of Automation for Men and Management*, New York: Harper and Row.

Sjöstrand, S.-E. (1978): Vem ska utforma framtidens organisationer? *Människan och organisationen*, Forsblad, P. et al. (Ed.), Malmö: Liber.

Slater, P. (1978): *Origin and Significance of the Frankfurt School*, London: Routledge and Kegan Paul.

Slater, P. and Bennis, W. (1964): Democracy is Inevitable, *Harvard Business Review*, March–April.

Smircich, L. (1983a): Concept of Culture and Organizational Analysis, *Administrative Science Quarterly*, 28, pp. 339–358.

– (1983b): Organizations as Shared Meanings, *Organizational Symbolism*, Pondy, L. R. et al. (Eds.), Greenwich, CT: JAI Press.

Smircich, L. and Morgan, G. (1982): Leadership as the Management of Meaning, *Journal of Applied Behavioral Science*, 18, pp. 257–273.

Taylor, F. (1912): Scientific Management, *Organization Theory*, Harmondsworth: Penguin 1977.

Therborn, G. (1970): A Critique of the Frankfurt School, *New Left Review*, 63.

– (1971): Jürgen Habermas: A New Eclectic, *New Left Review*, 67.

- (1981): *The Ideology of Power and the Power of Ideology*, London: New Left Books.
Thierry, H. and Koopman-Iwena, A. (1984): Motivation and Satisfaction, *Handbook of Work and Organizational Psychology*, Drenth, P. et al. (Eds.), Chichester: Wiley.
Thompson, P. (1983): *The Nature of Work*, London, McMillan.
Thorsrud, E. and Emery, F. (1969): *Medinflytande och engagemang i arbetet*, Stockholm: Utvecklingsrådet för samarbetsfrågor.
Thunberg, A.-M., Novak, K., Rosengren, K.-E. and Sigurd, B. (1978): *Samverkansspiralen*, Stockholm: Liber.
Van Maanen, J. and Barley, S. (1984): Occupational Communities. Culture and Control in Organizations, *Research in Organizational Behavior*, 6, Staw, B. and Cumming, L. (Eds.), Greenwich, CT: JAI Press.
Viklund, B. (1976): Att stoppa cancer en fråga om politik, inte forskning, *Arbetsmiljö*, 15.
Volmerg, B. (1977): Samfundsmässiggörelsen av psykopatologiske strukturer i produktionsprocessen, *Produktion, arbejde, socialisation*, Leithäuser, T. and Heinz, W. (Eds.), Copenhagen: Progressiv Bogklub.
Volmerg, U. (1979): Om förhållandet mellan produktion och socialisation med det industriella lönearbetet som exempel, *Tekla*, 6, April.
Vollpert, W. (1979): Der Zusammenhang von Arbeit und Persönlichkeit aus Handlungspsychologischer Sicht, *Arbeit und Persönlichkeit*, Groskurth, P. (Ed.), Reinbek: Rowohlt.
Walton, R. (1979): Work Innovations in the United States, *Harvard Business Review*, July–Aug.
- (1985): From Control to Commitment in the Workplace, *Harvard Business Review*, March–April.
Westlander, G. (1976a): *Arbete och fritidens innehåll*, Stockholm: PA-rådet.
- (1976b): *Arbete och livssituation*, Stockholm, PA-rådet,
Westlander, G. and Baneryd, K. (1970): *Att ha en sund själ ... Några synpunkter på mental hälsa och alienation i samhälle och arbetsliv*, Stockholm: Tiden.
Westley, F. and Jaeger, A. (1985): An Examination of Organizational Culture: How is it Linked to Performance?, paper, Faculty of Management. McGill University Montreal.
Whishler, T. (1970): The Impact of Computers on Decision Making, *Readings in Managerial Psychology*, Leavitt, H. and Pondy, L. (Eds.), Chicago: The University of Chicago Press 1973.
Willmott, H. (1984): Images and Ideals of Managerial Work: A Critical Examination of Conceptual and Empirical Accounts, *Journal of Management Studies*, 21, pp. 349–368.
Wilson, C. (1974): *New Pathways in Psychology. Maslow and the Post-Freudian Revolution*, London: Gollancz.
Wilson, H. T. (1983): Anti-Method as a Counter Structure in Social Research Practice, *Beyond Method*, Morgan, G. (Ed.), Beverly Hills: Sage.
Wood, S. (1982): Introduction, *The Degradation of Work?*, Wood, S. (Ed.), London: Hutchinson.
Wood, S. and Kelly, J. (1982): Taylorism, Responsible Autonomy and Manage-

ment Strategy, *The Degradation of Work?*, Wood, S. (Ed.), London: Hutchinson.

Woodward, J. (1958): Management and Technology, *Organization Theory*, Pugh, D. S. (Ed.), Harmondworth: Penguin 1977.

von Wright, G. H. (1978): *Humanismen som livshållning*, Stockholm: Rabén and Sjögren 1980.

Zetterberg, H. and Winander, B. (1983): Cheferna och organisationskulturen, *Våga leda!*, Arvedson, L. and Ryden, B. (Eds.), Stockholm: SNS.

Zey-Ferrell, M. (1982): Criticism of the Dominant Perspective on Organizations, *Traditions and Trends in Organization Theory*, Vol. 2, Berg, P. O. and Dandi, P. (Eds.), Lund: Studentlitteratur.

Zey-Ferrell, M. and Aiken, M. (1981): *Complex Organizations: Critical Perspectives*, Glenview Ill.: Scott, Foresman and Co.

Ziehe, T. and Stubenrauch, H. (1982): *Plädoyer für ungewöhnliches Lernen. Ideen zur Jugendsituation*, Reinbek bei Hamburg: Rowohlt, Taschenbuch Verlag.

Zimbalist, A. (1975): The Limits of Work Humanization, *Review of Radical Political Economics*, 7, (Summer).

– (1979): Introduction, *Case Studies on the Labor Process*, Zimbalist, A. (Ed.), New York: Monthly Review Press.

Yorks, L. and Whitsett, D. (1985): Hawthorne, Topeka, and the Issue of Science Versus Advocacy in Organizational Behavior, *Academy of Management Review*, 10, pp. 21–30.

Åberg, R. (1984): Teorierna om arbetets degradering och arbetsmarknadens dualisering – ett försök till empirisk prövning, *Sociologisk Forskning*, 2.

Author Index

Subject Index

de Gruyter Studies in Organization

An international series by internationally known
authors presenting current research in organization.

The Japanese Industrial System
By *Charles J. McMillan*
2nd revised edition
1985. 15,5 x 23 cm. XII, 356 pages. Cloth DM 88,-   ISBN 3 11 010410 5

Political Management
Redefining the Public Sphere
By *Hall Thomas Wilson*
1984. 15,5 x 23 cm. X, 316 pages. Cloth DM 98,-   ISBN 3 11 009902 0

Limits to Bureaucratic Growth
By *Marshall W. Meyer* in Association with *William Stevenson* and *Stephen Webster*
1985. 15,5 x 23 cm. X, 228 pages. Cloth DM 88,-   ISBN 3 11 009865 2

Guidance, Control and Evaluation in the Public Sector
Edited by *F. X. Kaufmann, G. Majone, V. Ostrom*
1985. 17 x 24 cm. XIV, 830 pages. Cloth DM 198,-   ISBN 3 11 009707 9

International Business in the Middle East
Edited by *Erdener Kaynak*
1986. 15,5 x 23 cm. XVI, 278 pages. Cloth DM 114,-   ISBN 3 11 010321 4

The American Samurai
Blending American and Japanese Managerial Practice
By *Jon P. Alston*
1986. 15,5 x 23 cm. XII, 368 pages. Cloth DM 105,-   ISBN 3 11 010619 1

Organizing Industrial Development
Edited by *Rolf Wolff*
1986. 15,5 x 23 cm. XI, 391 pages. Cloth DM 128,-   ISBN 3 11 010669 8

WALTER DE GRUYTER · BERLIN · NEW YORK

European Approaches to International Management

Edited by *Klaus Macharzina* and *Wolfgang H. Staehle*

1985. 15,5 x 23 cm. XIV, 386 pages. Cloth DM 128,–
ISBN 3 11 009827 X

Management Under Differing Value Systems

Political, Social and Economical Perspectives in a Changing World

Edited by *Günter Dlugos* and *Klaus Weiermair*

1981. 17 x 24 cm. XIV, 868 pages. Cloth DM 148,–
ISBN 3 11 008553 4

Studies in Decision Making

Social, Psychological and Socio-Economic Analyses

Edited by *Martin Irle* in collaboration with *Lawrence B. Katz*

1982. 17 x 24 cm. XVI, 917 pages. Cloth DM 176,–
ISBN 3 11 008087 7

The State of the Masses

By *Richard F. Hamilton* and *James D. Wright*

1986. 16,5 x 24,2 cm. XII, 470 pages. Bibliography, indices.
Cloth DM 148,–   ISBN 3 11 010819 4
For USA and Canada:
Cloth $39.95   ISBN 0-202-30324-1 (Aldine de Gruyter, New York)

Management Dictionary

By *Werner Sommer* and *Hanns-Martin Schoenfeld*

English-German:
1979. 12,2 x 18,8 cm. 621 pages. Cloth DM 58,–   ISBN 3 11 007708 6

German-English:
1978. 12,2 x 18,8 cm. 542 pages. Cloth DM 58,–   ISBN 3 11 004863 9

Prices are subject to change without notice

WALTER DE GRUYTER · BERLIN · NEW YORK